GOVERNMENT
AND
POLITICS
in the Evergreen State

GOVERNMENT
AND
POLITICS
in the Evergreen State

EDITED BY

David C. Nice • John C. Pierce • Charles H. Sheldon

Washington State University Press
Pullman, Washington

Washington State University Press, Pullman, Washington 99164-5910
©1992 by the Board of Regents of Washington State University
All rights reserved
First printing 1992

Library of Congress Cataloging-in-Publication Data
Government and Politics in the Evergreen state / edited by David C. Nice, John C.
  Pierce, Charles H. Sheldon.
      p. cm.
    ISBN 0-87422-085-8
    1. Washington (State)–Politics and government. 2. Local government–
Washington (State) I. Nice, David C., 1952-   . II. Pierce, John C.,
1943-   . III. Sheldon, Charles H., 1929-   .
JK9216.G68 1992
320.9797–dc20   92-8476
                                                                      CIP

We dedicate this book to Walfred Peterson, esteemed colleague and close friend, on the occasion of his retirement as professor of political science from Washington State University. For over two decades, Walfred Peterson instructed thousands of Washington State University students in the structure and processes of civil liberties, public law, and American politics. His scholarship illuminated our knowledge about Washington politics, and his personal endeavors contributed to the richness, diversity, and vitality of the university and the state. He has been a driving force in bridging the gap between the potential sterility of the classroom and the reality of the political arena. Walfred Peterson served his university and department in some of the most sensitive and difficult of positions and times. His several years as university ombudsman attest to the confidence and trust in which the university community has held him. His recent tenure as interim chair of the department of political science illustrated his capacity for good will and common sense. His scholarly work exhibits uncommon intelligence and insight into issues of church and state relations, while his personal relations with colleagues and friends reveal his openness, sensitivity, good humor, and honesty. In many ways our continuing interest in the central political issues of the state grow from Walfred Peterson, and we hope this book will be a continual reminder of his contributions.

Table of Contents

Acknowledgments

In any project such as this, editors accrue considerable debts. We could not have put together such a timely collection without the most able and always friendly efforts of Lynda Billings. In preparing the manuscript, she more than occasionally spotted mistakes and provided us with useful suggestions for correcting and improving the content as well as the form of the manuscript. The editors at Washington State University Press were always encouraging and patient. Glen Lindeman urged us to undertake the project and Keith Petersen's careful editing enhanced the book considerably. Finally, we are, of course, indebted to the authors of the individual chapters. They were patient with our often-petty requests, prompt with their drafts, and, as readers will discover, astute in their analysis.

Introduction

THE GOVERNMENTS OF WASHINGTON state and its localities affect our lives in many ways, from deciding levels of taxation and reforming education, to shaping relations with Pacific rim countries. In this volume we offer an overview of the institutions of government in Washington state and the broader environment in which they operate. We explore the ways in which people try to influence governmental decisions and the efforts of public officials to cope with a very complex world.

The present volume is more than a revision of 1985's *Political Life in Washington: Governing the Evergreen State* (Pullman: Washington State University Press). For the most part, new authors are involved and new chapters included. Some of the traditional chapters have been updated and present new and different materials. Nevertheless, the authors of this volume owe a large debt of gratitude to the authors of *Political Life In Washington;* their efforts made our task much easier.

We have written this book for two different types of readers. First, students who are learning about state and local government will find a broad-ranging discussion of the major features of Washington's political system and references to other studies that can provide more in-depth information on specific topics. Second, citizens who no longer think of themselves as students will find the book a useful guide to our state's government. The arrival of many people from other states and countries has fueled Washington's rapid growth. We hope this book will help them learn about distinctive aspects of the state.

We have organized the book in a sequence that begins with the setting of Washington state politics. We then examine modes of citizen involvement and the institutions that make public policy choices for the state. Chapter one presents an overall view of the prevailing social, economic, and political forces that have characterized Washington. The constitutional framework (chapter two) then provides boundaries within which those socioeconomic and political forces interact. Interest groups and political parties, as explained in chapters three and four, act as the channels through which public concerns are presented to decision-makers in the legislative (chapter five), executive (chapter seven), and judicial (chapter eight) branches. The agencies of direct democracy (chapter six)—the initiative, referendum, and recall—permit the people to take into their own hands responsibility for legislating. Washington's residents have been willing to exercise those options. Local government relies upon actions at the state level but has problems and opportunities of its own, as explained in chapter nine. Of course, any analysis of government would be incomplete without a discussion of the revenues and taxes which keep government running and are the focus of much political maneuvering. Chapter ten provides that discussion. Finally, chapter eleven provides the linkage among the forces, institutions, and policies emanating from governmental and political institutions.

Yet that which is presented here is only the beginning. We hope the reader will be encouraged to delve more deeply into these topics.

Nighttime view of the new capitol building in Olympia, c. 1930. Vibert Jeffers photo. *Susan Parish Collection*©

Chapter One

The Political Setting

Terrence E. Cook

ALTHOUGH NATIVE AMERICANS had long inhabited the region and Spaniards had explored it, the origin of Washington state can be traced to English-speaking explorers, especially the 1792 expeditions of British Captain George Vancouver in what he named Puget Sound and American Captain Robert Gray along the Columbia River. Even after the Louisiana Purchase in 1803, British and Americans disputed the northern half of what they called the Oregon territory. But in 1846 the British finally accepted American authority from the Columbia River north to the forty-ninth parallel. This section became separately administered in 1853 as Washington territory. White fur traders, missionaries, farmers, and gold seekers had long entered the area. Yet as late as July 4, 1876, the first centennial of the American Declaration of Independence, only some 3,500 whites lived in Seattle, while a mere 50,000 resided in the territory. Under rules Congress laid down, a portion of the Washington territory, excluding land east of the present Washington-Idaho boundary, emerged as Washington state in 1889, the forty-second state of the union.[1] Upon these early beginnings Washington evolved its sometimes singular political culture.

In the case of Washington state, we may raise some intriguing questions of contrasts with other states: Why has this population grown more rapidly than most other states? Why is the ethnic minority population less than the national average, yet growing very rapidly? Why is the population in general younger than average? Why is the juvenile suicide rate above average? Why do Washingtonians have one of the lowest levels of religious affiliation among the states? Why is trade protectionist sentiment apparently so low? Why has the state electorate, since the 1930s, repeatedly voted against any kind of personal income tax, making the state one of only a handful without one? Why is there no corporate profits tax? Why does the state retain a relatively long constitution which imposes many restrictions on policy choices as well as on political procedures? Why are state political party organizations so weak? Why, nevertheless, is state voter turnout somewhat higher than the national average?

Why have Washingtonians preceded the national trend toward more independence and split-ticket voting? Why do they traditionally avoid elevating lesser statewide elective officials to the governorship? Do votes, campaign contributions, or expert advocacy best predict Washington public policy choices, and what does a place called "Ulcer Gulch" have to do with it all?

This book does not pretend to have all of the answers, but its chapters offer a background for discussion of many such questions. The task of the present chapter is to speak broadly of Washington's political setting.

Politics is choice, but in Washington state, as in any other political system, current politics is shaped by a number of constraints, usually legacies of past choices made by other people. Sometimes these people may have lived in distant places.

Constraints on current choices include 1) the ecological setting (geography and related economy); 2) population characteristics (numbers, distribution, and political divisions); and 3) rules of the political game that have been imposed from without or that have arisen from within (the U. S. Constitution's requirement that each state have "a republican form of government").

The Ecological Setting: Washington's Geography and Economy

Hawaii excepted, Washington has the smallest territory of any Western state, consisting of some 67,000 square miles. It spans 340 miles east to west and 230 miles north to south.

As in the cliche of promotional brochures, this is certainly "a land of contrasts," especially on the east-west dimension as divided by the Cascade Mountain range. The west side has about one-third of the land and three-fourths of the people while the east has two-thirds of the land but only one-fourth of the people. As later shown, this contributes to a number of public-policy tensions.

The state's geographic characteristics influence the nature of the economy in various ways and, as a result, also influence the distribution of the population. An economy can be described in terms of three kinds of activity: 1) primary (extractive); 2) secondary (manufacturing, construction, related transport); and 3) tertiary (services).

The Primary Sector

The primary or extractive sector pulls something from nature. The first white settlers in the region encouraged Native Americans to extract sea otters and other furbearing animals from nature, then sold many of the skins to China. While one cannot neglect Washington's salmon, bottom fish, and crabbing industries, including its being the home port for many boats working Alaskan waters, most present primary sector employment involves the growing and harvesting of fibers and foods.

With a marine climate, western Washington is moderate in temperature range and relatively moist, with annual rainfall approaching 150 inches in a few places on the west side of the Olympic Peninsula—although that same deluge results in a drier area in the Olympic Mountains' rain shadow around Sequim, Port Townsend, and Whidbey Island. Elsewhere, the moist climate produced the original forests of great trees such as Douglas fir and western red cedar. Even after extensive harvests of such giants, abundant forest greenery led Washington to call itself the "Evergreen State." Seattle, more recently, named itself the "Emerald City." The forest products industry, which at times employs as many as 40,000 people statewide, has long been important to the Olympic Peninsula and the western Cascades, although there are also some tree-growing areas in eastern Washington.

Exhaustion of most old growth timber on private lands, combined with increasing environmental restrictions on the logging of old growth on public lands (including controversies over survival of the spotted owl and marbled murelet) have brought economic strain to many communities. Such strain becomes severe during lows in the business cycle, when curtailed construction activity reduces demand for lumber.

The Canadian-American free trade agreement seems destined to aid many aspects of the extractive Washington economy, perhaps especially grape growing because of increased sales of Washington wines. However, low stumpage fees for public timber sales in Canada have in the past irritated the timber industry of Washington state, as is evident in a temporary protection of cedar shake mills from Canadian competition.

Turning from forestry to farming, generous moisture has also contributed to western Washington's dairy industry, centered along many meandering river valleys and on the northern fringe of the Olympic Peninsula, as well as truck gardening and flower bulb-raising along the Skagit Valley and other regions north of Seattle. But recurrent overproduction plagues the dairy industry, and Puget Sound urban sprawl crowds western agriculture no less than forestry. Especially in that region, both farmers and timber companies such as Weyerhaeuser and Simpson have a continuing interest in retaining a special, lower property tax rate on their lands, based on current use rather than development potential. The timber companies also favor tax exclusion of the value of standing timber until it is cut and sold.

In eastern Washington the climate features greater winter and summer temperature extremes. Aside from bands of forest along the east slopes of the Cascades, in the Blue Mountains in the southeast, and in a northern tier of counties, lower rainfall and higher sunshine due to the Cascades' rain shadow has limited the forestry zone. The Columbia River descends southward from Canada about halfway across the state, and arid areas of the Columbia Basin, with summers of hot days and cooler nights, depend on irrigation for most of the orchards (such as the famous Washington red delicious apple), hops, wine grapes, carrots, potatoes, and other crops grown there. Toward the southeast, near Walla Walla and Dayton, onions, asparagus, and peas become the principal crops. In the higher lands of the Palouse country, consisting of the gently rolling hills between Clarkston and Spokane, wheat, peas, and lentils are the main concerns. While rich loess soils of the Palouse offer some of the nation's highest per-acre yields of wheat, problems include severe erosion, crop failures from weather or pests, abandonment of rail lines long used to ship some crops to market, as well as volatility in agricultural commodity prices due to uncontrolled supply and demand.

While the territory experienced gold rush prospectors from its early years, the hardrock mining industry has not been as important to this state as in nearby Idaho, where major lead, zinc, silver, and other operations are found. Base-metal mining has declined in Washington state, notwithstanding recent projects to reopen some older zinc and gold mines. As for fossil fuels, most Cascade Mountain coal mines have been abandoned because they have played out or because their soft coal cannot be burned without excessive pollution, although a revitalized coal operation is underway near Black Diamond. Nor is the state endowed with proven natural gas or oil deposits worth commercial exploitation, although scattered gas deposits exist on the northern fringe of the Olympic Peninsula, and traces of oil or gas have been found in exploratory wells just east of the Cascades.

Secondary Sector

While the primary sector pulls things from the land, the secondary sector works them or moves them. It encompasses manufacturing, construction, and related transportation. Manufacturing is quite varied in Washington state, but a few industries stand out in value of product. Some industries, such as food processing or milling of timber and paper making (especially Weyerhaeuser, which has its corporate headquarters north of Tacoma), are obviously closely linked to the primary sector. One perennial issue among timber interests has concerned export of logs from public lands: federal government policy prohibits exporting raw logs cut on federally owned lands, but the status of state forest logs has been long debated. Weyerhaeuser has invested heavily in seaborne export operations, and hence favors such exports, often joined by some public educators concerned about state log sale revenue, which helps pay some of the state's school bills. Major opponents include both environmental groups and small wood products firms which depend upon a steady supply of economically priced logs. Many have sought a total ban on log exports, arguing that without such a ban, a firm harvesting both private and public logs will simply boost exports of the former. Recently, heeding these arguments, a federal judge upheld a law banning the export of 75 percent of the timber from state trust lands.

Turning to other manufacturing, private shipbuilding has steadily declined since World War II due to lower labor costs in Asia or loss of navy business. Paccar Corporation builds heavy trucks in Bellevue. In aircraft, the Boeing operations, chiefly in civil aviation, have long proven vital to the state's economy, since Boeing employment may exceed 100,000. While a Boeing plant has opened in the Spokane area, most of the immediate job production has concentrated around Puget Sound, principally from Everett to Renton, with a few plants further south in Pierce County. Much additional area employment arises from smaller firms selling goods or services to Boeing. Among its political concerns, Boeing has tended to prefer the present low tax on the gross receipts of its business rather than a possible corporate profits tax, since its high-profit aircraft sales would mean a larger tax burden. Also, Boeing has opposed any sales tax on the component parts of its production, sharing that concern with Paccar. In order to protect its interests, Boeing in 1990 spent nearly a half-million dollars lobbying in the state.

Remembering Boeing's hard times in the early 1970s, many Washingtonians are interested less in simple growth than in diversifying the economic base toward less dependence on Boeing-related manufacturing. Although Boeing slumped in the early 1970s and slowed again in the severe recession of 1981-1983, a strong backlog of aircraft orders moderated the impact of the 1991 national recession in Washington.

As in forestry and agriculture, manufacturing in Washington state depends heavily on exports abroad. Hence a free trade, rather than a protectionist, outlook dominates the state. Washington is one of the leading states in per capita value of exports. In 1990 it led all states in value of trade with China, in large part due to Boeing aircraft sales.

Other manufactured export goods have included test and measuring equipment, medical equipment, and certain computer components, as illustrated by Key Tronics in the Spokane area, which employed some 1,700 workers in 1991.

Some industries, such as aluminum smelters, have heretofore depended heavily on the state's relatively cheap hydroelectric power, produced by the region's dams, many of which market their power under authority of the Portland-based Bonneville Power Administration. Fear of an insufficient power supply (brownouts) spurred hydroelectric firms to promote a public/private project of near-simultaneous construction of five nuclear power plants, three at the mid-state Hanford Reservation and two near Satsop west of Olympia. But when many industrial and private consumers responded to sharply higher costs of power with greater conservation, a surprise power glut halted construction of all but one, and cost-overruns and stoppages led to the 1983 bond defaults of the Washington Public Power Supply System, or WPPSS, which critics pronounced to rhyme with "oops." A catastrophe to some bond investors, a disaster to some utility share owners, this also proved very costly to regional electric power consumers and taxpayers. But the debacle at least inspired a more cautious, regionally coordinated approach to area power planning.[2]

While Puget Sound residents worry about fluctuations in Boeing aircraft orders (meticulously reported in the area's newspapers), the expansion of manufacturing activity preoccupies eastern Washington. Especially in such metropolitan areas as Spokane, Yakima, and the Tri-cities (a state and local phrase for the clustered cities of Richland, Kennewick, and Pasco), there has been much interest in increasing the numbers of manufacturing enterprises. While Spokane was delighted to start the 1990s with its first Boeing plant producing fiberglass aircraft interiors, local economic development agencies also tried to lure firms from high-cost areas outside the state, such as California. In such places as Seattle and Spokane, the state has also committed funds to encourage academic research oriented toward high-tech manufacturing. The University of Washington medical school has already stimulated nearby start-up firms in related technologies, but bio-tech manufacturing lags behind expectations elsewhere in the state.

The major cities of Washington state such as Seattle, Tacoma, and Spokane largely arose as farming, logging, and industrial transportation hubs, especially during the unchallenged primacy of railroads. The first two cities expect continued major gains in their port activity from the burgeoning trade of the United States with the Pacific rim, including pass-throughs of truck and/or rail containers of manufactured goods originating from other states or nearby areas of Canada.

The Tertiary Sector

As in the nation as a whole, while primary sector employment has steeply contracted, and while secondary sector employment has peaked, tertiary or service sector employment has grown dramatically. This sector includes many relatively low-skill service jobs in such areas as restaurants, hotels, tourist travel, retail trade, real estate, insurance, and banking. But most better-paying service employment arises in higher-skill jobs in fields like education, public administration, business management, medical care, and computer software production (especially Microsoft Corporation of the Redmond area, which employs over 8,000 persons).

With some obvious exceptions, most skilled service-sector jobs involve the manipulation of symbols, as in the provision of specialized sorts of information. Obviously, high school dropouts are handicapped in such a world, and Washington shares this problem with other states. The future of higher skill service jobs in Washington state depends not only on an attractive lifestyle environment permitting Washington to import more highly educated people, but also on the strength of post-secondary education systems, both public and private. When compared with other states, these after-high school educational institutions are most satisfactory at the vocational and two-year college levels, but more underdeveloped at the four-year and especially graduate education levels. Many urban areas have charged that they are inadequately supplied with higher educational institutions at all levels. In partial response to such political pressures, Seattle's University of Washington has begun branch campuses in Tacoma and Bothell, while Pullman's Washington State University has launched campuses near Vancouver and in Richland, while participating in a research center and opening a graduate education campus in Spokane.

The People of Washington State

Washington's population in 1990 was 4,866,692, but it has since exceeded five million. This makes it the most populous state in the Pacific Northwest. It is comparable in population to such nations as Haiti or Denmark. Further, Washington's population has grown rapidly. Results of the 1990 national census netted the state a new seat in the United States House of Representatives, its ninth.

To use the language of demographers, populations increase because of either "net migration" or "natural increase," and both have been important in Washington's recent growth.

Net migration, or in-migrants minus out-migrants, has been more important than natural increase. During the 1980s roughly two persons moved into the state for every person moving out, frustrating the "Lesser Seattle Movement," whimsically launched by Seattle journalist Emmett Watson. When not artificially driven or blocked by political constraints, migrants everywhere tend to move from places of lower economic opportunities to places of higher ones. Hence Washington's in-migrants were disproportionately young adults in quest of job opportunities concentrated primarily in the Puget Sound region, and often linked to Boeing aircraft production. While folklore claims that most in-migrants came from California, in fact only about one-fourth did so.

Natural increase, local births minus deaths, has also bolstered population growth. State mortality rates are comparable to those of other states, with some exceptions. To a lesser extent than elsewhere, the population is aging. The percent of state residents under 19 has been shrinking, from 38 percent in 1970 to a projected 26 percent in 2010.[3] Yet local birth rates have increased somewhat faster than the national average. While the state is also above national averages in single adult households, such as the never-married, divorced, or widowed, higher birth rates are largely due to the disproportionate youth of the in-migrant population: more young couples now live in Washington and are ready to build their families. The state's comparatively healthy economy in the later 1980s and early 1990s further encouraged those already settled in Washington to have more babies. Some observers have prophesied the start of a local baby boomlet in the 1990s.

Another important dimension of Washington's population increase is the higher growth among several ethnic minorities. While census figures often undercount urban ethnic minorities, in 1990 the state had at least 214,570 persons of Spanish origin, 210,958 Asians or Pacific Islanders, 149,801 African Americans, and 81,483 Native Americans. With about 11.5 percent of its population made up of such minorities (compared with only 8.5 percent in 1980), the state still falls below the national average. But minority population groups are rapidly increasing, with Asians and Hispanics eclipsing the growth of African Americans. Minority population growth overall is about four times that of whites.

Distributions of these minority populations can have political significance. About half the black population is in Seattle, and concentration there permits African Americans to elect one or two members to the state legislature. Seattle also entered the 1990s with a black mayor, Norman Rice. Asians may join blacks in winning some Seattle city council seats. In Columbia Basin municipalities, the number of Hispanics is relatively high; yet their political success seems uneven, perhaps due to failures of effective organization and voter turnout. Native Americans find that their low numbers and wide dispersal weaken them in electoral politics, although on such issues as off-reservation fishing and hunting rights, they have won compensatory gains in the courts.

Aside from greater population growth, the relative youth of the population, and relatively low numbers of ethnic minorities, the state's population is similar to that of most other states.

The Ends of Politics: Consensus and Cleavage in Washington Politics

While we may dream of an ideal politics of rational persuasion, real life politics can be roughly defined as that sphere of life where people may be forced to "cooperate" by a last recourse to official coercion. Thus, we may stop at stoplights or pay taxes out of habit; but would these habits arise or persist without the threat of arrest and punishment?

What do people want out of politics? Most public policy matters ultimately aim at 1) physical security; 2) economic advantage; and 3) group status or prestige. The vanity of would-be political leaders aside, political power is sought only to attain such goods. But motives seem doubly mixed.

First, if anyone pursues any one goal too far, it tends to interfere with the attainment of others. Rational people may not try to "maximize" either political power or any single goal, but perhaps rather the total value of a mix of goals which matter to them.

Second, in pursuit of their various goals, it is arguable that most live neither wholly for others, nor wholly for themselves. The assumption of saintlike altruism is an implausible predictor of normal political behavior. But the opposite assumption of the narrowest egoism of individual self-interest may also be given more than its due. While individuals can readily confuse what is good for themselves with what is good for everybody, usually they are looking for choices which seem to combine some kind of good for themselves with some kind of good for others.

These "others" who matter will not be the whole of society so much as immediate kith and kin or somewhat larger social subgroups of special concern. Since not all of our group memberships matter in politics, and since sometimes a non-membership group becomes the focus of a politically relevant loyalty, estimation of individual group identities is difficult. It seems that *who* political actors favor shapes *what* they favor in the way of ultimate outcomes and related policies.[4]

As argued in chapter three, if there is any ideological division of note it is that King County and its leading city, Seattle, are more liberal than the rest of the state, especially relative to the cordon of affluent, conservative suburbs near Seattle. But let us briefly survey the mentioned substantive policy concerns and address a few matters of policy tension.

Status Policies

Status policies do not concern tangibles, such as security or economic advantage, so much as enhancement of prestige. Matters of group rather than individual prestige are especially likely to enter the public arena. Often, status politics can be a means to attain security or economic goals. But when these are at satisfactory levels, status concerns can become an end in itself. People want favored groups celebrated, not denigrated by public action. They become vigilant as to how their groups are doing in such things as designation of holidays (such as Martin Luther King Day), naming of places, honorific gubernatorial appointments, and the speech of elective officials or other public employees. Although Washington state, as noted, has a lower than average presence of racial minorities, most white public officials have seemed sensitive toward them. In 1885, just prior to statehood, a menacing Tacoma mob forced Chinese laborers to flee the city. But, notwithstanding a more recent period of tension regarding Indian fishing rights, for the most part the state has lacked the nasty mutual hatreds among ethnic or other groups which may divide nations or even other states. The legislature has enacted a law against malicious harassment of certain minorities. Questions of racial sensitivities seem to have little prominence apart from public school grounds and university campuses.

If racial symbols carry little political charge in Washington, that of religious groupings also seems of low prominence. Worldwide, status politics has often been linked to religious identities. But Washington state has one of the lowest levels of religious affiliation of all 50 states—perhaps in part because of the in-migration of young people. Nationwide, about 49.3 percent of the population are churchgoers; in Washington only about 30.9 percent attend, with only Alaska and Nevada being lower.[5] Christian fundamentalists moved to capture the presidential convention delegates of the state's Republican party, making use of the caucus system to back evangelist Pat Robertson in 1988. But religious politics has not been prominent, and no one religious sect predominates over dimensions of policy. While some will regard the abortion question as an issue of privacy and personal choice, it has been strongly influenced by religious organizations. As elsewhere in the nation, Washingtonians are divided between the "right to life" position and the "right to choice" view, although the latter outlook is locally ascendant, possibly because of the population's low church involvement and relative youth. In 1991, a pro-choice initiative measure barely passed and then only after all absentee ballots were counted.

Rather than being agitated by racial or religious identities, most Washingtonians attentive to politics at all seem more concerned about their security from crime and their economic standard of living.

Physical Security: Law Enforcement and Corrections

Quite obviously, state government has little to do with military defense. The shared authority of the governor with the president over state national guard units only becomes important in natural disasters such as the eruption of Mount St. Helens, or in potential civil disorders. However, Washington state is affected by unusually high levels of federal military expenditure, typified by such bases as Fairchild near Spokane, McChord and Fort Lewis south of Tacoma, the Puget Sound Naval Shipyard at Bremerton, and the Bangor submarine base northwest of Bremerton. As the Cold War began to recede, a 1991 federal list of military bases for recommended closure first mentioned but later spared the naval bases on Whidbey Island and at Everett.

Turning from military to non-military security, law enforcement and corrections are primarily state and local concerns in the United States. It is worth noting that, misdemeanors aside, street crime rates vary with the percentage of a population who are young men. As in the nation, Washington state has found some relief from rising crime rates as the baby boom generation has aged. While *absolute* numbers of serious crimes still rose in 1990, this was largely due to increased population, since the actual crime rates per 100,000 population fell.[6] A 1991 Federal Bureau of Investigation study of the 50 states, plus the District of Columbia and Puerto Rico, ranked Washington thirtieth in violent crimes. But unlike other issue areas, almost all groups of society put a high priority on crime control, differing only on relative emphases in how to accomplish it.

A related problem concerns the system of punishment. The state has reenacted capital punishment for specified categories of murder, but defendant appeals have delayed executions of those on death row. As in much of the nation, more convictions and longer sentences prove more popular with voters than paying the bills to build new prisons and feed and retrain the inmates. But convictions so crowd prisons that the actual length of sentences served tend to be limited. In this state, prisons became so overcrowded that former Federal District Court Judge Jack Tanner ruled prison conditions had become "cruel and inhuman," in need of immediate correction. The state has sought to find locations for new prisons accessible to concentrations of population and unresisted by the not-in-my-backyard syndrome affecting location of many state institutions. The draw of new jobs has encouraged receptivity in some communities, such as Airline Heights west of Spokane. State facilities aside, city or county jail space has also been strained, notwithstanding the usually shorter terms given those incarcerated for traffic or other small offenses. Like absolute numbers of crimes, the prison space problem is largely a consequence of state population growth.

The Economic Problems: Questions of Inequalities by Region and by Socioeconomic Status

Speaking broadly, the largely "economic" policy problems of Washington's people grow out of uneven economic and population growth by regions of the state, and by uneven burdens among families and individuals of unequal earnings. Yet cleavages by region of residence or income tend to be softened, because for most Washingtonians, primary economic identity is by occupational category.

Uneven growth creates distinctive kinds of demands regarding economic issues (regulation, revenue, and expenditures) in different parts of the state.

As noted, growth has disproportionately concentrated on the west side of the Cascades around Puget Sound, from Olympia through Tacoma and Seattle to Everett. Because this growth area is hemmed in on the west by the waters of Puget Sound and on the east by the Cascade Mountains, there are consequent problems of traffic congestion and unaffordable housing. Although voters on both sides of the Cascades soundly defeated a growth regulation initiative proposal, western Washingtonians seem more willing to talk of regulating development than eastern Washingtonians. The state legislature and governor responded to such concerns in 1990-1991 with new planning laws imposing constraints on development projects.

Another issue of regulation intersects health, safety, and economics, for west-side cities have found themselves without enough landfill space and in need of new places to dump garbage and toxic substances. Seattle has considered long-line rail shipments of garbage to a new landfill in eastern Washington. Some people have also proposed a toxic waste landfill for the mid-state region near Vantage. While some communities have a tradition of receptivity, such as the Tri-Cities with its low-level nuclear waste disposal at Hanford, many plans to ship wastes galvanize environmental opponents who reply that recycling makes more sense.

Uneven regional development can also affect tax issues. Especially in the Seattle area, soaring property values up to 1991 led owners of rapidly appreciating homes to demand special property tax relief, such as a freeze or even retroactive refunds, which opponents regarded as efforts to shift the tax burden elsewhere.

Uneven development affects issues of budget expenditure. In eastern Washington, the leading metropolitan area is Spokane, comparable in size to Tacoma, with an economy based largely on medical and other professional services, local retail trade, and its function as a distributional hub for a large region called the "Inland Empire." Other metropolitan areas include the Tri-Cities, historically dependent on the nuclear operations of the nearby Hanford Reservation, and Yakima, with its surrounding base in agriculture. As in many other communities in eastern Washington, residents in these cities worry less about being choked by too much growth than being starved for lack of it. They do not sense the urgency of west-siders' transportation problems. Aside from relatively isolated problems, such as Spokane's congested north Division Street, the most severe traffic blockages clearly afflict the east-of-Cascades region, especially in the metropolitan areas near Seattle and Tacoma, where in the 1990s many major traffic arteries became severely clogged during rush hours. Even the vital north-south conduit of the interstate (I-5) is often reduced to standstills.

Correcting such traffic bottlenecks will be very costly, especially when combined with the broader problem of aging highways and bridges, which the state shares with the rest of the nation. But the much smaller population of eastern Washington gives its own pet proects high priority, as if greater distances between places compensated for lower population pressures. Eastern Washingtonians' desire to retain a major voice in state highway expenditure priorities seems excessive to many western Washingtonians trapped in an ever-graver traffic gridlock.

A related issue concerns appropriate relative expenditure on highways or on mass transit. Already, eastern Washingtonians who rarely use it question the high costs of the 25-boat state ferry system in the Puget Sound area, while western Washingtonians not only emphasize the high, daily numbers of job commuters (33,000 in 1991), but also the ferries' summer season draw as a top tourist attraction for the state. Many planning experts believe that light rail system development has become imperative in the Puget Sound region, perhaps eventually extended northward to Bellingham and southward to Vancouver.

While Spokane's airport capacity seemed adequate after construction of a new wing, the Seattle-Tacoma International Airport has outgrown its facilities. Most public officials and planners assume that another major airport must be built, but it is not yet clear where. Other kinds of capital expenditure projects have touched the east-west rivalry within the state. When Seattle received state funds to complete a major conference center around and over I-5, Spokane demanded and got an agricultural trade center as a comparable expenditure to boost its own economic base.

Even labor policies may experience east-west contrasts. The state is not a "right to work" state, whereby a majority of workers voting in a firm can bind the minority to make financial contributions to a union for its non-political expenses. Still, the Washington state labor force is more unionized than the national average. On some questions, such as permitting private companies to compete with the state for workers' compensation for smaller firms, organized labor, fearing lack of generosity, has opposed organized business, which hopes for lower insurance bills. The state allows most state employees the option of voting for collective bargaining, excepting only four-year and research university professors. Kindergarten through high school teachers are quite highly unionized. But even they often split on a regional basis, since many western Washington teachers plausibly claim higher costs of living and are more likely than those in eastern Washington to turn to strikes to secure wage increases.

Beyond such regional tensions, the costs and benefits of growth may fall differently on those of varying levels of income, education, and occupational status, which, combined, constitute socioeconomic status. The state is relatively prosperous and outperformed the national economy in the 1980s. In

1990 the U. S. Department of Commerce ranked it fourteenth highest among the 50 states with a per capita income of $18,858.

One impact of socioeconomic inequality may concern physical and mental health care. As with crime, the population's shared vulnerability to health problems tends to make this a high priority concern. The people of Washington take pride in their participation in healthy outdoor recreation. State laws curtail smoking in most public buildings and require catalytic devices on wood stoves to limit one source of growing outdoor air pollution. Enactment of a seat belt law in 1986 moved usage from just over a third to about two-thirds. But speaking broadly, mortality rates are comparable to those of other states. There seem to be few unusual health problems in the state, aside from higher presence of a few kinds of cancer in parts of the Puget Sound and an unusual rate of multiple sclerosis in eastern Washington. The possibility of thyroid and other problems linked to past nuclear operations of the Hanford Reservation or downwind from the Tri-cities has been under close study. Washington's children seem on most measures to have physical and mental health exceeding national averages, save for a few disturbing anomalies: there are somewhat higher than normal levels of deaths in the one to twelve month age group and considerably higher levels of adolescent suicides.[7] While about half of infant deaths arise from sudden infant death syndrome, one suspects that at least some may arise because of low-income ethnic minorities living some distance from health care centers. As in much of the country, many Washington rural areas are underserved by doctors and medical facilities.

During the 1970s the state seemed to underfund mental health facilities. This has since improved, but there are persistently recurring problems concerning the quantity and quality of staffing. But unemployability, often due to mental health problems or alcohol, has swelled the homeless population in some places, particularly in Seattle.

While estimates of numbers of homeless vary wildly, we do know that there are over 131,000 low-income Washingtonians using food stamps.[8] Although Medicaid (medical care for the indigent) has relieved medical problems of the poor, in 1991 a federal judge ruled that the state did not pay enough to cover real costs to medical providers who were forced to bear the burden themselves or pass it on as higher fees to other, paying patients.

A problem varying with the business cycle, statewide unemployment reached 12 percent in the 1982 recession, but showed wide variation among counties, ranging from a low of about 3 percent in Whitman County, with its stable employment base in wheat farming and Washington State University, to highs nearing 20 percent in Skamania or Pend Oreille counties, where volatile construction and logging jobs dominate.

As explained in chapter ten, the state's high reliance on the sales tax (which exempted food after a 1978 initiative) as well as other revenue sources—such as the lottery—has arguably given Washington one of the nation's most regressive revenue systems.

Most national studies show that education reinforces rather than overcomes the advantages of higher family income. But if better access to education does not affect inequalities among *groups*, it is still important for *individual* life chances. Without it, hope of equal opportunity seems an idle dream. Recognizing inequalities in local property tax bases, Washington state's supreme court ruled that the state, rather than the localities, had primary responsibility for funding basic education. Normally, issues in state education have been less concerned with content than with levels of funding, including teacher salaries and possible merit pay, the latter questions being influenced by the high presence of school teachers in the state legislature as well as by the vaunted prowess of teachers' union lobbyists.

In higher education, the state has a system of community or two-year colleges, important for vocational education for many lower-income people. However, the system seems overbuilt in some regions of less population growth while underbuilt in places with unusually strong growth, such as the suburbs north and east of Seattle. The state has four public four-year regional institutions, with base campuses at Cheney, Ellensburg, Bellingham, and near Olympia, but these have not reached all students desiring bachelor's or master's degrees, and many are unable to find a private college or university within the reach of distance or financial means. The recent development of branch campuses by existing universities may aid educational access for "place-bound" students, such as older students already tied to house, family, and job. But some faculty—especially at the research universities of the University of Washington and Washington State University—have feared a drain on resources needed by the home institutions.

Washington's Politics: Selection of Means

We have discussed how people choose their ends in politics, illustrating policy concerns of distinctive groups regarding status, safety, and economic advantages. There are no group minds or group actors, but reference to group categories often pervades the thoughts of the individuals who act. If so in choice of political ends, it is even more obviously true in the selection of political means.

In this, politics is not so much an individual as a team sport. Joining others is the name of the game. If politically engaged individuals normally favor some groups over others, they are naturally selective in choosing their coalition partners. They only rarely ally with traditional rivals. "Strange bedfellow" coalitions are usually temporary, with limited political aims.

In most coalitions, one pools resources—energies, votes, expertise, money—to seek greater success in policy aims. Often, partners have complementary resources. One may have strong finances and another expertise. But in other cases, coalitions form merely to attain some threshold of a resource, as in aligning enough votes to win an election.

Those unable to form a coalition with clout may find their political options narrowed to what can be called "strategic choices of the politically weak." The politically weak adapt to adverse authority rather than attempting to control it: enduring (somehow accept it), exiting (move somewhere else), or evading (hiding who you are or what you are doing, as in the obvious case of illicit tax evasion). Note that often in such choices, one acts alone, refusing to join a coalition or unable to form an alliance.

While an interest group normally has a narrower purpose and does not run candidates for public office under its own label, a political party tends to have larger aims and employs its label principally to harvest votes for favored candidates. As discussed in chapter four, business and other advantaged interests tend to be more conservative, and tend to give disproportionate backing to the Republican party, whereas labor and certain disadvantaged groups have tended toward liberalism and more often lean toward the Democrats.

Once aligned with an effective interest group or a mainstream political party, one may attempt to secure actual control of political authority by a trio of strategies—structuring, recruiting, and influencing. Modern democratic norms require that we limit any power struggle to peaceable, recurring competitions among institutional forms (structures), candidates for office (recruitment), or ideas (influence). The definition of acceptable competition is further specified in Washington's constitution, statutes, court decisions, or even customary ethical expectations. For example, as explained in chapter six, the initiative process often reflects competition among ideas.

In the structures field, groups attempt to influence decisions by controlling the governing agency or structure responsible for particular decisions. The author has elsewhere elaborated nine subfields of structures maneuvers.[9] But the basic premise is: remove decisional powers from agencies where you expect to lose; keep or place power where you and your pals can prevail.

Unlike Yertle the Turtle in the Dr. Seuss story, no one in a democracy is supposed to monopolize all powers. The 1889 Washington Constitution codified more specific structural restraints, broadly imitating the U. S. Constitution with some local modifications. Thus there is a constitutional principle of separation of powers among the governor, the legislature, and the courts. As shown in chapter two, it is extremely difficult to make politically sensitive structural revisions in the state constitution, and many structural changes are politically sensitive.

There are other fields for structural maneuver, especially in the state bureaucracy, court systems, and varying government levels (see chapters five, seven, and eight). For example, as noted in chapter seven, some reformers would like to increase the ability of governors to appoint top agency officials or to consolidate bureaucratic units as they please. But with a politically baleful eye, state legislatures often block any change on either score. Sometimes the state electorate may become the favored arena, as in recourse to direct votes, called initiatives and referenda (see chapter six).

Let us turn to the recruitment field of political means for those attempting to control political authority. While it sounds a bit military, "recruitment" is political science jargon for selecting persons to fill offices. Here, one attempts to shape policy by controlling which persons get into the specific offices that control the political decisions of concern. The recruitment field of action touches rules regarding formal and informal criteria of eligibility, who selects, numbers of incumbents, conditions of tenure (such as the term limitation initiative of 1991), and the like, but the main idea is simple: to get your way in public policy, get *their* rascals out, put *your* good guys in!

While recruitment politics can involve favorable appointments (see especially chapter seven), it more familiarly involves winning elections (see especially chapters three, four, and eleven). In regard to elections, the state has some history of "third party" strength up to the 1920s, and it remains easy for third parties to get on the ballot and even briefly state their views in the state voter pamphlet.[10] But, perhaps in large part due to the plurality voting rules of the electoral system, the state has settled into a closely competitive two-party system. This system is complicated by much independence and split-ticket voting, both in primary and general elections. The state has an open or blanket primary election system which encourages cross-overs of party identifiers. State voter turnout has been somewhat above national averages.

Finally, in the influence field, powers and personnel remain constant, but policy is ultimately controlled by shaping the minds or wills of those in office. The influence strategy includes three broad subfields of action: framing of persuasive messages, effectively delivering them, and then reinforcing them with hints of rewards for compliance or punishments for non-compliance. But the main game is clear: regardless of who is in office, how can I get my way with them?

Direct means of influence may include legislative lobbying, but indirect means may turn to mass media to influence public opinion (see chapters three and four). A state voters' pamphlet assures the possibility of at least basic competitiveness of messages regarding issues placed before the electorate in initiatives and referenda, since it invites pro and con essays. As elsewhere in the nation, Washington's major newspapers and television stations tend to have rather conservative owners and editors, but this is partially offset by some relatively liberal reporters. More "balance" in coverage is also encouraged as newspapers consolidate in urban markets, with hopes of placating Republican, Democratic, or independent subscribers.

Structures, recruitment, and influence are the main games of political means, although they are often obscured under many kinds of justificatory languages.[11] While courteously considering such varied arguments, it is important to look beyond words to ask what political agents are really after in the way of ends, and what they are really doing in the way of means. How would it make a difference and who would win or lose? Politics is not very complicated if one keeps that simple question in mind, even when one duly listens to all the fine rhetoric.

The structures, recruitment, and influence games are usually played in Washington state with civility and good humor. Modern Washingtonians have been militantly committed to moderation, which usually bodes well for majorities. But let us exit with provocative questions. Do moderate politics always imply that no one gets hurt? What of those who are weak on votes, campaign contributions, or articulate expertise? Must they be excluded from the benefits of democracy?

Notes

1. See Mary W. Avery, *Washington: A History of the Evergreen State* (Seattle: University of Washington Press, 1965), and Paul L. Beckett, *From Wilderness to Enabling Act: The Evolution of the State of Washington* (Pullman: Washington State University Press, 1968). Chapter two offers more detail on the origin of the state constitution.

2. By 1991, surplus power capacity was disappearing due to economic growth-induced demand. Some urged completion of at least one of the two "mothballed" reactor projects, whether Satsop No. 3 (76 percent completed) or Hanford No. 1 (63 percent finished). Transmission lines carrying power from east to west over the Cascades also neared maximum load capacity. A new threat to generating capacity arose from pressures rising from threatened extinction of Snake River salmon runs unless more water was allowed to slip past dams without power generation. Some proposed construction of a parallel channel to ease downstream migration of young salmon (called smolts), which have suffered high mortality from predator fish, as well as warming water in the reservoir pools.

3. See the Washington Child Health Research and Policy Group report, "The State of Washington's Children," 1991, reported in *Spokane Spokesman-Review*, 14 Je. 1991.

4. Political scientists face formidable problems in measuring and explaining group identities, although the consequences of such identities in shaping policy preferences seem obvious enough. Yet because people have a multiplicity of possible group identities, and also because of informational problems on how policy alternatives may impact such groups, most individual social characteristics at best weakly predict policy preferences, as is apparent in chapter three. A rare exception is that lower income strongly predicts demand for more government services, which is not unexpected.

5. *Statistical Abstract of the United States* (1990).

6. Report of the Washington Association of Sheriffs and Police Chiefs, *Spokane Spokesman-Review/Chronicle*, 22 Je. 1991. The FRI study is reported in the same newspaper, 11 Aug. 1991.

7. Washington infant deaths of 4.5 per 1,000 live births compare with 3.5 in the nation. In the case of suicides, the per 100,000 rates for adolescent girls was 2.5 in the nation, but five in Washington; for boys, it was less than 10 in the nation but 15 in Washington. See *Spokane Spokesman-Review*, 14 Je. 1991.

8. *Seattle Post-Intelligencer*, 22 Nov. 1990. One article suggests that the numbers of homeless could reach as high as 170,000 in Washington state. See *Spokane Spokesman-Review*, 29 Mar. 1991.

9. Terrence E. Cook, *The Great Alternatives of Social Thought: Aristocrat, Saint, Capitalist, and Socialist* (Savage, Md.: Rowman & Littlefield, 1991).

10. Prior to the 1920s, Washington state had a history of rather radical labor movements (such as the Industrial Workers of the World, or Wobblies) and political parties (such as the Socialist party). A Democratic party chairman, James A. Farley, once spoke in jest of "the forty-seven states and the soviet of Washington."

11. On the varieties of arguments and how they are used, see Cook, "Political Justifications: The Use of Standards in Political Appeals," *The Journal of Politics*, 42 (1980), pp. 511-537.

James A. Huntgate of Pullman attended Washington's constitutional convention in 1889, but had to leave before signing the document. In 1931 the *Seattle Times* staged this ceremony, allowing Huntgate to become a signer. "It is not many men who have signed a constitution 42 years after its adoption," he said. Vibert Jeffers photo. *Susan Parish Collection*©

Chapter Two

The Washington Constitution: Fundamental Law and Principles for the State

Linda Louise Blackwelder Pall

CONSTITUTIONS DEFINE THE NATURE of government—its structure, powers, limitations, and relations between government and the governed. Whether for a nation or a state, a basic task of constitutional construction is to provide a fundamental framework for governmental operation. The compact between government and its citizens, resting on the premise that "we, the people" are the creators and crafters of government, frames the conditions for lawful governance as set forth in the constitution.

The United States Constitution sets out a structure of limited government, with a limited grant of authority to the federal government for the enumerated powers set forth in the document. The states, by contrast, possess all other powers not defined and delegated within the federal constitution. This makes each state a semi-autonomous entity with a broad range of powers. While the federal government is limited by being allowed to do only what the constitution expressly permits, state governments can do anything unless specifically denied that power in the constitution. The Tenth Amendment of the U. S. Constitution gives to the states this breadth: "The powers not delegated to the United States by the Constitution, nor prohibited by it to the States are reserved to the States respectively, or to the people."

Since state government possesses all powers not given to the federal government, state constitutions do not grant power but rather structure and limit it. Even though constitutions are supposed to confine themselves to fundamental law and only the most essential aspects of governmental power, state constitutions are almost all longer and more detailed than their federal model.[1] Washington's state constitution is a contorted combination of basic law with dozens of specific provisions that are the functional equivalents of legislative enactments at the constitutional level. This excessive detail, running to some thirty thousand words, operates as a check on legislative authority and as a practical obstacle to flexible, modern government. Washington's constitution-crafters and other late-nineteenth century constitution authors sought to curb legislative power in the face of their distrust of the legislature. By the excessive, specific, and detailed approach to constitutional prohibitions, procedures, and propositions, the emerging constitutions became snapshots of the politics and culture of their period, providing serious drawbacks for future generations and for constitutional interpretation. Consequently, constitutions from this period have been the subject of frequent amendment activity; in Washington's case, 82 times during its first one hundred years.[2]

With all of these problems, the Washington Constitution remains a vital, important, even progressive document which serves as the foundation of state government and the touchstone of citizens' rights.[3]

Understanding how a state constitution functions involves reviewing the circumstances of drafting and adopting the document; examining the text itself; and looking at the state supreme court's interpretation of constitutional principles in various substantive areas of the law. Using this method to examine the Washington Constitution provides a route through controversial, complex, and even incomprehensible arguments over application, interpretation, and continued relevance of the document. The continuing vitality and centrality of the Washington Constitution unfolds with this examination.

Washington: The Constitutional Struggle, 1869-1888

For a territory to become a self-governing state, moving from federal to local control, the territory needed to authorize a constitutional convention and petition Congress for statehood. From 1869 through 1874, the question appeared on the Washington territorial ballot in each election—and failed each time. However, in 1876, when it appeared that the Walla Walla country might be lost to Oregon, voters authorized a constitutional convention by a vote of 5,698 to 1,530. The first of Washington's two constitutional conventions followed.

In June 1878, the first convention opened in Walla Walla. As there was substantial interest in reuniting the panhandle counties of Idaho with eastern Washington, the 15 delegates selected in April 1878 were joined by a non-voting member from northern Idaho. The convention worked 40 days, then adjourned with its constitutional product complete. It was typical for the period: long, detailed, and distrusting of power from any source.

On the whole, the territorial press and public received the document well, and approval followed in November 1878—in Washington by a vote of 6,537 to 3,236 and in Idaho by 737 to 26. Separate articles on women's suffrage and a woman's right to hold elective office failed by wide margins. Unfortunately, statehood was not forthcoming. The territorial delegate to Congress proved unsuccessful in getting a statehood bill passed in each and every Congress through the 1880s.

After years of struggle and partisan balancing between Republicans and Democrats in the post-Civil War years, the Republicans won both houses of Congress and the presidency in 1888. The Democrats, who held congressional power through most of the 1880s, had been loath to admit a state, with its new congressional representatives, from Republican ranks. Republicans, in control of the senate for most of the period, were similarly unenthusiastic about admitting Democratic party power bases in other territories. But in the waning days of Congress, following the 1888 election, the logjam broke and an omnibus statehood bill passed. President Grover Cleveland signed it on February 22, 1889, authorizing Washington, North Dakota, South Dakota, and Montana to hold conventions and proceed through the congressional hoops to statehood.

Constitutional Convention: Again

With the congressional mandate, Washington convened its second constitutional convention on July 4, 1889.[4] The Enabling Act balanced representation, making one-party domination difficult. In the Washington convention, Democrats provided more than a third of the delegates and chaired some of the important convention committees, including the Preamble and Bill of Rights Committee, the State, County, and Municipal Indebtedness Committee, and the Education and Educational Institutions Committee.[5]

What were the most important political, legal, and social concerns for convention delegates more than a hundred years ago? Many have a contemporary ring: distrust of government, fear of unbridled legislative power, concentration of political power inside and outside government, concern about the excessive power of corporations and other private entities that could shape governmental actions, and a deep and abiding concern for individual rights and liberties. The delegates of more than a century ago grappled with opposite ends of a problem that persists today: how can the individual and the state be protected from powerful, well-financed business interests, while at the same time the state tries to attract investment and business activity to develop its natural resources?

In 1889, many people believed it desirable—indeed necessary—to lure powerful financial interests into the state to enhance economic development. Railroads, timber interests, mining companies, and other businesses were an essential element of the partnership that would bring financial success to the new state. Yet, reformers could see great potential for abuse of power with the individual and small business concerns engulfed by the larger, more powerful, better-financed interests. The constitutional convention debate over the corporations article is an excellent example of this conflict.[6]

The Committee on Corporations Other Than Municipal addressed these issues by attempting to place significant constitutional limits on corporations. Opponents of this course argued that much of the corporations article really did not fit the fundamental constitutional framework and that such matters were better left to the legislature. Proponents had substantial, well-grounded fears of powerful economic interests controlling the legislature so that no effective or meaningful legislative measures of control would ever emerge, given the power of such economic lobbies in legislatures of the time. As a result of this division, the Committee of the Whole failed to adopt a number of significant measures proposed by the Committee on Corporations, including restriction of corporate activity to charter-authorized activities, requirements to maintain open records and a corporate office in Washington, and establishment of a constitutionally authorized railroad commission to regulate common carriers. Post-statehood life with the article presents a mixed review. Many matters were left to the legislature for enactment. The authorized, but not established, railroad commission of Article XII, Section 18, waited until 1907 to come into existence.[7] National legislation had more effect on the control of monopolies, trusts, and railroads in Washington than did state constitutional provisions and state legislation.

Though the framers of the Washington Constitution reflected a desire to control corporate interests, they attempted to balance this control against the need to attract business and capital. Frankly, the constitutional effort largely failed. Comparing the frequency of citation of Article XII with other constitutional provisions reviewed by appellate courts, it becomes clear it did not provide the pivotal tool that the framers may have had in mind. The article has been cited in a little more than 90 cases, most of which were determined on statutory grounds, according to a 1989 review.[8] By contrast the eminent domain provision of the Washington Constitution, Article I, Section 16, has been a direct subject of discussion in nearly 300 cases. Though the framers exhibited deep distrust of corporations, Washington came to grips with the uneasy relationship between governmental and corporate power through legislative means rather than constitutional principle. The ambivalence of 1889 remains alive and well more than a hundred years later, and more flexible and useful tools for dealing with corporate power are found outside the constitutional structure. The constitutional provisions on corporations, despite the compromises and legislative character of many of the sections, give a clear and unambiguous direction to public policy: protect individual rights, curb corporate power, and keep government in a close regulatory role with respect to its corporate creations.[9]

Fundamental distrust of legislatures was another theme of concern ingrained in the Washington Constitution. The constitution contains numerous restraints on legislative action and constitutional amendment, as well as a provision for municipal home rule to curb legislative intrusion. As a direct check on the legislature and its actions, the convention adopted a gubernatorial veto of broad and comprehensive scope. Washington's governor gained the power to veto entire sections or line items of any bill containing more than one item, whether for appropriations or not. Only a two-thirds vote of both houses of the legislature could override the governor's veto. Effectively, the governor could legislate with only one-third of the legislature supporting his or her position. In 1974, voters approved the 62nd amendment to Washington's constitution, restricting the item veto to appropriation measures, rather than sentences and phrases that could change the substantive meaning of legislation. With the amendment, the governor could still veto portions of non-appropriation bills, but had to negate "entire sections."[10] But the original framers of the constitution had viewed governors as more responsible, trustworthy repositories of public trust than the venal, easily swayed, part-time, non-professional legislators who would populate the halls of Olympia. In 1889, attendees of the constitutional convention had few concerns about executive power and its potential for abuse. Though the essence of this constitutional provision creates a problem of separation of powers, the 1889 convention did not flinch in providing the broadest possible opportunity for governors to become "super-legislators."

The amendment process the convention adopted resides first with the legislature. As outlined in Article XXIII, Section 1, any member of the legislature may propose an amendment; it must then be approved by a two-thirds majority of both houses before being referred to the electorate at the next general election. A simple majority of those voting on the amendment adopts it. Piecemeal revision via the legislature has thus been the rule since 1889.

The constitution does not provide for direct popular amendment. Indirect popular amendment can occur through an arduous process resulting in a constitutional convention. This process begins with the legislature. Both houses must approve a call for a convention. This is then submitted to the voters. A majority of all those voting in the election, not merely those voting on the constitutional convention measure, must approve the proposal. If the proposition survives to this point, the legislature must provide for the convention, delegates must be elected, the convention must meet, and its product must be submitted for voter approval.

The only time in Washington history that a constitutional convention proposition made it to the ballot box came in 1918 when voters decisively refused to take up the legislature's invitation to wholesale constitutional revision. Efforts to revise the constitution via convention surfaced again in the era of Governor Dan Evans. Even with the support of highly influential political players, numerous citizens' groups, and endorsements throughout the state, the effort failed. As in 1918, special interests that saw some advantage in the current constitutional framework feared losses if elected delegates wrote a complete revision. Also, citizens felt no great urgency to change. Constitutional revision will remain a piecemeal process and the legacies of 1889 will remain Washington's fundamental law.

Those attending the 1889 convention constructed Washington's constitution similarly to others crafted during the same period. The separation of power into three branches (with the gubernatorial veto exception discussed above) was standard fare, as was a two-branch legislature with biennial sessions of no more than 60 days. The executive branch had, in addition to the governor, a bouquet of other constitutionally enumerated administrative officers: lieutenant governor, secretary of state, treasurer, auditor, attorney general, superintendent of public instruction, and commissioner of public lands. The framers copied the judicial article of the constitution (Article IV) from California's judicial structure, providing in exquisite detail the structure and activities of the judiciary.

When all was said and most was done, two topics of extreme controversy remained outside the constitution for independent consideration and approval by the voters: women's suffrage and prohibition. The territorial legislature of 1883-1884 had granted women the right to vote and to serve on juries. But the territorial supreme court eliminated those rights in 1887 and 1888.[11] Constitutional conventioners came under considerable pressure from women's suffrage advocates. However, in a move that echoed the actions of Washington's first constitutional convention, the delegates voted to submit a separate article to the voters. The same sidestepping came with an article prohibiting the sale, manufacture, or "disposal of" alcoholic beverages. The delegates wanted to assure passage of the constitution and hence statehood. These two highly controversial topics would have placed that in jeopardy. Considering the vote tallies, the framers may well have been right. On October 1, 1889, Washington voters approved the constitution: 40,152 to 11,879. Yet they defeated the women's suffrage article, 34,513 to 16,527, and prohibition 31,487 to 19,546.

President Benjamin Harrison proclaimed Washington's statehood on November 11, 1889, and the 42nd state became a star on the flag. With statehood came interpretation and modification of Washington's constitution.

Washington judges have the final say on constitutional meaning through their exercise of judicial review. As explained in chapter seven, when a judge decides that a law conflicts with the constitution, he or she declares it null and void. Such declarations may have a profound impact on the state. But applying the constitutional compact to legislative enactments or executive actions requires considerable research and contemplation, for the meaning of constitutional provisions is not always obvious.

Several approaches are available to judges as they apply the constitution to the resolution of important economic and social conflicts. Throughout more than 100 years of state history, *textual, intentional, doctrinal, structural,* and *political* approaches have provided judges with guides in resolving constitutional disputes.[12]

Constitutional Analysis: The Text and the Framers' Intent

To understand the meaning of constitutional provisions, citizens, scholars, and judges must begin with the text of the constitutional provision itself. The language can be self-evident. To say that "the governor's item veto must be exercised within 20 days from the passage of the bill by the legislature" is relatively unambiguous language and does not need extensive interpretation. If, however, the constitution's words require interpretation, they must be given their common and ordinary meaning.[13] Additionally, since the meaning of such words may have changed over a hundred years of history and linguistic arabesques, the interpretation must take into consideration the meaning of the words at the time of the constitution's writing. This does not mean the usage of only those learned lawyers and professionals who were delegates to the convention; the meaning must be that of the ordinary citizen who voted to ratify the document.

Textual constitutional analyses at the state level is also constrained by higher law, such as the United States Constitution. Any construction of Washington state constitutional principles cannot be in conflict with the U. S. Constitution or federal laws in effect at the time of the state constitution's adoption. Any interpretation of the Washington Constitution would have to be in harmony with the provisions of the 1889 Enabling Act which authorized the writing of it in the first place. An interesting aspect of this can be found by looking at Section 4 of the Enabling Act which states that "provision shall be made for the establishment and maintenance of systems of public schools which shall be open to all children of [Washington], and free from sectarian control."[14] Whatever state constitutional interpretation is made concerning public schools, it appears that the Enabling Act would restrict any constitutional interpretations that would open the way to sectarian practices in public schools in Washington. Of course, there is considerable latitude available to jurists when they are faced with interpretation of what is and is not sectarian, starting with the "common and ordinary meaning" of "sectarian" in 1889. The constitutional framers incorporated this proviso into Washington's constitution in Article IX, Section 4.

History is more than footnote material in the interpretation of constitutional provisions. The *intent of the framers,* as well as the intent of the people adopting the document, must always be considered. Many have offered arguments advocating adherence to the text of a constitution and the framers' intent in the guise of getting back to the real foundations of the constitutional document.[15] More often than not, these arguments seek to constrain more liberal, progressive, and modern interpretations of constitutional provisions.[16]

To balance these perspectives, understanding the sources and intellectual context of the constitutional convention is valuable information, but should not be the end of the search and analysis of constitutional structures and limits. The next step toward understanding and interpreting constitutional principles is to look at what courts have, in fact, done over the years to interpret the state constitution.

Constitutional Analysis: *Stare Decisis,* Structures, and Politics

The moment Washington adopted its constitution and the day after it became a state, things were already changing. Change is a constant factor in human history, and resistance to change is one constant factor in judicial reasoning. The law is built upon prior decisions (*stare decisis*), consistency, predictability, and stability. The very essence of much legal thought and philosophy relies upon a strong notion of conservatism, adherence to precedent, and incremental change, if change there be at all. Such is the basis for the *doctrinal approach.*

The *structural* perspective permits judges to interpret the constitution in terms of its general principles, such as separation of powers, federalism, or the idea of a constitution as a contract between the people and their government. Should, for example, a legislative act seriously damage relations between the executive and legislative branches, it would be invalidated.

As the word implies, judges taking a *political* perspective would base their decisions on the prevailing political mood of the state. They would largely ignore the text, intent, doctrine, and structure of the fundamental law.

Textual, intentional, and doctrinal approaches to understanding and applying constitutional provisions assure a judiciary that tends to leave change largely to the political branches of government. Such a judiciary is *restraintist.* However, the political branches may be unable or unwilling to bring about change in order to confront pressing economic, political, or social problems. Judges may intervene, by means of a political and sometimes structural perspective, and change constitutional applications on their own as they decide cases brought to their courts. Such judges are *activists.*

Activism and restraint, or independence and accountability, as explained in chapter eight, are the two extremes of constitutional interpretation. Resistance to change or modernity in the face of significant social forces can undermine respect for law and the courts, as well as generate potentially debilitating conflict with the other branches of government. The conjuring trick that appellate courts must perform is striking a balance between a hide-bound, historical, or precedent-driven philosophy, resistant to social change or economic necessities, and the politically rudderless approach that is too often ignorant or disparaging of that which has gone before. The balance between judicial restraint and judicial activism is often a matter of considerable argument, cast in the language of "framers' intent" versus "progress."

There are few courts at either end of this spectrum. Most, including Washington's supreme court, have a tradition of balancing constitutional interpretation with the needs of a modern, changing society. Much of what government and private individuals must now contend with lay outside the realm of even adventure novels in 1889. For example, in 1889, no one considered questions of privacy about computer data, yet the people of that era widely accepted the general principle of protection of individual rights against intrusion of government. Can state constitutional interpreters of the 1990s craft a right for citizens to maintain privacy in light of the vast array of private computer data now available about each of us? Or must citizens resort to legislative protection alone?

Looking at how the Washington Supreme Court has treated important constitutional issues gives an understanding of how important the Washington Constitution remains as a source of fundamental law and personal protection of civil rights. The Washington court has been, on the whole, generous in its expansive view of constitutional protections for the people of the state, bringing through to the 1990s a keen appreciation of the framers' advocacy of personal rights and liberties, a healthy skepticism of governmental power, and an understanding of the ever-changing threats to personal rights.

Free Speech

The Washington Constitution's Declaration of Rights provision on freedom of speech, contained in Article I, Section 5, is broad and expansive: "Every person may speak, write, and publish on all subjects, being responsible for the abuse of that right."

Federal constitutional language in the First Amendment focuses on governmental action: "Congress shall make no law." Interpretation of the First Amendment free speech guarantee has focused on state action, i. e. there must be some governmental attempt to limit or curtail speech or expression for the First Amendment to encompass the matter. Private activity restricting speech must be dealt with other than in the analysis of constitutional rights. Statutory or common law restrictions may apply, but constitutional-level protections against private intrusions are inapplicable at the federal level. One prime example of this in federal constitutional jurisprudence can be found in *Lloyd Corp. v. Tanner.*[17] The question presented to the U. S. Supreme Court was whether a private shopping center could restrict access of private individuals who wanted to protest the war in Vietnam. The court found that the shopping center could be restrictive, since it involved no state action. Tanner could find no solace or protection in the First Amendment.

However, free speech under the Washington Constitution has been treated differently. In *Alderwood Associates v. Washington Environmental Council,*[18] a four-judge plurality using a structural approach based on federalism found that shopping center owners are required to accommodate reasonable free speech and petitioning on their property so long as the private property interests do not outweigh the exercise of free speech. Federalism permits state constitutional provisions to replace their counterparts in the federal constitution if they grant more freedoms. A fifth justice joined the plurality, concurring in the result but arriving at it via a different analysis involving the state's police powers with respect to collection of initiative signatures.[19] Four other justices, fearing activism of the plurality, objected vigorously to the elimination of a "state action" requirement for application of constitutional protection.[20]

This sharply divided court chose a route of accommodation and balance between the rights of the speakers and the private property owner. Private actors who seek to restrict speech will have to demonstrate that the expression does not merit protection. Rather than requiring state involvement directly or via a surrogate, the plurality chose to reject "state action" directly and evaluate the merit of each case in order to protect free speech values.

The decision resulted in a running feud in law reviews over the extent to which the state action requirement had really died, since *Alderwood* was only a plurality and has been limited to initiative petition efforts. Justice Robert F. Utter, author of the *Alderwood* decision, has encouraged a strong and independent view of Washington's Declaration of Rights and constitutional protections. Federalism is a viable principle to Utter:

> An independent interpretation and application of the Washington Constitution is not just legitimate, historically mandated, and logically essential; it is, in the words of the Washington Supreme Court, a "duty" that all state courts owe to the people of Washington.[21]

In 1986, James M. Dolliver, then chief justice of the Washington Supreme Court, strongly criticized the Utter plurality in *Alderwood* for dispensing with the state action requirement and related analysis. Dolliver's structural approach using the idea of the contract leads to different results:

> The fundamental fact is that a constitution is a compact between a united people and their new government. . . . The power the state uses to defend its citizens from each other, however, is its police power . . . which is exercised by the legislature, not the courts.[22]

Because of the centrality of free speech values to democracy, whether the Washington Supreme Court takes an expansive or a narrow view of its state constitutional provisions affecting free speech is a question with practical impact on every Washington citizen. Can you solicit for your favorite political candidate at your local shopping mall? Can you collect signatures for an initiative campaign there? Will you be protected if you want to distribute literature on a private college campus? What about exercising your free speech rights in private, "planned" communities? Will the Washington Constitution protect you if you want to collect petition signatures in a migrant labor camp? What about access to a nursing home? Or while you are on the job? Can your condominium association prevent you from using the recreation facilities for your political meeting?

Whether you, as a Washington citizen, will receive protection from those who would seek to curtail your free expression will depend upon whether the Washington Supreme Court takes the broad, expansive view of the plurality in *Alderwood* or whether the court takes its policy lead from analysts of the federal constitution and requires state action before constitutional protection is extended.

Church and State

Religion is addressed in three places in the Washington Constitution: first, in the preamble where gratitude to the "Supreme Ruler of the Universe" is extended for our liberties; second, in the Declaration of Rights which provides for free exercise of religion and prevents state sponsorship of religion via establishment language;[23] and third, in a special section of an article which tracks language from the Enabling Act authorizing Washington to seek statehood and requiring public schools to be "forever free from sectarian control and influence."[24]

To understand these provisions, one can look first at the intent of those who drafted them. It is clear that the framers were not hostile to religion. The constitutional proceedings detail substantial references to the benefits and importance of religion.[25] Though the delegates did not intend to prohibit the discussion of religion or religious influences in schools, for example, there was specific antipathy to sectarian influence and sponsorship. The delegates were familiar with anti-Catholic, and to a lesser extent anti-Mormon, sentiments, though they did not universally embrace them. Washington's neighbor, Idaho, successfully adopted a number of anti-Mormon state constitutional provisions, among them denial of suffrage and the right to hold office.

Washington's strong constitutional provisions in this area provide a fertile source for state constitutional analysis and protection of religious civil liberties.

Instead of reflecting federal jurisprudence in this area, the Washington Supreme Court has firmly staked out its own territory, interpreting the provisions of Article IX, Section 4 of the state constitution prohibiting state funding of sectarian education.

In Weiss v. Bruno,[26] the issue revolved around public funding for needy students in public and private schools from kindergarten through twelfth grade and in higher education. The court unequivocally concluded that the state constitution provides for an absolute prohibition against using public funds in sectarian schools "regardless of whether that benefit is characterized as 'indirect' or 'incidental.'"[27]

Such a position is a great distance from the United States Supreme Court's willingness to retreat from a firm distinction between church and state matters into a nebulous analysis. G. Alan Tarr, a scholar who has written often on the matter of state constitutions and legal systems, argues that the inability of the U. S. Supreme Court to provide legal uniformity, consistency, and comprehensibility in church/state conflicts on federal constitutional grounds is justification in itself for the state supreme court to look to its own state constitution for instruction and direction.[28] At the federal level, the court is split between separationists who would preserve a high wall between church and state and accommodationists who appear to be gaining the upper hand by allowing and even promoting religious practices in conjunction with government under certain circumstances. State constitutions like that of Washington, with relatively clear and unambiguous language on church/state relationships, provide a more likely source of consistency and predictability than the federal constitutional seesaw of inconsistency.

The distinctive state constitutional perspective of Washington provides a source for a clean division between church and state, especially in the public schools. As former Justice Hans Linde of the Oregon Supreme Court advocated, first address state law – including state constitutional provisions – for an answer to the speech or religion issue; failing that look to the federal constitution.[29] The clearer sources of many state constitutional provisions, including those of Washington, plus their clearer language, provide a more direct avenue for solution of many questions of religious liberty and practice arising in the context of state law.

Criminal Justice Issues: Search and Seizure

In the world of constitutional rights, nothing is more troublesome than extending constitutional protections, whether federal or state, to the accused. For the most part, law-abiding citizens regard the accused as, at best, unworthy, and, at worst, outright dangers to the rest of us. The notion of spending time and money through the courts on prolonged cases involving the accused strains the patience of many upstanding citizens. When the drug lords, the street gangs, and violent, sadistic thugs are at large in our society, many, perhaps even most, citizens agree with the broad latitude the U. S. Supreme Court has granted police and law enforcement agencies through a paring away of Fourth Amendment guarantees against unreasonable searches and seizures and Eighth Amendment protections against cruel and unusual punishment.

Again, state constitutional analysis in Washington has provided a different avenue. In the context of Article I, Section 7, "No person shall be disturbed in his private affairs, or his home invaded, without authority of law," the Washington Supreme Court has sharply limited a police officer's warrantless search of an automobile in *State v. Ringer*.[30] In 1984's *State v. Williams* it required officers to limit detention of a suspect to questioning and to use the least intrusive means available to investigate in.[31] In *Ringer* the court required the officer to weigh whether the exigent circumstances existed to justify an immediate search of the vehicle without a warrant against the suspect's privacy interests. In *Williams* the court placed similar decisional and procedural strictures on the officer. Neither of these decisions met with much support from the public nor from the law enforcement community. Both were roundly criticized despite their adherence to the text and the intention of the framers of Washington's constitution.

New, more conservative justices on the Washington Supreme Court prompted the court to revisit both of these cases. In 1986, the court overruled *Ringer* on the grounds that requiring a police officer to balance privacy interests on a case-by-case basis would be too difficult a rule.[32] Instead, the court paid lip service to the Washington Constitution's greater privacy rights and adopted a "balancing" standard where officers should be permitted to search a car following arrest but should not be able to gain access to any locked compartments, since the owner reasonably expected the contents of the locked compartment (or container) to remain private.

In *State v. Kennedy*,[33] not only did the court reject the *Williams* procedural direction, but also the independent state constitutional analysis. In *Kennedy* the court adopted the federal standard in stop-and-frisk cases that has created a line of cases wherein the person's privacy interests are entirely outweighed by the police officer's balancing of law enforcement necessity.[34] The Washington court adopted the federal demise of privacy rights under the Fourth Amendment for stop-and-frisk cases.

In *State v. Gunwall* the Washington Supreme Court has fashioned a set of neutral criteria to consider when the question of greater rights and liberties should be extended under the state, rather than the federal, constitution.[35] The neutral criteria include questions of constitutional text, constitutional structure, textual differences between state and federal documents, doctrinal and legal history within the state, and whether the rights at issue are of particular interest to state or local concerns.

Arbitrary governmental power can intrude upon anyone. The Washington Constitution's privacy protections can be a powerful source of defense of individual rights in the face of governmental criminal prosecutions.

Washington's ERA

Women's rights were not uppermost in the minds of those who gathered in Olympia in 1889 to draft Washington's constitution. Some of the same people who proposed strong religious liberty and a high wall between church and state did not mind using Scripture to oppose any constitutional provision supporting women's suffrage.

By 1972 many minds had changed. Women voted, served in the legislature, and were still victims of stereotypical views, some of which remained in the *Revised Code of Washington*. On November 7, 1972 the state constitutional amendment authorizing the Washington Equal Rights Amendment passed by a hair: 645,115 for and 631,746 against.

The Washington Supreme Court took an initially strong stand interpreting the state ERA, prohibiting all sex-based discrimination. It applied a strict scrutiny standard to all sex-based distinctions, requiring that an overwhelming state interest in the distinctions be proven. However, in several subsequent cases, the court backtracked, ruling that the state ERA only prohibited "harmful" discrimination. It even refused to apply the state ERA in a "ladies night" case where the male plaintiff complained he was not accorded the same admission privilege, in contravention of the ERA.[36] However, in a college athletics case, the court appears to have returned to its strict scrutiny standard. In *Blair v. Washington State University*[37] it found that the Whitman County trial court had improperly excluded football from its injunction requiring WSU to correct its inequities between men and women in the athletic program. The court reasoned that leaving football out would have perpetuated the discrimination and inequities suffered by women athletes and their coaches.

The changes wrought by *Blair* have meant much more than burgundy-colored cars for women coaches and letter jackets for female athletes. The prohibition of considering separate sex-based athletic budgets has forced WSU and every other state university in Washington to treat men and women equally and expand opportunities for women athletes in areas previously closed to them.

Questions remain, however, given the court's past rulings on the ERA. Will the court extend *Blair* to private institutions? Even though many jurists have argued for a "state action" requirement, the ERA's broad language points the way to extension to private institutions: "Equality of rights and responsibility under the law shall not be denied or abridged on account of sex."[38] Will the absolute standard be adopted in circumstances other than athletics, such as employment, for example? Arguably, *Blair* again points the way affirmatively, since this case involved the employment of staff.

Here, under state law, Washington citizens are able to secure rights which they would likely be denied under federal law. The Washington Constitution assures the protection of personal rights superior to those enjoyed under the U. S. Constitution as interpreted by the present supreme court.

Vitality of State Constitutions: "Not-so-New" New Federalism

Studying the Washington and other state constitutions is not a backwater of jurisprudence or a procedural cul-de-sac for scholars of dim imagination. In a time when the United States Supreme Court is paring away constitutional rights and liberties once thought to be obvious and secure, from free speech to defendants' rights, state constitutions are achieving far more prominence in civil rights cases with some state-connected component to them. What was once a question of mild academic interest has become a burning issue of primary importance for litigants: does the state constitution provide protection for fundamental rights in the case under consideration?

The federal constitutional rights embodied in the U. S. Constitution are treated as minimal standards—the floor, not the ceiling. State supreme courts, like Washington's, have been willing to read the state constitution carefully and with attention to the background, language, and subsequent court interpretations of constitutional provisions and have broadened and deepened, on the whole, the protections of life, liberty, property, privacy, and other fundamental rights enjoyed by citizens.

This analytical shift has touched almost everything, even the tort reform crisis. Can the legislature place a monetary cap on damage awards? No, according to the Washington Supreme Court, because that interferes with the state constitutional right to a jury trial and the scope of the jury's duties.[39] Can citizens circulate initiative petitions at their favorite shopping mall? Yes, according to the state supreme court's interpretation of the free speech rights found in the state constitution's Declaration of Rights.[40]

Constitutional amendments have added substantive law in public finance, gender equality, and dozens of other areas. Attempts at constitutional revision on a grand scale have failed, but efforts by the courts to enhance state constitutional jurisprudence have succeeded on a significant scale, where a broader grant of rights is recognized under the state than the federal constitution. For 20 years, those urging the "new federalism" and a revitalized view of state constitutional jurisprudence have worked in state supreme courts, law schools, and law offices, with some spectacular results. The extension of personal liberties has not been one vast, extended wave of triumph for the individual. Rather, state supreme courts in general, and Washington's in particular, have traveled this route in fits and starts.

The great message of it all is not complicated. The Washington Constitution derived from a convention more than a hundred years ago, populated by white males, most with social and economic privilege and most without a clue about the tremendous social, economic, and perceptual changes that would accrue to this state and her citizens in the coming century. Even so, that constitution contains powerful, effective checks on government's power over the governed, making the compact between state and citizen one of limits, with the interest of the citizen at heart.

The impact on ordinary Washington citizens will continue on a daily basis, whether citizens realize it or not. Can you walk, without police interference, in Washington's cities and towns? Can you go to a state university and expect to obtain the same benefits as other students, regardless of sex? Can you expect that the state will prohibit school districts from teaching the tenets of the Church of Nothing in Particular? Yes. You have several to thank for this: the delegates to the 1889 convention, the voters who approved the constitution, the voters who continue to amend and adjust it, the legal scholars who comment on it, the lawyers who litigate it, the judges who interpret it, and, vital to this chain, the courageous—or possibly foolish—citizen who will not roll over and give up when his or her rights may have been impaired.

The process has been long and still continues. The twists and turns are not always elegant. The process is human, capable of error and prejudice. Yet, it is also filled with people of courage, acting in good faith and with a deep commitment to the framers' intent as well as to changing facts, circumstances, judicial interpretations, and theories, in what Justice Dolliver calls "that glorious adventure of self government."[41] As he also says, "may it always be so."[42]

Notes

1. Only Vermont's constitution is shorter. The average state constitution is three times longer, including many specifics which would normally be thought of as legislative matters, such as Louisiana's designation, Article 19, Section 22, of Huey Long's birthday as a perpetual state holiday. See B. Alan Tarr and Mary C. A. Porter, *Supreme Courts in State and Nation* (New Haven: Yale University Press, 1988).
2. James M. Dolliver, "Condemnation, Credit and Corporations in Washington: 100 Years of Judicial Decisions – Have the Framers' Views Been Followed?" 12 *University of Puget Sound Law Review* 162 (1989). Hereafter cited as "Dolliver."
3. See William Brennan, "State Constitutions and the Protection of Individual Rights," 90 *Harvard Law Review* 489 (1977).
4. Idaho, without authorization from Congress, did the same. The four Enabling Act states were admitted in November 1889, while Idaho followed in July 1890.
5. For an analysis of the push toward statehood, see Paul L. Beckett, *From Wilderness to Enabling Act: The Evolution of the State of Washington* (Pullman: Washington State University Press, 1968). For a record of the constitutional convention, see Beverly Rosenow, *The Journal of the Washington State Constitutional Convention, 1889* (Seattle: Book Publishing Co., 1962). The original record was destroyed.
6. See Dolliver, pp. 190-195.
7. The commission has metamorphosed over the years into the Utilities and Transportation Commission.
8. Dolliver, p. 194.
9. See *American Export Door Corp. v. John A. Gauger Co.,* 154 Wash. 514, 519, 283 P. 462, 463 (1929).
10. Washington Constitution, Amendment LXII, Article III, Section 12.
11. *Harlan v. Territory of Washington,* 3 Wash. Terr. Repts. 131 (1887); *Bloomer v. Todd, et al.,* 3 Wash. Terr. Repts. 599 (1888).
12. For an analysis of decisional approaches to the exercise of judicial review see Charles Sheldon, " 'We Feel Constrained to Hold' . . . An Analysis of Judicial Review with the Washington Supreme Court," 27 *Gonzaga Law Review* 73 (1991/1992).
13. The Washington Supreme Court has set this standard in *State ex. rel. O'Connell v. Slavin,* 75 Wash. 2d 554, 557, 452, P.2d 943, 945 (1969).
14. Act of Feb 22, 1889, Ch. 180, Section 4, 25 Stat. 676, reprinted in Washington Revised Code at 19 and quoted in Justice Robert F. Utter's excellent article, "Freedom and Diversity in a Federal System: Perspectives on State Constitution and the Washington Declaration of Rights," 7 *University of Puget Sound Law Review* 491, 511 (1984).
15. See Robert Bork, "The Constitution, Original Intent and Economic Rights," 23 *San Diego Law Review* 823 (1986); H. Jefferson Powell, "Rules for Originalists," 73 *Virginia Law Review* 659 (1987); Philip Kurland, "History and the Constitution: All or Nothing at All?" 75 *Illinois Bar Journal* 262 (1987); Edwin Meese, "Addresses – Construing the Constitution," 19 *University of California Davis Law Review* 22 (1985); or William Rehnquist, "The Notion of a Living Constitution," 54 *Texas Law Review* 693 (1976).
16. For a stimulating attack on the intentionalists in the Washington context, see Pierre Schlag, "Framers' Intent: The Illegitimate Uses of History," 8 *University of Puget Sound Law Review* 283 (1985).
17. 407 U.S. 551 (1972).

18. 96 Wash. 2d 230, 635 P.2d 108 (1981).
19. See Justice Dolliver's concurring opinion, 96 Wash. 2d 230, 252, 635, P.2d 108, 120.
20. 96 Wash. 2d at 247, 635 P.2d at 118.
21. Utter, "Freedom and Diversity in a Federal System: Perspectives on State Constitutions and the Washington Declaration of Rights," 7 *University of Puget Sound Law Review* 491 (1984). See also Utter, "The Right to Speak, Write and Publish Freely, State Constitutional Protection Against Private Abridgment," 8 *University of Puget Sound Law Review* 157 (1985).
22. "The Washington Constitution and 'State Action': The View of the Framers," 22 *Willamette Law Review* 445, 456 (1986).
23. Utter and Edward Larson, "Church and State on the Frontier: The History of the Establishment Clauses in the Washington State Constitution," 15 *Hastings Constitutional Law Quarterly* 451, 468 (1988).
24. Washington Constitution, Article IX, Section 4.
25. See Utter and Larson, "Church and State," note 23, for an excellent historical analysis.
26. 82 Wash. 2d 199, 509 P.2d 973 (1973).
27. 82 Wash. 3d at 211, 509 P.2d at 981.
28. G. Alan Tarr, "Church and State in the States," 64 *Washington Law Review* 73 (1989).
29. Hans Linde, "Without 'Due Process'–Unconstitutional Law in Oregon," 49 *Oregon Law Review* 125 (1970).
30. 100 Wash. 2d 686, 674 P.2d 1240 (1983).
31. 107 Wash. 2d 733, 689 P.2d 1065 (1984).
32. *State v. Stroud,* 106 Wash. 2d 144, 720 P.2d 436 (1986).
33. 107 Wash. 2d 1, 726 P.2d 445 (1986).
34. This line of cases begins with *Terry v. Ohio,* 392 U.S. 1 (1968) and is popularly known as the *"Terry* stop," allowing an officer to stop a suspect on less than probable cause under certain circumstances. The exceptions allowing the stop now engulf the original *Terry* rationale.
35. 106 Wash. 2d 54, 720 P.2d 808 (1986).
36. *Seattle v. Buchanan,* 90 Wash. 2d 584, 584 P.2d 918 (1978) (an ordinance prohibiting exhibition of female breasts in public was not unconstitutional) and *MacLean v. First Northwest Industries,* 96 Wash. 2d 338, 635 P.2d 683 (1981) ('ladies night' at basketball games does not violate the state ERA).
37. 108 Wash. 2d 558, 740 P.2d 1379 (1987).
38. Washington Constitution, Article XXXI.
39. *Sofie v. Fibreboard Corp.,* 112 Wash. 2d 636, 771 P.2d 711, *amended,* 780 P.2d 260 (1989).
40. See *Alderwood,* 96 Wash. 2d 230, 635 P.2d 108 (1981).
41. Dolliver, p. 196.
42. *Ibid.*

Hunger march at the state capitol, 1932. Vibert Jeffers photo. *Susan Parish Collection*©

Chapter Three

Interest Groups in Washington State[1]

Elizabeth Walker

ISSUES REFLECTING THE INFLUENCE of various state and national interest groups have dominated the recent political agenda of Washington state. Spotted owls, reproductive choice, teachers' salaries, euthanasia, toxic waste incinerators, and the control of urban sprawl represent only a few of the topics on the minds of voters and elected officials. Issues such as these represent the conflict between, perhaps, inevitable antagonists – environmentalists and the timber industry; abortion opponents and supporters – but they also indicate the extent to which interest groups are active at the state government level. But not every issue confronting the legislature, on the governor's desk, or before the courts, reflects interest group activity. To understand the role of interest politics we need to agree on some definitions.

Interest Groups Defined

David Truman has defined an interest group as any collection of persons which is based on one or more shared attitudes and which makes certain demands upon other groups or organizations in society.[2] That is, an interest group comprises individuals who band together to protect their interests. Some authors argue that such a group must be organized in some manner, while others suggest that formal organization is not a prerequisite in order to qualify: any association of individuals, formally organized or not, that attempts to influence public policy is an interest group. The breadth of this definition would include groups such as labor unions, Realtors, and teachers but also "hidden groups and lobbies" which are not ordinarily required to register under state law.[3]

Interest groups became an important focus in political science immediately after World War II, when political scientists adopted a "group theory of politics."[4] By the 1950s, groups were considered primary actors in the policy-making process.[5] Political scientists, however, fail to agree on whether these groups are good for the political system. Many are suspicious of these organizations, in light of the increased financial clout they wield during election campaigns. In 1988, interest group contributions to congressional candidates amounted to almost one-third of all funds raised.[6] People have criticized interest groups for pursuing their own immediate agendas while paying little attention to the needs of the nation or state as a whole. Furthermore, it is recognized that not all groups are of equal power. Inequality of results inevitably occur in a system when financial and political resources available to groups are uneven.

On the other hand, these same groups are identified as sources of continuity in a constantly changing system. Groups become surrogates for individuals. Where single persons or even a few individuals lack political clout, an interest group draws the attention of policy makers. In the give-and-take of politics, policy decisions reflect compromises among many separate interests. For each group which develops to support one position, a comparable group usually emerges to represent the opposite view. This is part of the pluralist political system in the United States.

In any case, interest groups influence public policy. This can be accomplished in at least two ways. First, many interest groups, but not all, become involved in election campaigns. They help recruit candidates and offer financial and technical assistance. They may also expend considerable financial resources to defeat candidates whom they oppose.

Second, on a more continuous basis, groups become directly involved in the policy-making process. By utilizing salaried lobbyists and volunteers who are group members, organizations provide technical information to policy makers, testify at public hearings, and engage in social activities such as golf or expensive dinner parties. All of these activities are undertaken with one purpose in mind – to achieve a climate favorable to legislation or regulations which will be in the groups' interests.

Washington state has traditionally been classified as a state with a strong issue group system.[7] But categorizing Washington as a strong group system state is overly simplistic. According to Ronald Hrebenar and Clive Thomas, the extent to which groups interact with other policy makers is of most importance. In this schema, Washington is listed as a "dominant/complementary" state whose group systems alternate between two situations. This means that although groups have an overwhelming and consistent influence on policy, they have to work in conjunction with, or are constrained by, other parts of the political system.[8] For example, in Washington state, manufacturers, health practitioners, and trade unions wield considerable power, but all must operate within very stringent public disclosure requirements which constrain their activities.

The "dominant/complementary" schema provides a useful analytical framework for thinking about the role of interest groups within a particular state.

The Hrebenar and Thomas guidelines are helpful in analyzing the *types* of groups most likely to be active, the *methods* utilized by them in pursuing their goals, and the *power* exerted by these groups. Furthermore, they suggest that the *policy process* within an individual state will significantly condition the strength of groups within that particular geographic area.[9] Policy process includes the strength of political parties, the power of the governor, and the presence or absence of the initiative and referendum.

Factors Affecting Group Activity

The *constitutional and legal authority* of a state will affect which groups become politically active. All states share public policy responsibility for the health and welfare of their citizens. Therefore, it is expected that groups will emerge which have a vested interest in issues such as education, social services, and health. The states are responsible for the regulation of many business practices, such as liquor sales, banking, and insurance, as well as for the regulation of utilities, and they share with the federal government the responsibility for regulating the environment and labor practices. Of necessity, one would therefore expect interest groups which reflect these myriad issues to develop and exert some measure of influence in each state.

In addition to these policy areas which are uniform across the states, individual states have the flexibility to emphasize topics which may be unique to their particular state or region. Because of its bifurcated nature (see chapter one), Washington finds itself focusing on agricultural issues in the eastern part of the state and timber/industrialization in the western section. Therefore, one expects that groups related to these segments of the economy will wield considerable influence within the state.

A second consideration involves the political attitudes which exist within a state, particularly the *political culture and political ideology*. Political cultures vary in terms of the beliefs and values of the citizenry concerning the appropriate goals of a political system, the acceptable roles of the political parties, and the appropriate political activities of the citizens and professional politicians.

Daniel Elazar identified three basic political cultures within the states — traditionalistic, individualistic, and moralistic.[10] Washington has been identified as a moralistic/individualistic state. In other words, the political system's goal is to achieve the broadest good for the community with or without public pressure. Political parties are competitive but not necessarily controlled by professional politicians, and common citizens are viewed as the primary political actors.

In terms of ideology, Washington state has been most consistently categorized as a moderately liberal state. This designation reflects an ideological identification that was measured by asking respondents whether they considered themselves liberal, moderate, or conservative. Additionally, liberalism of state policy was measured by examining existing policy on a series of eight issues which ranged from public expenditures for education to the number of years since the state had ratified an Equal Rights Amendment. On both indices of liberalism, Washington was clearly "left of center." Only 16 states, most of them in the Northeastern region of the country, significantly exceeded the degree of liberalism found among the electorate and as reflected in state policies in Washington state.[11]

States with predominantly moralistic political cultures will have governments that take an active role in solving social and political problems. They will also place greater restrictions on acceptable group tactics and have more extensive and stringently enforced public disclosure laws. In contrast, predominantly traditionalistic political cultures tend to be more conservative, with less activist governments.

Evidence concerning a moralistic political culture is certainly found in Washington state. Beginning as early as 1970, concerned citizens began demanding more public information related to financing political activity in the state. In 1971 citizens made an unsuccessful attempt to force the legislature to act. Another attempt in 1972 resulted in two referenda going before the voters. Referendum 24 dealt with lobbyist registration and expenditure reporting, while Referendum 25 required campaign finance disclosures.

Concerned citizens, subsequently operating as the Coalition for Open Government, felt that neither measure went far enough.[12] So they wrote Initiative 276, gathering the requisite number of signatures in time for it to appear on the November 1972 ballot with the two referenda. Initiative 276 required personal financial disclosure for candidates and elected officials, but also included the creation of an independent administrative and enforcement agency—the Public Disclosure Commission. All three measures passed by large margins. Initiative 276 became the Washington Open Government Act and took effect on January 1, 1973. Washington became a true pioneer—the first state to create a single agency responsible for collecting information on lobbying expenditures and contributions/expenditures related to election campaigns. The newly created Washington Public Disclosure Commission subsequently became a model for many other states. This commission is a classic example of the type of activity one would expect to find in a moralistic political subculture that emphasizes restricting interest group behavior.

A third factor to be considered when examining the strength and scope of interest groups within a state is the level of *integration* or *fragmentation* of the *policy process*. The more integrated the system, the fewer the options available to groups in terms of access points. The level of policy integration depends upon the structure of government and the strength of political and governmental institutions.

One component of policy integration is the strength or weakness of the political parties. The stronger the party system, the more limited the avenues of access open to groups. Washington state has consistently been identified as, at best, a moderately strong party state. One's conclusion depends on whether one looks at organizational strength of the parties or how competitive they are in terms of election returns, particularly for the gubernatorial race. Washington has been ranked as a highly competitive state. Over the years the difference between the winner and loser in gubernatorial races—whether Democrat or Republican—is slight. However, there is less evidence that the parties are organizationally strong.[13] Strength of organization includes variables such as size of budget and staff, breadth of recruitment activity, and services to candidates, including public opinion polling. Some scholars suggest that, based on indicators such as these, the Democrats in Washington state would be classified as organizationally weak while the Republican party is the ninth strongest in the country. Sarah McCally Morehouse concludes that Washington is among the moderate party/strong interest group states. Her analysis infers that as the strength of party organization increases, that of pressure groups diminishes, and visa versa.[14]

A second component of the concept of integration of the policy process includes the power of the governor. This includes institutionalized powers as well as the number of directly elected cabinet members and the number of independent boards and commissions. With a more tightly integrated executive, there are fewer opportunities for groups to lobby this branch of government. Washington's governor is particularly weak in terms of appointment powers over six key state agencies, the authority of the legislature to change the governor's recommendation regarding the budget, and the ability of the governor's political party to control both chambers of the legislature.[15]

In addition to fairly weak institutionalized powers, it should be noted that the governor's cabinet includes eight other statewide officials—all of whom are elected by the voters. With the exception of the superintendent of public instruction, all of these positions are partisan. Consequently, many of the highest-level executives in the state frequently come from the governor's opposition party. The constitution established all of the offices, except that of insurance commissioner. Thus there is little likelihood that bureaucratic reform would permit the appointment of some or all of these policy makers. Currently, the Washington executive branch reflects a very fragmented political system with many opportunities for interest group impact at the highest level.

A final component of fragmentation within the political system includes the elaborate configuration of initiative and referenda available to the states.[16] States that provide generous opportunities for citizens to make law through the initiative process also afford interest groups the opportunity to support, oppose, or in some way significantly impact these legislative proposals.

In summary, the political process in Washington state may be characterized as fragmented rather than integrated. With competitive but weak political parties, moderate institutional power on the part of the governor, an extensive elected cabinet, and an active initiative history, Washington provides many opportunities for interest groups to wield their power.

A fourth factor within the Thomas and Hrebenar framework for examining interest group activity at the state level is the degree of *professionalization* of the legislature (see chapter five). Many observers believe that groups have their biggest influence where legislatures are the least professional, because amateur legislators, depending on limited staff support, necessarily rely on outside sources of information. The lawmaking body in Washington state has not yet approached professional status. Legislators take considerable pride in being designated "citizen legislators," but this status leads inevitably to more interest group influence over the decision-making process.

It has also been suggested that the *economic development* of a state will influence the number and scope of interest groups within that state. With increased economic diversification, a more competitive group system will develop which will be accompanied by more sophisticated techniques of lobbying and a general increase in the professionalization of lobbyists.

Although Sarah Morehouse suggests that states with strong pressure groups will also be states in which a single major economic enterprise dominates the economy, this is clearly not the case in Washington. Here, the large number of competing groups reflects a diversified economy. Based on surveys sent to state legislators in 1976 and 1982 asking respondents to list the four most powerful groups in the state, Walfred Peterson discovered not only a broad range of important groups but also that perceptions of group influence varied depending on whether a campaign was in progress or a legislative session underway.[17]

Included among the most powerful groups during both time frames were the Washington Education Association, Washington State Labor Council, Washington Federation of State Employees, Boeing Corporation, the banking community, forest products firms, developers, environmentalists, utilities, the agriculture industry, business, insurance, contractors, and various professional groups.

Diversification of interest group influence has been accompanied by a parallel growth in the number of lobbyists. According to Public Disclosure Committee documents, there are approximately 900 registered lobbyists in the state.

In addition, there are at least 45 lobbying firms that have two or more lobbyists on their payroll.[18] The lobbyists in the state capital increasingly include "contract lobbyists," i. e., independent operators who represent as many as a dozen different clients at any one time.

Traditionally, most lobbyists came to the capital on behalf of a single corporation or labor union. Contract lobbyists, or super lobbyists, represent a new breed. They are younger, more issue-oriented than their predecessors, and increasingly likely to be members of large, politically active law firms. Their strategies rely less on plying legislators with food and drink and more on grassroots organizing and involvement in political campaigns. In the seven-year period from 1979 to 1986, the number of contract lobbyists increased by 100 percent, according to the Public Disclosure Commission.[19] Thus, Washington state has experienced economic diversification with a corresponding growth in the number and sophistication of professional lobbyists. Clearly, this development facilitates more interest group participation in the political process.

A final factor to be considered when analyzing the scope and influence of groups within state government is related to the escalating *costs of election campaigns* and the role which interest groups have played in providing these funds. Even in states where parties are strong and make major contributions to campaigns, candidates are relying increasingly on interest group money and political action committee (PAC) contributions, as are the parties themselves.[20] By 1980, PACs provided 45 percent of all contributions over $100 to California state legislative candidates, while PACs in New York state accounted for 60 percent of contributions to the legislative campaign committees of both major parties.

Washington state appears to be no exception to a national trend of rising election costs. In 1974, the first regular election year for which campaign contributions and expenditures were publicly reported under Initiative 276, total spending by all candidates for the legislature amounted to $1.57 million. Table One illustrates increases in total expenditures in each subsequent election. In four years, spending had nearly doubled, and doubled again four years later. Ruth Jones discovered that PACs in 1980 provided 37 percent of the contributions to legislative races in Washington state. In 1988 interest groups picked up approximately 40 percent of the costs of political races. By 1990 the percentage for legislative races had increased to 60 percent.[21]

By 1990, state legislative candidates reported spending nearly $12 million, while total contributions to legislative races reflected similarly large increases. The average amount spent by successful legislative candidates increased from $7,000 in 1974 (both house and senate) to $43,000 in 1990 for winning house of representative candidates and $133,000 for victorious senate candidates.[22]

Table One

Total Contributions and Expenditures of Legislative Candidates, 1976-1990
(dollars, in millions)

Category	1976	1987	1980	1982	1984	1986	1988	1990
Total Contributions	$2.25	$3.05	$4.65	$5.94	$6.53	$7.62	$9.18	$12.57
Gain over previous election year	31%	35%	52%	28%	10%	17%	20%	37%
Total Expenditures	$2.07	$2.79	$4.29	$5.56	$6.03	$6.97	$8.38	$11.53
Gain over previous	28%	35%	54%	29%	8%	16%	20%	38%

Source: *1990 Election Financing Fact Book* (Olympia: Washington State Public Disclosure Commission, 1991), p 37.

In 1990, nonpartisan judicial races cost over $1.4 million, and state ballot propositions $2.8 million. Candidates for local offices spent in excess of $3 million.[23] In total, the 1990 election cost over $19 million.

Clearly, election expenditures are increasing at a very rapid rate. At the same time, there is evidence to suggest that the proportion of funds originating from interest groups – at least for legislative races – has also increased dramatically. Although it is an oversimplification to conclude that there exists a direct relationship between expenditure of money and influence, evidence from an exhaustive study of Western states strongly suggests that contributions to campaign chests lead to success in the political system.[24]

Money and Politics: PACs

The remainder of this chapter will present information relative to the financial resources available to various groups in Washington state. Expenditures will be examined during two discrete time periods – the legislative session, when monies are spent in an attempt to impact policy formulation, and the election campaign, when candidates and ballot issues are supported or opposed depending on the perspective of various interest groups.

Although it is not required under state law, most interest groups in Washington form political action committees. The proliferation of PACs at the federal level can be attributed at least in part to election reform under the Federal Election Campaign Act of 1972. State law, however, does not prohibit individuals, government contractors, labor unions, or corporations from making direct contributions to candidates from corporate funds. There are no ceilings on the amounts that individuals or organizations, with or without political action committees, may contribute directly to state campaigns.

Nonetheless, Washington's law does require full and timely disclosure of campaign contributions by candidates and campaign committees. One incentive for PAC formation in some states is a desire to remain anonymous or to obscure the source of a contribution by creating a committee that may not necessarily reflect in its name the actual source of funds. However, since all contributions to committees are public record under Washington state law since 1973, that incentive is not likely to be a strong one here.

Typical names found among the biggest contributors are Washington Medical PAC, Realtors' PAC, and Washington Federation of State Employees. Some of the other names are not as descriptive. The Political Unity of Leaders in State Education, PULSE, is comprised of members of the Washington Education Association, a teachers' group. United for Washington, one of the largest PACs, receives its money from the business community. The Washington Affordable Housing Council is affiliated with the Home Builders Association.

The greatest number of PACs are business-related. There were 127 business-related committees in 1984, from ABCPAC-Washington, affiliated with Associated Builders and Contractors of the Inland Empire, to the Washington Medical PAC Tort Reform Fund, affiliated with the Washington State Medical Association. Thirty-three PACs had union connections, in addition to the 29 local units of the Washington Education Association. In 1984, only 19 PACs appeared to have no connection to business, professional, or labor groups. The majority of these were ideological groups, such as the Washington Environmental Council and the Human Life Committee. Of the twenty PACs with the largest amounts of receipts and expenditures, sixteen had business connections and four were affiliated with unions.[25]

Figure One represents total expenditures from 12 of the 39 major interest group categories in the state during two time periods. The left portion of each bar indicates lobbying expenditures during the 1989 legislative session, while the right side indicates money contributed to legislative and executive races, initiative drives, and political parties. Approximately five-and-a-half million dollars were spent during both periods by the group categories included in this figure.[26] However, in many cases, a particular preference in spending pattern can be noted. Manufacturing interests, health practitioners, transportation interests, the insurance industry, and water/waste utilities prefer to spend their money during the legislative session, although, in all cases (with the exception of the latter), interest groups spent sizeable amounts during election campaigns.

Both forms of expenditures are considered by interest groups to be financial investments. Candidates for office, especially in the legislative and executive branches, are carefully screened for appropriate responses to key political and economic issues. Once a group has determined that a particular candidate reflects the "appropriate viewpoint," financial contributions are likely to be forthcoming. In this manner, the Washington Labor Council generously assists

Figure One

Political Spending by Major Interest Groups, 1988-1989*

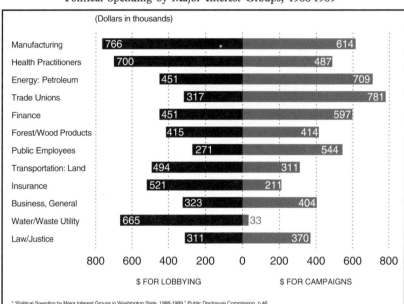

* "Political Spending by Major Interest Groups in Washington State, 1988-1989," Public Disclosure Commission, p 46.

candidates who are usually Democrats but always pro-labor, while United for Washington identifies candidates who are usually Republican but always pro-management. Groups such as these devote as many financial resources as possible to the election of candidates who are perceived as supporters of the groups' agendas.

Support from special interests does not end with the elections. Both forms of activity—campaign contributions and lobbying expenditures—are devoted to the same end, i. e., the continuation or creation of public policies that will benefit the numerous interest groups in the state.

The Boeing Company led the manufacturing group, both in lobbying expenditures and political contributions. Other manufacturing groups that made large expenditures included Kaiser Aluminum and Chemical, Aluminum Company of America, the Tobacco Institute, and Philip Morris USA. Health Care practitioners include the Washington State Medical Association, the leader in this group with a total of $280,000 spent for lobbying in the first nine months of 1989. This total exceeded any other lobbyist in the state. Safeco Corporation led the insurance category, another that emphasized the lobbying aspect of its activities. The Washington Citizens for Improved Transportation, including contractors, construction firms, Boeing, Sea First Bank, Security Pacific

Bank, US West, Sabey Corporation, and Puget Power, spent considerable funds on lobbying.

To an extent unmatched by any other interest category, the finance group concentrated its effort on executive elections, being the largest of Governor Booth Gardner's major contributors and supplying about half of the interest group money state treasurer candidates received. These contributions reflect the fact that key financial policies of the state, such as developing the budget, originate within the executive rather than the legislative branch.

Public employee unions concentrated on state legislative races and provided 10 percent of the total of major contributions of $150 or more reported by legislative candidates. The leading member of this group, the Washington Federation of State Employees, distributed 95 percent of its funds to Democratic candidates, parties, and caucuses. Some of the smaller police guilds and deputy sheriffs' associations proved more supportive of Republican candidates.

Trade unions led all other contributors to legislative candidates. Democratic legislative candidates received 20 percent of their major contributions from trade unions. These unions also provided the biggest single source of contributions to Democratic caucuses and the second highest to executive candidates.

Table Two illustrates the campaign contributions made by the ten largest categories of groups in the state in 1988, a year when all statewide executive offices were on the ballot. In addition to the governor, Washington voters elect seven other executive officers in partisan elections every four years and a nonpartisan superintendent of public instruction. Candidates for these executive positions raised $2.9 million dollars in contributions of $150 or more. Slightly more than $1 million of that amount came from individuals. The largest interest categories contributing the remaining funds to these candidates included financial institutions, trade unions, teacher unions, and forest/wood products companies.

Only a few categories spread their contributions among candidates for a variety of offices. Most concentrated on a single office whose functions most related to the activities of the interest group. For example, groups in the forest/wood products category provided 54 percent of the interest money reported by candidates for commissioner of public lands, the executive officer who manages more than 2,000,000 acres of state forest land. Banks and other financial businesses gave just over half of the total money received by state treasurer candidates. The state treasurer is the custodian of all funds in the state treasury and is the disbursement officer for the state. Teacher unions provided nearly one-fourth of the major contributions reported by candidates for superintendent of public instruction. The law and justice category, which includes the state association of trial lawyers as well as many law firms, was the

Table Two

Sources of Major Contributions to Candidates and Committees in 1988*

	To State Executive Candidates	To State Legislative Candidates	To Initiative Committees	To Caucuses and State Parties	Totals
Manufacturing	81,924	195,286	298,200	39,480	614,890
Health Practitioners	39,665	406,596	0	40,233	486,494
Petroleum	25,181	149,164	503,553	32,826	710,724
Trade Unions	172,486	449,973	85,493	74,275	782,724
Finance	265,781	193,897	59,000	78,275	596,953
Forest/Wood Products	129,157	103,352	145,385	37,494	415,388
Public Employees Unions	94,198	405,370	8,000	36,780	544,348
Transportation/ Land	91,921	124,561	64,600	28,580	309,662
Insurance	66,681	91,266	10,500	42,203	210,650
Business, General	3,088	384,226	10,960	5,890	404,164
Water/Waste Utility	1,950	22,000	4,000	5,335	33,285
Law/Justice	93,692	224,976	28,470	22,740	369,878
Totals	1,065,724	2,750,667	1,218,161	444,111	5,478,663

* Major Contribution = $500 or more to gubernatorial candidates and $150 or more to all others

Source: *Political Spending by Major Interest Groups in Washington State, 1988-89* (Olympia: Washington State Public Disclosure Commission, 1990), p 59.

largest single contributing group in the attorney general campaigns. The attorney general is the chief legal advisor for the state and for all state officers.

Table Two also indicates the major contributors to the statewide initiative campaigns. Such contributions are clearly issue-oriented and no pattern of funding is evident.

In summary, major interest group categories within Washington state make significant expenditures of money—in excess of $11 million in 1988/1989—as they lobby the state's policy makers and as they participate in the campaign election process. While some groups choose to equitably divide their resources during these two periods of time, others make conscious decisions to specialize in campaign politics or legislative lobbying.

Groups and Campaigning

Tables Three and Four provide more detailed information about contributions from interest groups to candidates for legislative seats during a ten year period.

Table Three

Top Contributors to 1980 Legislative Candidates

	Total Contributed	Total to Democrats	Total to Republicans	% of Their Candidates Who Won
United for Washington	$ 339,695	$ 15,600	$324,095	74.3%
PULSE–WA Education Assn	142,545	138,541	4,004	58.2%
WA Federation of State Employees	111,812	110,312	1,500	53.9%
WA State Dental PAC	73,125	26,400	46,725	90.9%
WA State Labor Council	62,959	62,559	400	48.8%
First Associates	44,890	10,940	33,950	84.9%
Affordable Housing Council	37,067	100	36,967	66.7%
Fair Competition Council	54,675	13,375	41,300	79.8%
WA Optometric PAC	54,460	35,735	18,725	74.3%
WA Assoc of Realtors	46,920	10,600	36,320	75.8%
LAW-PAC (WA St. Trial Lawyers)	42,991	33,566	9,425	69.1%
WA Affordable Housing Council	41,324	7,600	33,724	79.7%
Totals	$1,052,463	$465,328 (44%)	$587,135 (55%)	

Source: Washington State Public Disclosure Commission and Walfred H. Peterson, "Washington: The Impact of Public Disclosure Law," in Clive Thomas and Ronald Hrebenar, eds., *Interest Group Politics in the American West* (Salt Lake City: University of Utah Press, 1987), p 127.

In these tables, specific associations that make significant contributions during campaigns have replaced interest group categories. Table Three shows that the 12 largest donors to legislative candidates in the 1980 elections gave a little over a million dollars. United for Washington, which includes business contributors who support the election of free enterprise legislators, clearly led the group of 12, with nearly all of its resources devoted to Republican candidates. First Associates, representing employees of Sea First Bank, supported maximum freedom in the banking industry and also favored Republican candidates. Seattle-based Affordable Housing Council and the statewide Washington Affordable Housing Council worked to reduce government regulations related to the construction business, while the Fair Competition Council, representing major utilities, favored the issuance of industrial revenue bonds to help business. In contrast to these organizations which focused on Republican candidates for state legislature, teachers, state employees, and the State Labor Council made significant donations to Democratic candidates. In 1980, the top 12 contributors to legislative candidates proved more generous to Republican candidates, giving 55 percent of total funds, than to Democrats.

Table Four

Top Contributors to 1990 Legislative Candidates

	Total Contributed	Total to Democrats	Total to Republicans	% of Their Candidates Who Won
United for Washington	$ 588,631	$ 34,000	$ 554,631	58.6%
WA Federation of State Employees	383,606	345,629	37,977	78.2%
Washington Medical PAC	230,674	64,438	166,236	84.4%
WA State Labor Council	219,429	219,179	250	66.4%
PULSE–WA Education Assn	210,658	202,958	7,700	78.1%
LAW-PAC–WA St Trial Lawyers Assn	197,379	189,379	8,000	77.2%
The Boeing Company	158,981	47,418	111,563	83.2%
Realtors PAC	149,925	37,600	112,325	75.3%
Atlantic Richfield Co.	138,118	60,158	77,960	85.9%
WA St Dental PAC	109,525	58,550	50,975	84.2%
IBEW Local #77– Elec. Workers	106,320	106,320	0	42.9%
WA Teamsters Legislative League	105,580	99,530	6,050	75.8%
Totals	$2,598,826	$1,465,159 (56%)	$1,133,667 (43%)	

Source: Washington State Public Disclosure Commission; personal correspondence from Paul Gillie.

By 1990, the total amount contributed by the 12 largest benefactors had more than doubled to over two-and-a-half million dollars. Each of the organizations reported contributions that exceeded $100,000. In contrast to the 1980 election, Democratic candidates became the primary beneficiaries.

Groups and Lobbying

As indicated on Figure One, interest groups in Washington state spend an equivalent, if not larger, sum of money lobbying elected officials during the legislative session than they do on all election campaigns combined. This fact reflects the political reality that all groups must face: political and economic policies that will have an impact on individuals and organizations are established during the legislative session, not during election campaigns. More financial resources are therefore expended during this period attempting to persuade legislators to a particular viewpoint or encouraging already sympathetic officials to maintain their policy positions.

Table Five compares the lobbying expenditures by interest group categories during two legislative sessions, 1980 and 1990. The first obvious difference

Table Five

Lobbying Groups Ranked by Expenditures for 1980 and 1990

Lobbying Groups	1980 Expenditure	Rank 1980	1990* Expenditure	Rank 1990
Banking and Finance	$ 523,000	2	$ 809,000	11
Business and Trade Assocs.	334,000	12	814,000	10
Business, Unclassified	111,000	19	814,000	10
Chambers of Commerce	25,000	26	814,000	10
Education	427,000	5	840,000	8
Insurance	408,000	8	987,000	5
Labor Unions	353,000	6	376,000	18
Manufacturing	327,000	7	1,461,000	3
Medicine and Health Care	623,000	4	2,155,000	1
Petroleum and Natural Gas	304,000	9	937,000	6
Public Employees	230,000	17	825,000	9
Timber and Forest Products	401,000	1	1,365,000	4
Transportation	366,000	10	903,000	7
Utilities (Public and Private)	599,000	3	1,973,000	2
Totals**	$6,623,000		$18,179,000	

* Several Interest Group categories for 1990 were combined in order to make the comparison between 1980 and 1990.

** Only groups ranked 1 through 10 in 1980 or 1990 are included in this table. However, the total expenditure figures reflect *all* lobbying groups in the state.[27] (Endnote 27 contains a complete listing.)

Source: Washington State Public Disclosure Commission.

comes in the total amounts spent by these groups during the two contrasting years. The grand total almost triples from approximately $6.5 million in 1980 to more than $18 million ten years later.

In 1990, the top four interest group categories—medicine, utilities, manufacturing, and timber—spent approximately $7 million in lobbying expenditures alone. Individual businesses within these categories included Northwest Pulp and Paper Association, Boeing Company, Washington State Medical Association, Puget Sound Power and Light, and Weyerhaeuser. Each of these lobbyist employers spent in excess of $250,000 in 1990.

Table Six summarizes the most current information available for interest group expenditures in Washington state. The totals represent contributions of at least $150 during the 1990 legislative races, and lobbying expenditures during the 1990 legislative session. Although there were no statewide elections in 1990 and only one initiative on the ballot, these expenditures represent a two-and-a-half million dollar increase in campaign spending over the 1988 totals. Additionally, the lobbying expenses represent a nearly $7 million increase over the 1989 session totals.

Table Six

Lobbying and Major Legislative Campaign Contributions by
Interest Group Category for 1990

Categories	$ Expended Lobbying *	$ Expended Leg Campaigns	Total $ Expended
1. Manufacturing	$ 1,461,123(1)	$ 305,212(5)	$ 1,766,335
2. Health Care: Practitioner	1,014,108(3)	595,925(4)	1,610,943
3. Forest/Wood Products	1,364,503(2)	178,662(14)	1,543,165
4. Unions: Public Employee	824,789(6)	616,896(2)	1,441,685
5. Unions: Trade	375,792(20)	880,269(1)	1,256,061
6. Energy: Petroleum	937,303(5)	286,757(8)	1,224,060
7. Business: General	611,336(10)	605,181(3)	1,216,517
8. Insurance	986,996(4)	211,519(12)	1,198,515
9. Finance	808,650(7)	298,385(6)	1,107,035
10. Food/Beverage/Lodging	684,899(9)	239,286(11)	924,185
11. Utilities: Electric	747,128(8)	127,866(17)	874,994
12. Construction	542,862(14)	290,702(7)	833,564
13. Unions: Teacher	469,413(17)	272,072(9)	741,485
14. Law/Justice	432,772(19)	259,801(10)	692,573
15. Government	243,149(7)	5,194(33)	248,343
Totals	$17,975,604	$6,529,826	$24,505,430

* Lobbying expenditures from employers' annual reports for 1990.
** Only groups ranked 1 through 10 in either category are included, although totals
include all interest group categories in the state. See endnote 27 for a listing of additional interest group categories in the state.

Source: Personal correspondence from Paul Gillie, research director, Washington State
Public Disclosure Commission.

The numbers in parentheses indicate the relative ranking of each interest
category in lobbying and campaign expenditures in 1990. Examination of these
rankings reveals that six groups appear among the top ten categories in both
areas of spending. These groups are manufacturing, health care practitioners,
public employee unions, finance, general business, and petroleum.

Even a cursory examination of the data in Table Six reveals evidence to
support the analytical guidelines suggested by Hrebenar and Thomas. Washington, as is true in every state, creates public policy that has an impact on health,
education, labor, banking and finance, the environment, and utilities. Interest
groups that represent these concerns are found among the leaders in financial
expenditures. The state's dependence on timber interests is reflected in the third
place which the forest products industry occupies. Tourism, agriculture, retail
sales, recreation, and fishing are other important economic interests in the state.
The specialized concerns of Washington, as well as the general concerns that
all states share, are both reflected in the financial resources expended by these
interests.

Table Seven

Sources of Major Contributions to Candidates and Committees, 1988*

	To State Executive Candidates	To State Legislative Candidates	To Initiative Committees	To Caucuses and State Parties	Totals
Interest Group & Lobbying Firms	$1,856,205 (29%)	$4,129,266 (47%)	$1,524,152 (86%)	$ 781,408 (31%)	$8,281,031 (43%)
Dem/Rep Parties & Party Caucuses	233,790 (4%)	757,922 (9%)	10,250 (1%)	613,829 (25%)	1,615,144 (8%)
Transfers	132,226 (2%)	583,842 (7%)	12,147 (1%)	84,576 (3%)	812,791 (4%)
Independent Donors	1,724,878 (27%)	739,701 (8%)	49,089 (3%)	1,013,161 (40%)	3,526,829 (18%)
Candidates' Own Funds	219,638 (3%)	225,884 (3%)			445,523 (2%)
Unanalyzed Small Contributions	2,218,502 (35%)	2,308,707 (26%)	167,283 (9%)		4,694,492 (24%)
					$19,386,409

* Contributions = $500 or more to Gubernatorial
$150 or more to all others

Source: *Political Spending by Major Interest Groups in Washington State, 1988-89* (Olympia: Washington State Public Disclosure Commission, 1990), p. 59.

In Table Seven it is possible to assess the relative influence of interest groups compared to individuals and other organized groups during election campaigns. This table indicates that a total of $19,386,409 was spent in all state elections in 1988. The data indicate that the proportion of funds coming from interest groups varies depending on the specific campaign, but nearly half (43 percent) of all major contributions for political races came from interest groups and lobbying firms. This percent clearly dwarfs all other contributions.

Funding Trends and Reforms

The tremendous size of interest group contributions causes political reformers to criticize the cash flow between affluent groups and elected officials. While historically the parties and wealthy individuals amassed large campaign war chests, today candidates look to the most powerful interest groups when planning their campaign treasuries. As reported in Table Eight, 1990 continued the trend.

Some very clear trends are reflected in regard to sources of contributions during legislative campaigns. Over the 16-year period detailed in the table, the proportion of candidates' own funds used, contributions from individuals, and contributions from the political parties and legislative caucuses has consistently declined. In contrast, significant increases are obvious for PACs and

Table Eight

Sources of Contributions Reported by Legislative Candidates

	1974	1978	1982	1986	1990
Candidates' own funds	7.1%	4.6%	6.8%	3.6%	2.3%
Individuals	36.4%	27.9%	31.5%	27.6%	19.6%
Political party organizations	15.8%	15.2%	11.4%	9.6%	6.9%
Business PACs	16.2%	22.8%	24.5%	26.3%	29.7%
Union PACs	14.5%	15.8%	11.5%	13.5%	15.5%
Businesses	6.7%	8.9%	10.9%	12.6%	15.4%
Trade and professional associations	1.1%	1.4%	1.2%	1.4%	
Miscellaneous organizations	0.2%	0.1%	0.9%	0.3%	2.6%
Other candidates	2.0%	3.2%	1.3%	5.1%	8.0%

Source: Washington State Public Disclosure Commission.

businesses. In 1990, these latter sources represent more than 60 percent of total contributions to legislative races. A much smaller increase is noted in the percent of money transferred from one candidate to another.

Legislative races set a new campaign spending record in 1990. Democrat Ray Moore spent $276,867 to keep his state senate seat, exceeding by $52,000 the previous record for a legislative post. Nine other candidates, all running for the senate, expended more than $200,000 during their campaigns, including five who lost. The average expenditure for winning legislative candidates in 1990 came to $62,581, a 39 percent increase from 1988. Winning senators spent, on average, $113,501 while winning house members spent $43,078. The average in losing legislative races totaled $45,142 — a 66 percent increase from 1988.[28]

These spending levels resulted in several concerns among voters. Despite the characterization of Washington as a state with a "citizens' legislature," most candidates are faced with the task of raising an amount of money double their prospective salary for house members and five times the salary of senators. Can candidates from all backgrounds still seriously consider a legislative candidacy, or are all but the well-connected now excluded from this level of office?

There is also concern over the source of contributions. Voters have a sense that PACs are now the primary financial backers of many legislative and executive candidates. The data presented in this chapter confirm these suspicions (see Tables Seven and Eight). As a result, to whom are state legislators and other elected officials accountable? Do they represent the constituents within their legislative districts or voters statewide in the case of an executive position, or have they become responsive to powerful interest groups from within and outside the state?

Both state and federal governments face the problem of ever-increasing campaign costs and voter skepticism about the legitimacy of the election system. Many acknowledge that something is wrong. U. S. Senator Robert Dole suggests that the solution is to encourage "good money" and to ban "bad money." He supports legislation encouraging contributions from individuals and political parties while banning interest group money in congressional races. In Washington, the citizens' group Common Cause echoes these sentiments. Unusual alliances are developing among groups who have worked unsuccessfully for many years to bring campaign finance reform.

The public increasingly perceives state legislators as "scumballs who are bought and sold by special interests," as stated by Representative Louise Miller in her testimony before the house Government Committee in Olympia. "The public is absolutely disgusted with the election process," agreed Representative Lorraine Hine.[29] Miller, a Republican, and Hine, a Democrat, co-sponsored a bill, HB 1434, that passed the state house of representatives on an 80 to 18 vote in the 1991 regular session. The measure would limit both the size of contributions and overall spending in political campaigns. It would limit contributions from individuals, unions, or businesses to $1,000 per legislative candidate and $5,000 per candidate for statewide office. Political action committees could give $3,000 to legislative candidates and $7,500 to statewide candidates. Political parties and legislative caucuses would be limited to $5,000 per legislative candidate and $10,000 for statewide candidates.

The plan also included voluntary spending limits of $55,000 for state house or senate races, $2.2 million for governor, and $800,000 for other statewide offices. A participating candidate whose opponent refused to limit spending could receive partial matching funds from the state. The bill would also charge higher filing fees for candidates and create a new fee for lobbyists, candidates, and officeholders who file public disclosure documents.[30]

Republicans immediately opposed this bill when it came to the senate. Linda Smith, sponsor of an alternative senate measure, declared it "dead on arrival." The senate bill, SB 5864, would impose much tighter individual contribution limits ($500 for legislative and executive races) and include a *total ban* on political action committee contributions. Political parties and caucuses could contribute up to $25,000 to each legislative candidate. However, there would be no overall spending limits on campaigns. Senate Majority Leader Jeannette Hayner objected strenuously to caps on total spending, while the house responded that without spending limits the bill would be meaningless.[31] The impasse between house and senate killed the measure.

The chair of the house State Government Committee immediately filed an initiative to take the issue to the people. The initiative included the contribution and spending limits agreed upon in the bipartisan house measure.

Backers of the senate alternative also filed an initiative. Both measures failed to garner sufficient signatures to make the November 1991 ballot.

At the same time, Common Cause of Washington State has spearheaded a statewide coalition operating under the title "Citizens United to Reform Election Spending," or CURES. The plan suggested by this group would further restrict individual and PAC contributions to $350 per candidate. Political party organizations would be limited to 40 cents per voter per campaign, with the stipulation that at least two-thirds of all contributions to candidates come from individuals and the parties. Under this proposal, not more than one-third of the money candidates accept could come from PACs, and only individual voters could form PACs.[32]

Washington is not the first state to consider dramatic campaign finance reform. Eight states currently have spending limits for executive and/or legislative candidates. Campaign contributions from individuals are limited in 23 states, while candidate contributions to one's own campaign are limited in only three. Corporate contributions are prohibited in 21 states and limited in 18, while union contributions are prohibited in 10 states and limited in 19. Contributions from political action committees are limited in 26 states.[33]

Although a very strong case can be made that interest groups have increasingly become significant political actors in both the policy-making process and in state-level election campaigns, it is less obvious what steps, if any, should be taken to alter this reality. When interest groups hire lobbyists to present their case to elected officials, valuable information is also provided that may assist in developing the most beneficial policies for the state. Given the fact that our state relies on an amateur legislature, this service is definitely a positive aspect of the lobbying process. Additionally, interest groups provide experts who are willing to testify at legislative hearings and therefore further educate elected officials and the general public.

However, the fact that lobbyists reported spending more than $18 million during only one legislative session causes some observers to question the extent to which interest group money influences eventual state policies. Do health care providers, trade unions, utility companies, manufacturers, and foresters wield greater influence in the state capital merely because they spend more money lobbying than any other groups in the state? Is there an inequality of result in our state government? If so, should any measures be taken to address this situation?

The role of interest group money during elections is even more controversial in the United States today. Many are quick to suggest the elimination of PAC money, or at the least, its severe restriction. On the other hand, PAC money reflects interest groups, and organized groups merely represent people. The U. S. Supreme Court has ruled that spending money during political campaigns is a form of freedom of expression.[34] Are political reformers any more justified in restricting the rights of speech of organized groups than they would be in restricting individual voters? Have researchers proven, beyond a shadow of a doubt, that campaign contributions are directly tied to votes cast by policy makers? Perhaps not beyond a shadow of a doubt, but a cause and effect relationship, however weak, remains.

Until such a connection is established scientifically, however, political reformers are faced with the "Madisonian Dilemma."[35] In the Federalist Papers, James Madison expressed his concerns about interest groups (factions), but he also strongly argued that within a democratic country, the cure would be worse than the affliction. Our constitutional freedoms preclude undue restrictions on the political activities of organized groups in the United States.

Notes

1. The author wishes to acknowledge the invaluable assistance of Paul Gillie, research director, Washington State Public Disclosure Commission.
2. David Truman, *The Governmental Process* (New York: Knopf, 1971), p. 33.
3. Jeffrey Berry, *The Interest Group Society,* 2d ed. (Glenview, Il.: Scott, Foresman, 1989), p. 4-5; Clive S. Thomas and Ronald J. Hrebenar, "Interest Groups in the States," in Virginia Gray, Herbert Jacob, and Robert Albritton, eds., *Politics in the American States,* 5th ed. (Glenview, Il.: Scott, Foresman, 1990), p. 124.
4. Arthur Bentley, *The Process of Government* (Cambridge: Harvard University Press, 1967); G. David Garson, *Group Theories of Politics* (Beverly Hills, Ca.: Sage, 1978).
5. Belle Zeller, ed., *American State Legislatures* (New York: Crowell, 1954) pp. 190-91; W. Duane Lockard, *New England State Politics* (Princeton: Princeton University Press, 1959); V.O. Key, Jr., *Southern Politics* (New York: Vintage, 1949); John C. Wahlke, Heinz Eulau, William Buchanan, and L.C. Ferguson, *The Legislative System* (New York: Wiley and Son, 1962); Harmon Ziegler and Michael A. Baer, *Lobbying: Interaction and Influence in State Legislatures* (Belmont, Ca.: Wadsworth, 1969); Hrebenar and Thomas, eds., *Interest Group Politics in the American West* (Salt Lake City: University of Utah Press, 1987).
6. Allen Cigler and Burdett Loomis, *Interest Group Politics,* 3rd ed. (Washington, D.C.: Congressional Quarterly, 1991), p. 3.
7. Sarah McCally Morehouse, *State Politics, Parties and Policy* (New York: Holt, Rinehart, and Winston, 1983), p. 109. Also see L. Harmon Ziegler and Hendrik van Dalen, "Interest Groups in State Politics," in Herbert Jacob and Kenneth N. Vines, eds. *Politics in the American States,* 3rd ed. (Boston: Little, Brown and Co., 1976), pp. 93-136.
8. Thomas and Hrebenar, "Interest Groups in States," pp. 147-48. This section of the paper will draw heavily on this discussion by the authors.
9. *Ibid,* p. 137, Figure 4.1.
10. Daniel J. Elazar, *American Federalism: A New View from the States* (New York: Harper & Row, 1984), defined political culture as "the particular pattern of orientation to political action in which each political system is embedded."

11. Gerald C. Wright, Robert S. Erickson, and John P. McIver, "Measuring State Partisanship and Ideology with Survey Data," 47 *Journal of Politics* 468-489 (1985). Gerald C. Wright, Jr., Robert S. Erickson, and John P. McIver, "Public Opinion and Policy Liberalism in the American States," 31 *American Journal of Political Science* 890-1001 (1987).

12. The Coalition for Open Government was made up of the American Association of University Women, League of Women Voters, Municipal League of Seattle and King County, Common Cause, Young Republicans of King County, Washington Environmental Council, Washington State Council of Churches, Seattle Press Club, CHEC (Choose an Effective City Council), and the Seattle-King County Bar Association, Young Lawyers Section.

13. Morehouse, *State Politics,* p. 147, ranks Washington as a strongly competitive party state; while Thomas R. Dye, *Politics in States and Communities,* 6th ed. (Englewood Cliffs, N.J.: Prentice Hall, 1988), p. 130, indicates that Washington's political parties are only moderately competitive.

14. Cornelius P. Cotter, James L. Gibson, John F. Bibby, and Robert J. Huckshorn, *Party Organizations in American Politics* (New York: Praeger Publishers, 1984) p. 28-29; Morehouse, *State Politics,* p. 147.

15. Thad L. Beyle, "Governors," in Gray, Jacob, and Albritton, *Politics in American States,* pp. 201-251.

16. Although both the Citizens for Balanced Growth and the Washington Taxpayers for Livable Communities were clearly pro-environmentalist, the former represented organizations that supported the initiative to restrict unplanned growth in the state and spent $431,186, while the latter groups spent $1,674,757 to defeat the initiative. More than 70 organized groups signed onto the campaign to oppose Initiative 547, including the Association of Washington Cities, the Association of Washington Business, the Washington State Transportation Commission, and the Washington State Association of Counties. See *1990 Election Financing Fact Book* (Olympia: Washington State Public Disclosure Commission, 1991), p. 7.

17. Morehouse, *State Politics;* Walfred Peterson, "Washington: The Impact of Public Disclosure Laws," in Hrebenar and Thomas, *Interest Group Politics in the American West,* p. 126. Also see the appendix of the same book, p. 150.

18. *Index of Registered Lobbyists* (Olympia: Public Disclosure Commission, 1990).

19. Quoted in *Seattle Times,* 11 Jan. 1987.

20. In Washington state, a political action committee is an organized political committee that receives contributions and makes expenditures to support or oppose more than one candidate. A group organized solely to support or oppose a specific candidate or ballot measure is not considered a PAC.

21. Larry Sabato, *PAC Power* (New York: Norton, 1985), p. 117; Thomas and Hrebenar in Gray, Jacob, and Albritton, *Politics in the American States,* p. 139; and Ruth Jones, "Financing State Elections," in Michael J. Malbin, ed., *Money and Politics in the United States* (Chatham, N.J.: Chatham House Publishers, 1984) p. 183, Table 6.3.

22. *1990 Election Financing Fact Book,* p. 36; and *The Increased Cost of Legislative Campaigns, 1974-1982* (Olympia: Public Disclosure Commission, 1984), p. 1.

23. *1990 Election Financing Fact Book,* p. 2.

24. Thomas and Hrebenar in Gray, Jacob, and Albritton, *Politics in the American States,* p. 140.

25. *Political Action Committees—Their Role in Campaign Finance in Washington State* (Olympia: Public Disclosure Commission, 1985), esp. Appendix B.

26. Note on Figure 1: these data represent only the major group categories. In total, $8 million were spent on elections by all interest groups, and lobbying expenditures exceeded $11 million. *Political Spending by Major Interest Groups in Washington State, 1988-1989* (Olympia: Public Disclosure Commission, 1990).

27. Other interest group categories include: telephone utilities, land transportation, law/justice, water/waste utilities, health care insurance, amusements, health care facilities, real estate, commercial services, education, agriculture, social/fraternal organizations, social services, outdoor recreation, marine transportation, retailing, health care products, fisheries, recreation/arts, religious organizations, broadcast utilities, advertising/print media, air transportation, and mining. The groups are listed here in order from most money expended to least money expended.

28. *1990 Election Financing Fact Book,* p. 36-38.

29. *Spokane Spokesman Review,* 10 Feb. 1991.

30. *Spokane Spokesman Review,* 1 Mar. 1991.

31. *Spokane Spokesman Review,* 13 Mar. 1991.

32. Information from correspondence received from Mr. Chuck Sauvage, Director, Washington State Common Cause, 22 May 1991.

33. Federal Election, "Campaign Finance Law 90," 33. *Buckley vs. Valeo,* 424 US 1 (1976).

34. C. Herman Pritchett, *The American Constitution,* 3d ed. (New York: McGraw-Hill, 1977), p. 316.

35. *The Federalist Papers* (New York: New American Library, 1961) pp. 77-84. On this point see Berry, *Interest Group Society,* chapter one.

Opening of the Olympia office of the "Dan Evans for Governor" campaign, June 1968. Vibert Jeffers photo. *Susan Parish Collection*©

Chapter Four

Political Parties in Washington

David C. Nice

John: "I vote for the candidate, not the party."
Marsha: "Who did you vote for?"
John: "Some Republican."

AMERICANS HAVE AN ambivalent relationship with political parties. On one hand, most feel some form of attachment to or favorable inclination toward one or the other of our major political organizations. On the other hand, few Americans think parties are very successful in making government respond to people's desires, in developing better solutions to policy problems, or in helping people understand the political world.[1]

Making sense of political parties is difficult, partly because we expect them to perform a variety of tasks and partly because parties have multiple facets not necessarily closely connected to one another. Political parties also vary considerably from one nation to another and, in the United States, from one part of the country to another and from place to place within individual states. This chapter will discuss the various tasks that parties perform, and will explore the different facets of the political parties of Washington.

Political Parties and What They Do

Because political parties vary considerably from place to place, scholars have struggled to develop a definition that can be used everywhere.[2] For our purposes a simple one will suffice. A political party is an organization (formal or informal) that runs candidates for office under the organization's name. The major parties in Washington are the Democrats and the Republicans, but a number of other parties have also run candidates from time to time. In 1980, for example, citizens in Washington cast votes for presidential candidates representing eight different political parties, as well as for John Anderson, who ran as an independent.[3]

The parties perform a number of different tasks, although not always with a high degree of effectiveness.[4] First, they help to *educate* the public about political issues and the political system. The parties use election campaigns, press releases, and a host of other approaches to distribute information about the condition of the state, proposals for dealing with state problems, and records of various candidates and officials. The messages are not always clear, and some information is certainly biased; we rarely hear party politicians admitting that positions they have held for years were, in hindsight, wrong. Many people pay little attention to the messages that parties send, but the parties do try to distribute information to the public from time to time. At least some of the information occasionally gets through. The parties' role in distributing information was more important prior to the development of modern systems of mass communication.

A second major task is *political recruitment.* The parties are involved in the selection of a wide range of public officials, from presidents, members of Congress, and governors, to county commissioners and a variety of other local officials. They may encourage people to run for office, assist in their campaigns, and sometimes try to steer potential candidates away from the political arena when their prospects seem poor. The parties' role in recruiting elected officials is fairly well known, but they are also involved in recruiting officials to appointive positions. A party may help a governor find suitable staff assistants, sift through potential appointees for executive branch positions, or screen possible replacements for a judge who has resigned before the end of his or her term.

A third party task is *interest aggregation,* the building of political coalitions large enough to exert significant influence on the political system. In a state as large and diverse as Washington, individuals and groups are likely to hold a wide range of opinions on many issues. A government bombarded by too many conflicting opinions at once may face deadlock, with smaller groups being ignored. The parties can help to overcome that problem by building alliances among individuals and groups with views that are broadly similar, but not identical. They can then press for the alliance's broad position. Bear in mind that developing a position on which different groups can agree is not necessarily easy and is sometimes impossible; it requires at least some willingness to compromise on the part of coalition members. That willingness is sometimes absent, especially on emotional issues like abortion. Nonetheless, some consensus is needed in order to win voter support and gain elections.

A fourth major task is *organizing the policy-making process.* Washington resembles other states in that decision-making authority is scattered across a variety of institutions, including the legislature, the governor, the courts, and a number of executive offices. Many policy issues cannot be resolved if those different institutions are not coordinated in some fashion. The governor may submit a budget proposal to the legislature, but the legislature may alter or reject it. The governor may veto the resulting budget and court rulings may generate additional state expenses, with the result that both the governor's and legislature's budgetary plans are rendered impractical. If a political party can gain control of the various branches and persuade the party's members to work together, the result *may be* more effective coordination of the various decision-making centers of government.

A final party task is *forging a link between citizens and the government.* The size and complexity of government might confuse and/or intimidate people. What are the many public officials doing? Which of the armies of candidates deserve my support? How can I make the government do what I want? Parties can help people become a part of the political system and help them to exert influence on the government. They can do that in many ways. They may work to register potential voters and remind them to vote on election day. They might simplify the voters' job by assembling teams of candidates rather than placing voters in the extremely difficult position of trying to remember dozens of individual candidates for office. The parties also give people opportunities for involvement in election campaigns: people may be asked to donate money, distribute campaign literature, or perform any number of other tasks.

Political parties may not necessarily perform these functions very effectively and are not the only organizations working on these tasks. Politicians may sometimes prefer to avoid issues rather than send the public clear messages. The parties may be unable to control the political recruitment process very effectively, and organizing the policy-making process is rarely easy. Linking a large, diverse population and a large, complex political system presents enormous problems.

The parties face a number of major competitors when attempting to perform these tasks. Political information is distributed by the news media, interest groups, and many other sources. Candidates may prefer creating a personal organization to handle the campaign rather than working with a party. Interest groups try to organize the policy-making process on specific issues, and individual public officials may have personal beliefs that do not agree with their party's positions. The parties do not always have the upper hand in dealing with their competitors.

Note, too, that parties face considerable controversy over how these tasks should be performed. Supporters of the *responsible party model* believe that each major party should adopt a set of party principles or policy positions that all members of the party support. The party should then assemble a team of candidates, each of whom believes in the principles, and each party and its candidates should clearly communicate the party's positions on the issues to the electorate. Each voter will assess the party's positions and vote for the candidates from the party with the most attractive position package. The winning party should have the discipline and strength to deliver its policy commitments, and the losing party should serve as a constructive critic, keeping an eye on the politicians in power and developing positive alternatives to the choices the party in office makes.[5]

Critics of the responsible party model generally doubt that a large, diverse political party can develop a number of specific policy positions without angering many people and, consequently, damaging the party's chances of winning elections. Sometimes the only way to keep a party together is by avoiding divisive issues entirely or dealing with them only in broad, vague terms. Moreover, the structure of our political system does not give the parties very dependable control over what sorts of candidates win the party's nominations. In addition, if each major party adopts a set of positions to which it is rigidly committed, what happens if one party wins control of the governor's office and another the legislature? The result could be deadlock or an unmanageable level of political conflict. Changing conditions, such as a sudden recession, may render a party's campaign promises impractical and force abandonment of some proposals.

The responsible party model tries to establish a firm linkage between a majority of voters and government policy decisions. If each major party takes a clear stand on the issues, if voters cast their ballots based on the party position they support, and if the winning party can deliver on its promises, then the resulting policies should be at least broadly in step with the views of most of the electorate. Critics of the responsible party model are generally concerned that the result could be a neglect of the needs of small groups. Moreover, if a party takes positions on 20 or 30 different issues, different people may vote for the same party for very different reasons. One person may vote Republican because of the party's position on tax policy, but another person may vote Republican based on its environmental position. A party may win an election without gaining majority approval for any of its policy positions.

A useful approach to exploring political parties is to examine three different facets: the party organizations, the party electorate, and the party in government. Each presents a somewhat different set of issues, and relationships among the different facets cast considerable light on the distinctive nature of individual political parties and party systems. In some political parties, for example, organization exerts substantial control over the party in government, but in others, the party in government has a great deal of autonomy.[6] We will begin with party organizations.

Party Organizations

Washington political parties have a number of organizational components, including precincts (the lowest level), legislative district organizations (in counties with more than one legislative district), counties, and the state central committees. The ideal precinct worker becomes acquainted with people in the precinct, encourages those sympathetic to the party to register and vote, and persuades people to cast ballots for the party's candidates. The precinct worker organizes the precinct caucuses, the first step in selecting Washington's delegates to the presidential nominating conventions. They also make up the county central committee, or legislative district committee, and select its officers, including a county chair and members of the state central committee.

The state central committee in turn chooses the state party chair and has a number of other duties, including fundraising, filling vacancies on the party ticket (for offices covering more than one county), and calling state conventions, which meet every two years. The state conventions draft a platform identifying policies that members support.

On paper, the organizational units form a roughly pyramidal, tightly linked organization that effectively performs a variety of tasks, from raising campaign funds and recruiting candidates to contacting the public for a variety of purposes, such as determining public beliefs and turning out the vote on election day. In practice, however, people who hold party offices are not always very conscientious about performing these tasks, and in some areas, party offices remain vacant because no one is interested in the job.[7] Maintaining a high level of discipline is difficult when few people in the party are highly motivated, and those who are not prove very difficult to remove.

Available evidence comparing Washington's party organizations with their counterparts in other states presents a mixed pattern. Some studies report that Washington's organizations are weaker than are those in most other states. Surveys of state legislators and county party officials in the early 1970s found that they believed party organizations in Washington were weaker and less influential than the organizations elsewhere.[8]

By contrast, evidence from the late 1970s indicates that the Washington Republican organization was one of the 10 strongest state party organizations in the country and that the Democratic state organization was only slightly weaker than the national average for both parties and somewhat stronger than the average state Democratic party organization. Washington's local party organizations are stronger than their counterparts in most other states, as measured by party budgets and staffing, services provided to candidates, and issue leadership.[9] Keep in mind that party organizations in many states are not terribly strong; consequently, being stronger than average is not necessarily a sign of great strength.

One of the chief difficulties facing Washington party organizations is the blanket primary, the state's main nominating mechanism. The blanket primary permits voters to switch from one party to another as they go down the primary ballot. A voter can, therefore, vote for a Democrat for governor, a Republican for the state senate, and a Democrat for attorney general. In most other states voters can only participate in one party's primary during a given election. The blanket primary enables voters who feel no attachment to a party to participate in the selection of that party's candidates for office. A candidate with no connection to the party thus may win the party's nomination by appealing to voters who may have no party connections. Not surprisingly, primaries in Washington tend to have more candidates and a more splintered vote than those in most states.[10] As a result, party organizations have a difficult time controlling which candidates win their nominations.

More generally, the state organizations operate in a legal environment less supportive of party influence than is the case in most states. Washington laws do not provide for the use of conventions for nominating state or local candidates, or for formal party endorsements of preferred candidates. The laws do not restrict participation in party primaries to voters with a genuine party commitment, nor does Washington allow a ballot that enables voters to cast a straight party ticket (that is, to vote for all of the Democratic candidates or all of the Republican candidates) with a single motion, such as pulling a voting machine lever or punching a single spot on a punch card.[11]

In one respect, however, Washington laws make the job of party organizations easier than in many other states. Campaign finance laws in Washington place fewer restrictions on contributions by corporations, unions, individuals, or political parties than do most states.[12] The Washington party organizations have, therefore, more options in financing campaigns than do most state parties. That comes at a price, however; candidates also have considerable flexibility in raising campaign funds, and they may use that flexibility to finance their campaigns independently of the party organizations.

Party organizations have had a difficult time controlling the political recruitment process in recent years. Candidates may raise substantial sums directly from contributors and use those funds to create personal organizations that gather information about public concerns, prepare media advertisements, and mobilize volunteers. Modern technologies, including television, public opinion polling, and computerized direct mailings, enable candidates to build political support without working through party organizations. Many candidates continue to receive significant help from party organizations, but most find

Table One
Party Loyalties in Washington and Nationwide

Washington	1976-1982	1983	1988
Republican	21%	19%	32%
Independent	48%	54%	37%
Democrat	31%	28%	31%
Nationwide	1982	1984	1988
Republican	24%	28%	28%
Independent	30%	34%	36%
Democrat	44%	36%	35%

Sources: Washington figures are from Ross Anderson, "Republicans and Democrats," *Pacific* (21 Oct. 1990), p. 16; William Mullen and John Pierce, "Political Parties," in Thor Swanson, et al., *Political Life in Washington* (Pullman: Washington State University Press, 1985), p. 67; Malcolm Jewell and David Olson, *Political Parties and Elections in American States*, 3rd ed. (Chicago: Dorsey, 1988), p. 38. Nationwide figures are from William Flanigan and Nancy Zingale, *Political Behavior of the American Electorate*, 7th ed. (Washington, D.C.: CQ Press, 1991), p. 37.

that they need more campaign assistance than party organizations alone can provide. If the party organizations cannot control who wins the party nomination, and if nominees can win election with relatively little help from the party organizations, the party is not likely to have much influence over that official's behavior in office.

Party Electorates

Political parties' largest single component is the party electorate—the voters from whom they draw support. Election researchers have long known that most Americans have some degree of attachment to one or the other of the major parties, although loyalties are considerably weaker than they were in the 1950s. Party identification, that sense of psychological attachment to a political party, is one of the guiding principles of much modern research on voting decisions. Many controversies surround party identification (how it should be measured and how durable it is are two major examples), but most scholars agree that party loyalties are an important influence in elections.[13]

The distribution of party loyalties in Washington generally resembles national patterns, but the resemblance is far from perfect (see Table One). Washington residents in the late 1970s and early 1980s were more likely than people in most states to be political independents lacking a firm attachment to any political party. As in most states, Democrats outnumbered Republicans in the early 1980s, but the Democrats' numerical advantage was somewhat smaller in Washington than nationally.

By 1988, survey evidence revealed virtual parity between Democratic and Republican identifiers in Washington, a pattern that resembled the broader

Table Two

Presidential Elections in Washington and Nationally

| | *Democratic Percentage of the Two-Party Vote* | |
	Washington	Nationally
1988	51%	46%
1984	43%	41%
1980	43%	45%
1976	48%	51%
1972	40%	38%
1968	51%	50%
1964	62%	61%

Source: *World Almanac* (New York: Pharos Books, 1990), pp. 442, 425.

Republican surge nationwide. The lasting significance of that surge remains to be seen; the historical record shows that decisive presidential victories sometimes produce a short-term boost in the proportion of people claiming to belong to the winning party and a corresponding decline in the number of people identifying with the losing party. At any rate, the evidence clearly indicates that each of the major parties has a substantial group of supporters. Still, there are large numbers of citizens with no particular loyalty to either party.

One consequence of the broad similarity of party loyalties in Washington and nationwide is that national political tides are reflected in Washington voting decisions. A comparison of presidential election results in the state and nationally reveals that the two sets of results are quite similar (see Table Two). The percentage of the two-party vote for the Democratic presidential candidate in Washington was within two percentage points of the national percentage in five of the seven presidential elections between 1964 and 1988. Only once, in 1988, was the gap as large as five percentage points.

The large proportion of independents in Washington and the relatively close proportions of Democrats and Republicans combine to produce a fairly competitive political environment, at least from a statewide perspective. Studies of party competitiveness based on legislative and gubernatorial elections generally classify Washington as a reasonably competitive state but one that leans somewhat toward the Democratic party,[14] as would be expected from the Democrats' advantage in party identification statewide, at least through the mid 1980s. Other evidence points to a similar conclusion.

For example, in the 1990 U. S. House of Representatives elections in Washington, Democratic candidates received 54 percent of the total votes cast, and Republicans 46 percent. However, the division of the vote varied greatly from one part of the state to another. In one district, the Republican candidate received 70 percent; in another district, the Democrat received 75 percent.[15] Competition on a statewide basis does not assure competition everywhere within the state.

The competitiveness of Washington party politics contributes to the state's relatively high levels of voter turnout. During the 1980s, Washington ranked 15th nationally in voter turnout for presidential, congressional, and gubernatorial elections. Here, too, there was variation: nearly 59 percent of the voting-age population turned out in gubernatorial elections, but less than 43 percent cast ballots in U. S. Senate races.[16] Washington's voter turnout is considerably lower than rates of many countries, but is moderately high by United States standards.

The combination of high voter turnout, competitive parties, and large numbers of political independents presents candidates and public officials with a difficult task. Major elections bring out large numbers of voters, many of whom have no firm party loyalties. A substantial number of the voters who have party ties are affiliated with the opposition party. Candidates find that loyal supporters are difficult to find, and winning candidates discover that they must devote considerable effort to retaining the support that helped them to win initially. The tasks are not impossible; note, for example, that all of Washington's members of the U. S. House of Representatives won reelection in 1990. Retaining political support is difficult, however, when large numbers of potential voters have no firm party loyalty or prefer the opposition party.

Parties in Government

Discussions of the actions of political parties in public office frequently raise a number of questions. Do Democratic public officials behave any differently than Republicans? Do the structures of political institutions enhance or limit party influence over public policies? Do political parties actually have any impact on governmental policy decisions? These questions are more easily raised than answered, but available evidence casts some light on them.

Some of the most readily available evidence on the behavior of partisans in office comes from studies of congressional voting. That evidence reveals that Washington's Democrats in Congress are clearly more liberal than the state's Republicans, both in the house and the senate. There are also significant differences among members of the same party, however (see Table Three). Intraparty differences are especially pronounced among the Democrats, as the figures for the ranges of individual scores indicate. But Republicans also present noticeable diversity.

The results of voting studies also indicate that members of Washington's congressional delegations are ideologically similar to most members of their own parties on a national basis: Republicans vote similarly to other Republicans in the house and Washington Democrats vote as most other northern Democrats do.

Table Three

Voting Ratings of Washington's Members of Congress

House of Representatives	Conservative Coalition Support		Americans for Democratic Action	
	Mean	Range	Mean	Range
Republicans, 1988	81%	71-87	53%	45-60
Democrats, 1988	31%	17-53	87%	85-90
Republicans, 1986	72%	59-82	27%	20-40
Democrats, 1986	31%	6-46	81%	70-95
Senate				
Adams (D), 1988	18%		90%	
Evans (R), 1986	78%		35%	

Source: Norman Ornstein, Thomas Mann, and Michael Malbin, *Vital Statistics on Congress, 1989-1990* (Washington, D.C.: CQ Press, 1990), pp. 230, 250, 259, 266. High Conservative Coalition Support scores indicate conservatism; high Americans for Democratic Action ratings indicate liberalism.

Studies of voting by state party delegations to the presidential nominating conventions paint a somewhat different picture. However, one must keep in mind that party delegations to national conventions include public officials, party officers, and private citizens. From the 1940s through the early 1960s, Washington's Republican party occupied a moderately conservative position, as indicated by votes for presidential nominees and other party decisions (see Table Four). Since then, Washington Republicans have migrated from a more moderate position in the national party to being one of the most conservative Republican state parties in the country. Washington Democrats from the 1940s through the early 1960s were one of the most liberal Democratic state parties in the country. Since then, they have gradually moved to a comparatively middle-of-the-road position within the national party.

In some respects the institutions of Washington state government support party influence over policy decisions. Party caucuses in the state legislature are actively involved in selecting a number of legislative leaders. The caucuses also work to develop party positions on issues and to mobilize support for those positions, often with at least some success.[17] The governor has broad budgetary powers and can use them to support party programs.[18]

In other respects, however, the institutional setting presents major obstacles to party control over policy. One of the most obvious difficulties comes from the numerous centers of authority in state government. If a party has a clear set of principles and a team of candidates who support those principles, the party must win control of a number of different offices and branches in order to translate those principles into public policies. The Washington

Table Four

Party Ideology of Washington Delegations to the National Conventions

Republicans	Ideology Score (Low scores indicate conservatism)
1940-1964	2 (on a scale of 1 to 5)
1948-1972	3 (on a scale of 1 to 5)
1968-1976	1 (on a scale of 1 to 5)
Democrats	Ideology Score (Low scores indicate liberalism)
1940-1964	1 (on a scale of 1 to 6)
1948-1972	2 (on a scale of 1 to 5)
1968-1976	3 (on a scale of 1 to 5)

Sources: Frank Munger and James Blackhurst, "Factionalism in the National Conventions, 1940-1964: An Analysis of Ideological Consistency in State Delegation Voting," *Journal of Politics* 27 (1965), pp. 380, 383; Eugene McGregor, "Uncertainty and National Coalitions," *Journal of Politics* 40 (1978), pp. 1020-1023; David Nice, "Ideological Stability and Change at the Presidential Nominating Conventions," *Journal of Politics* 42 (1980), pp. 847-853.

parties have not been dependably successful in winning control of the various parts of the state government at the same time. In 1990, for example, the Democrats held the offices of governor, lieutenant governor, and treasurer, along with a majority of seats in the state house of representatives. Republicans held the offices of attorney general and secretary of state as well as a majority of seats in the state senate. Nor was 1990 terribly unusual; from 1965 through 1988 the same party controlled the governorship and both houses of the legislature for only eight years. For all the other years during that period, Washington governors faced legislatures with at least one house controlled by the opposition.[19]

Divided partisan control creates a number of difficulties for parties. First, if they come into office with different policy agendas, which is sometimes the case, divided partisan control often produces a great deal of wrangling between different parts of the government and, at times, policy deadlock. Governmental action will be slowed, and some problems may go unresolved. Second, if the two parties made conflicting promises to the voters during the election campaign, partisan control may force officeholders to compromise in order to accomplish anything. Voters may in turn feel that officeholders have reneged on campaign promises. In addition, divided control complicates the task of voters when the time comes to hold officials accountable for what they have done. When one party controls the entire state government, citizens unhappy with governmental performance can vote against that party's members. If one party controls the governorship and state house and the other the state senate and the attorney general's office, the voters' task of assigning blame and credit becomes much more complex. Officeholders of each party will blame the other for policy failures, and voters will have a difficult time sorting out the charges and counter charges.

Divided party control can have beneficial effects as well. A legislature controlled by one party may be more vigilant in overseeing the bureaucracy when the governor belongs to the opposition. If the electorate finds that Republicans are too conservative and Democrats too liberal, then divided control can help balance the two extremes and produce moderation in policy decisions. Policy proposals may receive more thorough scrutiny when examined from more than one point of view.

How much influence do the parties have on policy decisions in Washington? Many factors affect policy making, from the weight of past commitments and the performance of the economy, to interest groups and bureaucratic maneuvering. Studies of party influence on policy making have produced mixed results. The extent of Democratic or Republican control of state government in Washington appears to have relatively little influence on changes in welfare spending, but apparently has some influence on tax policy decisions. In addition, research on the ideological leanings of state parties reveals that they have considerable influence on state policy decisions. States with more liberal political parties tend to have more generous welfare programs, higher education spending, and lower reliance on sales taxes.[20] The parties must struggle with a host of other actors also attempting to influence policy decisions, but at least some policies bear the imprint of party influence.

Conclusion

America's political parties face a difficult period as they prepare for the twenty-first century. The challenges facing government are many and complex. Voter loyalty to parties has declined considerably since the 1950s, and most citizens do not believe parties perform very effectively. New campaign technologies enable candidates to run for office with little or no party help. If the party cannot control what sorts of candidates carry its label, it is likely to present the voters with a variety of different positions on some issues. The result may be an electorate that believes parties have no principles. If those candidates are elected, the party faces the daunting task of trying to weld them together into a force capable of governing.

The parties have tried to cope with those developments, particularly by strengthening their organizations and by trying to master new campaign technologies.[21] While there are clear signs of progress on both fronts, the parties are not likely to regain a dominant position in running election campaigns. If the parties cannot control the nomination and election phases of the process, then performing other tasks will also be very difficult. Parties of the 1990s face the prospect of being only one player in a crowded political arena, and not necessarily the most important player in many situations.

Notes

1. See Jack Dennis, "Trends in Public Support for the American Party System," 5 *British Journal of Political Science* 187-230 (1975).
2. For discussions of party definitions see Samuel Eldersveld, *Political Parties in American Society* (New York: Basic, 1982), pp. 7-12; and Frank Sorauf and Paul Beck, *Party Politics in America*, 6th ed. (Glenview, Il.: Scott, Foresman/Little, Brown, 1988), pp. 7-10.
3. *World Almanac* (New York: Pharos Books, 1990), p. 422.
4. Eldersveld, *Political Parties in American Society*, p. 14; Sorauf and Beck, *Party Politics in America*, pp. 13-16.
5. For conflicting views of the responsible party model see Pendleton Herring, *The Politics of Democracy* (New York: Norton, 1940); and E. E. Schattschneider, *Party Government* (New York: Rinehart, 1942).
6. The threefold division of parties is widely used. See Eldersveld, *Political Parties in American Society;* and Sorauf and Beck, *Party Politics in America.*
7. William Mullen and John Pierce, "Political Parties," in Thor Swanson, William Mullen, John Pierce, and Charles Sheldon, eds., *Political Life in Washington: Governing the Evergreen State* (Pullman: Washington State University, 1985), pp. 56-57.
8. Mullen and Pierce, "Political Parties," pp. 57-58; David Mayhew, *Placing Parties in American Politics* (Princeton, N.J.: Princeton, 1986), pp. 189-196, 337-338.
9. Cornelius Cotter, James Gibson, John Bibby, and Robert Huckshorn, *Party Organizations in American Politics* (Pittsburgh: University of Pittsburgh, 1989), pp. 28-29, 52-53. Their measures of party organizational strength are based on party budgets and staffing, services provided to candidates, and issue leadership.
10. Mayhew, *Placing Parties in American Politics*, pp. 337-338.
11. Timothy Conlan, Ann Martino, and Robert Dilger, "State Parties in the 1980s," 10 *Intergovermental Perspective* 12-13 (1984).
12. *Book of the States* (Lexington, Ky.: Council of State Governments, 1990), pp. 245, 251.
13. For a good overview, see Norman Nie, Sidney Verba, and John Petrocik, *The Changing American Voter* (Cambridge: Harvard University, 1976), chapters 1-4.
14. See John Bibby, Cornelius Cotter, James Gibson, and Robert Huckshorn, "Parties in State Politics," in Virginia Gray, Herbert Jacob, and Robert Albritton, eds., *Politics in the American States*, 5th ed. (Glenview, Il.: Scott, Foresman/Little, Brown, 1990), pp. 90-93, and the studies they cite.
15. *World Almanac*, pp. 81-82.
16. Bibby, et al., "Parties in State Politics," p. 89.
17. *Book of the States*, pp. 128-130, 167-168; Malcolm Jewell and David Olson, *Political Parties and Elections in American States*, 3rd ed. (Chicago: Dorsey, 1988), p. 237. A caucus is a meeting of all the party's members in a chamber of the legislature, such as all the Republicans in the state senate or all the Democrats in the state house.
18. Gray, Jacob, and Albritton, *Politics in the American States*, p. 570.
19. See Jewell and Olson, *Political Parties and Elections*, pp. 225-226; *World Almanac*, p. 95.
20. See Thomas Dye, "Party and Policy in the States," 46 *Journal of Politics* 1107-1109 (1984); Thomas Dye, *American Federalism* (Lexington, Ma.: Lexington, 1990), pp. 126-127; David Nice, "State Party Ideology and Policy Making," 13 *Policy Studies Journal* 780-796 (1985).
21. Bibby, et al., "Parties in State Politics."

Governor Clarence Martin, surrounded by state legislators, signs a bill into law in 1938. Vibert Jeffers photo. *Susan Parish Collection*©

Chapter Five

The Legislature

Kay Gausman Wolsborn

The Labors of Hercules involving the resolution of impossible tasks can be interpreted as a metaphor for the legislative process. The constant struggle to achieve results along with the constant possibility of experiencing defeat is explicit in the myth and implicit in the political process.[1]

T HE UNITED STATES tradition of representative democracy was born in colonial assemblies, adopted into the United States Constitution, and persists as "the guts of democracy"[2] in state legislatures. It is no accident that the branch in which democratic representation resides is not only described first in the U. S. Constitution, but at greater length than either of its two partners, the executive and the judiciary. The Washington Constitution article describing legislative responsibilities is preceded by a declaration of individual rights, reminding state legislators from the outset that the people of the state delegate, but do not relinquish, sovereign authority to their legislative representatives.

Like its national counterpart, the Washington legislature is the place where democratic representation unfolds in the management of state government and in the formulation of sovereign law. Article II, Section 1 of the Washington Constitution reads:

> The legislative authority of the state of Washington shall be vested in the legislature. . . but the people reserve to themselves the power to propose bills, laws, and to enact or reject the same at the polls, independent of the legislature, and also reserve power, at their own option, to approve or reject at the polls any act, item, section, or part of any bill, act, or law passed by the legislature.

Legislators may often disagree on the proper role, priorities, and size of government. They are besieged by influences both personal and political. Yet they must seek consensus even in the absence of agreement. Reaching decisions amid political conflict involves complex and reciprocal interdependence at every stage, and the task never ceases. Each decision, each resolution to a conflict generates new struggles—within the legislative branch itself, among the three branches of state government, among levels of the public sector, and throughout the private sector. Participation in the activities of legislative institutions can be addictive, but it is definitely not for the impatient or the fainthearted.

This chapter examines the Washington state legislature from the following perspectives:

- as a collection over time of *persons and groups* representing the interests of the state's populations,
- as a *complex process* resolving interdependent influences, and
- as an *institution* defining and serving the goals and traditions of state government.

These categories are not as perfectly distinguishable from one another as they appear. But a tripartite approach of focusing on persons, processes, and institutions provides a systematic way to study the many dimensions of what otherwise might appear to be a most confusing sector of state government.

The Legislature as Persons and Groups

Legislators

Geography and Population

The core group of individuals in the state legislature is its elected membership. The bicameral (two house) structure of the Washington legislature is patterned on the United States Congress, as are most other state legislatures.[3] One state senator is elected from each of 49 legislative districts for a four-year term. Senate elections are divided so that half the seats are up for election during each even-numbered year. Two representatives are elected from each legislative district (totalling 98) for two-year terms. Thus, all of the house membership and one-half of the senate membership stand for election during each even-numbered year.

Division of the state into legislative districts assures that each person within the state's geographic boundaries is represented. However logical the idea, the drawing of legislative district lines has nevertheless been politically controversial through most of the state's history. Although charged by the state constitution to "apportion and district anew [both chambers]. . .according to the number of inhabitants,"[4] the legislature has frequently stalled and evaded its responsibility, even as pressure mounted from federal courts against malapportionment during the second half of the twentieth century.[5] Twice, in 1930 and again in 1956, citizens used the initiative process to produce a redistricted state in spite of the legislature. Several federal court cases, beginning in the 1960s, specifically precluded legislatures from straying far from apportionment based on equivalent district populations.[6] In 1972, The U. S. District Court redistricted Washington, the legislature having failed to meet its obligation following the 1970 U. S. census. After the 1980 census, the legislature completed its task in a timely fashion, but then proceeded to shift responsibility for future apportionment into less partisan hands in the form of a special commission.

Most political party loyalists in government prefer that their favorite party control both legislative chambers and the governor's seat during the first session following the census. It would then be relatively easy to construct districts largely favoring the reelection of the incumbents who drew the lines.[7] In a state like Washington, however, where it is rare that a single party holds such complete control, a history of struggle has persisted on this issue. In 1983 legislators sought to reduce the future likelihood of partisan deadlock by winning the voters' approval of a constitutional amendment establishing an independent bipartisan redistricting commission, to be appointed following each federal census cycle.[8] The legislative leadership of the two major political parties selects two commission members each. The four appointed members then choose a non-voting chair.[9]

The 1991 commission published its guidelines for redistricting as follows, in abbreviated form:

- equal population as practicable;[10]
- no purposeful favoritism or discrimination toward any political party or group;
- lines to coincide with counties and municipalities wherever possible;
- districts to be as compact and contiguous as possible.

Once the commission adopts a redistricting plan, it is not subject to gubernatorial veto. The legislature may amend the plan, but only within the first 30 days of the next session, and then only by a two-thirds majority vote in each chamber. If this approach to redistricting operates as expected, majority parties will have lost an opportunity to strengthen their position following each census. Proponents generally see commissions as a means of reducing the politics involved in redistricting. Rather, political maneuvering may simply become less visible to the public. Commenting on the political weakness of the commission approach, one writer has cautioned that "appointed individuals obviously will never receive the pressure of public accountability which legislators must endure each election." [11]

Demographics

During the 102 years from 1889 to 1991, a total of 2,686 persons gained election to the Washington state legislature. They were men and women, but mostly men; of more than one race, but predominantly white; and in many occupations, but with higher proportions in business, law, and agriculture. A close review of the data, however, indicates that the Washington state legislature is not likely to enter the twenty-first century looking as demographically unrepresentative of the population as it was throughout most of the nineteenth and twentieth centuries.

Washington, like so many other states, has made little progress in achieving a racially representative legislature. Communities of color comprise approximately 12 percent of the state's population, but in 1991 were demographically represented by only about 3.4 percent of legislative membership. The composition of district populations, insufficient campaign funds, and inadequate party recruitment may be among the factors sustaining underrepresentation of racial groups. It remains to be seen whether the redistricting commission will address the former. The latter two factors deserve attention from the electorate as long as issues related to race are a part of the state's political agenda.

In his well-researched book on the Washington legislature, Edward Seeberger noted a dramatic rise in the number of women in the state legislature from 1973 to 1987. This pattern has continued into the 1990s.[12] In 1991, gender distribution in the state's population showed 50.3 percent women and 49.7 percent men. In the Washington senate, gender proportions were 24.5 percent women and 75.5 percent men. The proportion in the Washington house was closer at 35.7 percent women and 64.3 percent men. Moreover, women and men shared caucus and committee leadership in similar proportions (approximately one-third and two-thirds respectively). As a result, the Washington legislature, and the voters that elected it, ranked fourth behind New Hampshire, Colorado, and Maine as one of the most advanced states in the area of gender representation.[13]

Patterns of occupational identification have also changed, although not as dramatically as gender distributions. Increasingly, legislators identify themselves as retired, in education, or simply as "legislators."[14] This observation corresponds to a trend reported nationally toward professionalized legislative institutions with increasing proportions of full-time, career-focused legislators.[15] Washington's changing breed of legislative officeholders are less dependent than part-time legislators upon sources of income outside of their salaries. They are people with the time and flexibility to devote to government endeavors.

Legislative salaries are now set by a special nonpartisan state salary commission. In 1991 the commission raised basic legislative salaries from $19,500 to $25,900. The raise prompted a referendum drive to allow voters to decide whether legislators and other public officials deserved the raises. Per diem, transportation, postal, and other allowances provide supplementary compensation, defraying the expense of special sessions and interim committee work.

Nevertheless, legislative work is still considered "part-time," and many members find it necessary to maintain financial support from outside sources. The term part-time is deceptive, however. Work during legislative sessions frequently exceeds 40 hours per week. Moreover, committee responsibilities continue during the periods between sessions. A legislator is expected to serve on three or four standing committees, as well as on appropriate subcommittees, each requiring a considerable amount of time for meetings, homework, and hearing testimony. Meanwhile, casework for individual constituents takes a high priority among a legislator's responsibilities. Lobbyists and interest groups are ever anxious to offer information and support in return for the legislator's time and attention. And it is necessary to mix with constituents and maintain strong connections in the home district if an incumbent is to retain advantage on election day. Incumbents who choose to run for reelection are generally successful. Novices to the legislative process are not unknown, but they are unusual. Especially in the upper house, most first-term senators have had prior experience in the house of representatives or in local government.

The policy implications of change in the distribution of legislative demographics have not been thoroughly documented. It is easier to count the members' characteristics than it is to study the differences in policies and processes that may result from declining proportions of groups traditionally overrepresented. If demographic variables like gender, race, occupation, and socioeconomic class are politically relevant, and if legislators have traditionally represented their own demographic groups better than others, voters may expect to see revised policy agendas and decisions coming from legislatures that reflect their populations more accurately than they have in the past. The linkage, if any, between demographic representation and public policy output from legislatures deserves further exploration.

Partisanship

In contrast to demographic characteristics, partisanship is a powerful determinant of the roles and possibilities open to a legislator. Four party caucuses represent Republicans and Democrats in the house and senate. Political parties present, in their respective platforms, competing value statements concerning the proper role and priorities of government—a philosophical commitment that suggests that house Democrats, for example, collaborate with Democrats in the senate to achieve shared goals. But because political parties are no longer the most powerful force in Washington electoral politics (see chapter four), identification of a legislator's party affiliation does not automatically predict how he or she is likely to vote on a given issue. Concerns of district constituents may well prevail over partisan loyalists, with one exception. On matters of chamber leadership, legislators will vote in unity with their party.

When there is a relatively high turnover rate, a large contingent of freshman legislators arrive in the house after election. Partisans who seek chamber leadership recognize that a certain amount of political courting goes a long way toward winning the support of these newcomers to caucus meetings. Majority versus minority chamber status interjects strategic considerations that can interfere with legislative party cohesion.[16] And individual aspirations of party leaders to statewide elective office may strain intraparty unity across the chambers or even within a chamber.[17]

Yet, in spite of weak state parties, competing district needs, and conflicting party strategies, a legislator's party affiliation remains the single most defining characteristic throughout his or her legislative service.

Committees

Committees provide for a division of labor for legislative work. The trend toward professionalization has often localized expertise within specific committees, with farmers on agriculture committees and teachers on the education committees. A concentration of expertise may simultaneously look much like a concentration of special interests. Such restricted settings may not always fully consider broader needs, such as environmental protection and budgetary constraints.

There are three basic types of legislative committees: (a) ad hoc; (b) standing or permanent; and (c) joint. Ad hoc committees undertake a particular task. An interim committee, for example, might be appointed to study a specific issue during the period between sessions. These ad hoc committees are considered temporary, even though some tasks perpetuate a committee's existence well beyond expectations.

Standing, or permanent, committees are the legislative workhorses—established, modified, or terminated by statues. Each standing committee is chaired by a member affiliated with the chamber's majority party, working in consultation with the ranking minority member—the minority member with the greatest seniority.

The 50th legislature had 21 standing committees in the house. House leadership, in consultation with legislators, assigned each house member to about three committees. The numbers in parentheses represent the number of members assigned to serve on each committee:[18]

Agriculture and Rural Development (12)
Appropriations (30)
Capital Facilities and Financing (13)
Commerce and Labor (11)
Education (19)
Energy and Utilities (13)

Environmental Affairs (12)
Financial Institutions and Insurance (15)
Fisheries and Wildlife (11)
Health Care (11)
Higher Education (14)
Housing (9)
Human Services (11)
Judiciary (19)
Local Government (14)
Natural Resources and Parks (11)
Revenue (17)
Rules (19)
State Government (10)
Trade and Economic Development (13)
Transportation (27)

In the senate, members are usually assigned to three or four committees, depending on the committee workload, which may vary widely depending upon the issues and the member's leadership role. The senate's standing committee structure somewhat paralleled the house structure in the 50th legislature, with 14 standing committees:

Agriculture (7)
Children and Family Services (5)
Economic Development and Labor (11)
Education (11)
Energy and Utilities (9)
Environment and Natural Resources (9)
Financial Institutions and Insurance (11)
Government Operations (5)
Health Care and Corrections (7)
Higher Education (7)
Law and Justice (11)
Rules (17)
Transportation (14)
Ways and Means (23)

Finally, joint committees are, as the name suggests, made up of members from both chambers, and may be permanently defined by statute or short-term conference committees. Conference committees, on the other hand, are joint and ad hoc, charged with reaching an acceptable compromise on legislation which has passed in both chambers, but in different versions.

Committees provide important opportunities for individual legislators to influence public policies that the member or the member's constituents care about. As one of a small, motivated, informed group, the wise member will work hard to cultivate the respect and cooperation of committee colleagues.

Staff

Legislators have recognized the link between a professionalized approach to policy planning and the need for permanent staff with professional expertise. In a real sense, these full-time professionals represent the legislature's backbone, working year-round to maintain operations, conduct research, and provide information to standing committees. Their attention to the legislative process brings system and order to an annual cycle that appears to accelerate from a deceptive calm in August to near chaos by session's end in the spring. In addition to the permanent, nonpartisan professionals, several categories of session staff, partisans, and nonprofessionals cooperate to keep the legislature functioning well.

Partisan and personal loyalty is expected from those who serve on legislators' personal staffs. Many legislators must make do with a single all-purpose staff person. Caucus and committee leaders are generally supported by several staff, in addition to permanent nonpartisan committee professionals. With primary loyalty to their legislators, personal staff members serve as added eyes, ears, voice, and feet. Responding to constituents' requests, gathering information, maintaining calendars, drafting position papers, and monitoring bill progress are some of the tasks demanding immediate attention throughout a session. While tenure in Olympia may depend upon the boss's reelection, many staff members use what they learn to follow career paths into subsequent political and professional occupations of their own.

College students serving internships from schools around the state supplement regular staff. Their responsibilities vary from one office to the next, depending in part on the amount of initiative shown by the intern. Compensation consists of a modest stipend, college credits, and, usually, a well-founded respect for the legislative process and for those who make it happen.

Chamber officers serve in daily sessions as guardians of procedures in their respective chambers. In the house, these are the chief clerk, assistant clerk, minute clerk, and reader. In the senate are the secretary (who is chief administrative officer), assistant secretary, reading clerk, docket clerk, journal clerk, and sergeant-at-arms. Although serving at the behest of the majority political party, the primary responsibility of these officials is to their respective chambers. The house and senate each have security personnel posted at entrances to check credentials and bags. Friendly and casual, they and the capitol security staff provided by the state police are called upon to monitor and, if necessary, constrain the energies of visiting groups and constituents. Performers, protestors, advocates, and tourists keep the capitol buildings humming and the staffs busy all through the sessions.

Finally, high school students in colorful blazers serve as pages, stationed throughout the chambers and legislative office buildings. "Gofers" of the first order, these young people are recommended by their local legislator, trained to be quick and quiet and to respect capitol traditions. They serve no more than a few weeks in order to allow a maximum number of students to participate in this on-site introduction to legislative government.

The "Third House"

The "third house" is an informal association of the professional lobbyists who work the legislature. Many of the ideas associated with public policy formation originate from groups and individuals working outside the categories of elected legislature and publicly paid staff. Whether promoting preservation or modification of the status quo, lobbyists understand that information is their primary resource (see chapter three). Information about the interest they advocate, identification of those legislators and staff members supportive and those not supportive, and information on the progress of any item in the legislative pipeline relating to that interest—all are critical elements in making the best use of a lobbyist's time and energies. A single professional lobbyist may be employed by one or more clients. Likewise, a single organizational interest may choose to employ one or more lobbyists. Public Disclosure Commission (PDC) records indicate that, over the period covered by a legislative session, lobbyists are likely to outnumber legislators by three or four to one.[19]

With a few notable exceptions, interests represented in "ulcer gulch"[20] are as diverse as those extant in society. Business and education are represented by a variety of organizational interest groups as are utilities, labor, local government, churches, gambling, and health care. As explained in chapter three, techniques by which specific interests are served are as much a part of politics as are roll call votes in chamber.

Lobbyists often draft and propose bills to legislators for sponsorship. Testimony and background research are provided to staffs and committees. Lobbyists monitor the progress of bills and amendments, project potential impacts, and suggest alternative courses of action. And, of course, they may offer campaign support, usually funding and/or workers, to a legislator more favorably inclined than his or her opponent to the preferred issue positions of a given interest group, especially if that legislator is on a relevant committee or in a strategic leadership position. Equally active in pressuring or persuading legislators are numerous volunteer advocates who constitute an important part of legislative monitoring and campaign work for legislative candidates.

The impact on public policy of systematic promotion of particular interest preferences is difficult to assess. At the very least, such organized mobilization gains the attention of legislative decision-makers. It also allows for systematic feedback to district constituents on the voting behavior of their respective legislators. Interests lacking the advantage of group organization are less likely to be part of legislative consideration when policy choices are made. Noncitizens, Native Americans, the homeless, and the poor are examples of groups traditionally underrepresented in the dynamics of legislative lobbying.

In addition to the persons and groups discussed above, scholars, journalists, visiting dignitaries, and members of the executive branch frequent the capitol buildings on a consistent basis, mostly to observe legislative processes. Of these "others," however, the executive branch in particular interacts with, sometimes initiates, and often depends upon the decisions and activities of the legislative branch.

Legislative Processes

Policy choices are made and statutory law evolves by means of a systematic process. Putting legislative process into a broad framework, one could say that it begins with an issue of concern to one or more individuals, i. e., a "problem." Someone's idea of a proper solution is drafted into a bill to be processed by the legislature. A bill passed by both chambers becomes a legislative act. Signed by the governor, or at least not vetoed, the act becomes a part of Washington law. Bills are not the only routine items of business to come before the legislature. Resolutions, memorials, and appointment confirmations are among other business attended to by one or both houses during each session. But only bill proposals may come to impact public policy as expressed in statutory law.

Although the process is systematic, it is also complex, presenting formidable obstacles to each new proposal. Precisely because of its complexity, three observations should be made about legislative policy making. First, it is easier to delay, dilute, or defeat a bill than it is to pass it. Second, passage of a bill into law does not guarantee satisfactory resolution of the original issue. Administrative implementation and judicial interpretation of a statute may produce unforeseen and unintended consequences. Third, although a particular bill may die during a session, no issue need ever be considered permanently "dead." The basis for these observations become clear from the discussion in this section on house and senate procedures, committee work, and executive actions.

Sessions

Biennial elections set the stage for each new legislature. The 50th legislature followed the 1986 election and extended from January of 1987 through December 1989. Regular sessions of each legislature begin on the second Monday each January. The constitution stipulates that regular sessions are to be 105 days in length in odd-numbered years and 60 days in even-numbered

Table One

Margin of Control of Washington Legislature, 1941-1991

Year	Senate Democrat	Senate Republican	House Democrat	House Republican
1991		1	13	
1989		1	28	
1987		1	24	
1985	5		8	
1983	3		10	
1981		1		14
1979	11		0	0
1977	11		26	
1975	11		26	
1973	13		16	
1971		9		3
1969	5		13	
1967	9		11	
1965		15		21
1963	15		3	
1961	23		19	
1959	21		33	
1957		16		13
1955		2	1	
1953		4		17
1951	4		9	
1949		8	35	
1947	0	0		43
1945	18		27	
1943	8		15	
1941	28		37	

Source: *Members of the State Legislature by District, 1889-1987* (Olympia: Washington State Legislature, 1987).

years.[21] However, it is rare that the state's business is completed in a regular session. Special sessions can be called by a two-thirds vote of each house. More typically, the governor calls a special session for a specific purpose. Once in session, however, the legislature may set its own agenda.

The dynamics of conflict during each legislature are determined by which political party or parties wins control of each house, the size of the margin of control, and the party affiliation of the sitting governor. Table One shows the margin of partisan control for the senate and house of representatives for 50 years. Margins range all the way from zero (a tie)—once in the senate and once in the house—to a high of a 43 Republican margin in 1947 in the house and a 23 Democrat margin in 1961 in the senate. In 15 cases out of 100, the margin was five or fewer. In general, the larger the margin of control, the less

Table Two
State of Washington Legislative Activity
51st Legislature, 1989-1990

Activities	Senate		House	
Bills—	(no.)	(%)	(no.)	(%)
Introduced	1,912		2,039	
Passed in chamber of origin	685	35.9[a]	878	37.6[a]
Passed by legislature	388	20.3[a]	406	19.9[a]
Signed by governor	377	97.2[b]	391	96.3[b]
Vetoed by governor	11	2.8[b]	15	3.7[b]
Vetoed in part by governor	40	10.3[b]	62	15.3[b]
Veto overridden	1	(partial)		
Joint Resolutions—				
Introduced	41		31	
Passed in chamber of origin	7		6	
Passed by legislature	4		1	
Concurrent Resolutions—				
Introduction	50		48	
Adopted by chamber of origin	25		33	
Adopted by legislature	20		28	
Joint Memorials—				
Introduced	27		38	
Passed by chamber of origin	19		17	
Passed by legislature	11		6	
Floor Resolutions, single chamber—	187		203	
Gubernatorial government appointments—	267		N/A	

Source: Calculated from data reported in the final edition of vols. 1 and 2, *Legislative History and Digest of Bills of the Senate and House of Representatives* (Olympia: Washington State Legislature, 1990), compiled to and inclusive of April 25, 1990.

[a] Percentage of the total number of bills introduced in that chamber.

[b] Percentage of the total number of bills passed by the legislature (both chambers) and submitted to the governor for signature.

influence is wielded by the minority party—unless the governor is affiliated with the same party as a legislative minority. In such a case, the majority party can be forced, by the threat of veto, to negotiate in order to avoid stalemate.

In an effort to spread the workload somewhat evenly over the duration of the regular session, a session calendar announces in advance the cutoff dates for floor reading of committee reports, as well as consideration of bills from the house of origin and from the opposite house. Although several categories of business are exempt from cutoff dates,[22] the session calendar represents a shared plan by which to reach the end of the legislative business sometime near the constitutional limit of the legislative session.

The amount of business accomplished over the two-year period of a legislature is staggering. Table Two lists the official count of bills, resolutions, and memorials processed during the 51st legislature. Each tally represents varying numbers of hours in conference with colleagues, meeting with constituents and journalists, contacting executive branch officials, and listening to lobbyists. The result is that thousands of proposals are winnowed down to hundreds of official policy actions. The largest proportion of work is devoted to revisions in the statutory policies of the State of Washington. In the 51st legislature, for example, 3,951 bills were turned into 768 pieces of legislation in the house and senate combined.

Rules and Norms

Rules, behavioral norms, and leadership provide the lubricants for legislative decision-making. Each new legislature adopts and publishes its own set of rules, although there is substantial continuity from one legislature to the next. The legislative handbook provides predictability for a complicated process and is invaluable not only for legislators and their staffs, but also for lobbyists, the press, and constituents. Those who are familiar with the rules are able to work the legislative process to maximum advantage, adopting parliamentary maneuvers likely to succeed and avoiding those likely to fail.

Behavioral norms are the informal expectations of proper behavior, not so readily available in written form. Norms are, nevertheless, crucial to a smooth-running legislature. They set the standards for good manners that supplement rules by providing a protocol of diplomacy among legislative participants. In a political environment, differences of opinion can produce a stalemate. Colleagues who are foes on one issue may need to ally on another. Little would be accomplished without appropriate deference patterns, a willingness to negotiate, graceful compromises, and mutual respect.

Never was the importance of norms more clearly demonstrated than during the 1979 session, with the house of representatives evenly divided with 49 Republicans and 49 Democrats. Traditionally, the party with the most members controls leadership positions and committees. Assignments to committee membership generally reflect the ratio between the parties. Only because norms of diplomatic behavior had been passed along from one legislative generation to the next could special rules appropriate to the anomaly of an even split develop. As a result, some committees had co-chairs while Republicans chaired some and Democrats others. Because of the informal norms, the house largely ignored stalemates.[23]

House and Senate Leadership

The lieutenant governor serves as president of the senate, traditionally an office emphasizing fairness in the administration of rules of order and aloofness from partisan struggles. A president *pro tempore* from the senate serves in the lieutenant governor's absence. Partisan leadership is organized around majority and minority leader, whips, and caucus chairs chosen by the majority and minority party caucuses. In the senate, with its fewer members serving longer terms, rules are less specific than in the house of representatives. Norms and personalities are crucial to systematic proceedings. Since a relatively small minority can effectively obstruct the legislative process, the majority leader seeks amicable consensus within his or her caucus, as well as in negotiations with the minority leadership. This requires keeping careful account of how individuals plan to vote on a given issue, making sure that "friends" show up when the item is on the calendar, and arranging compromises and tradeoffs when necessary. The caucus chairs preside over their respective party caucuses where general policy and strategies are discussed. Party floor leaders coordinate policies through the senate. Information retrieval from individual senators is managed by the whips and their staffs. While discussions and preliminary votes may be held in caucus on controversial issues (during meetings closed to the public), such votes are generally not binding on caucus members, though pressure to conform may be intense.

Leadership in the house of representatives revolves particularly around the powerful position of speaker. The speaker's power stems from election by and support from the majority party, and is exercised by means of parliamentary dominance of the house sessions, a prominent role in making committee assignments, and chairing of the Rules Committee. Typically, the speaker is an experienced and respected—sometimes feared—legislator, a person of considerable political stature in the eyes of colleagues. Characterized by shorter terms, larger membership, and higher turnover, the house depends heavily on its leadership and rules to dispose of legislative business in a systematic way. As in the senate, house leadership also includes majority and minority leaders, whips, and caucus chairs. These positions are important, but not quite as powerful as their senate counterparts by virtue of the speaker's multiple power bases.

Literally thousands of proposals are filed each session with the secretary of the senate and the chief clerk of the house of representatives (see Table Two). While one or more legislators must sponsor a bill, the ideas—even the precise wording—for bill proposals come from a variety of sources. The governor's program, for example, takes the form of a group of bills, including the budget, and is traditionally introduced ("placed in the hopper") and given priority by the leadership of the governor's political party. Executive request bills are often closely followed by press and television news personnel as measures of the effectiveness of the state's chief executive.

Bill proposals originate from other government sources as well. Requests are received directly from individual agency administrators, county and municipal officials, and professional organizations. Moreover, court decisions, state agency policies, local government actions, and changing federal laws impact public policy. Changes in one aspect of policy often require legislative action to establish compliance by all offices and individuals affected by that policy. Lobbyists, public interest organizations, political parties, and political action committees constitute still other sources of bill ideas. Legislators and their staffs submit bill proposals from any or all of these sources, as well as generating their own.

Various strategies are employed in securing sponsorship for a bill.[24] Prestige, acknowledged expertise in a particular issue, and a breadth of ideological perspectives are among factors sought in sponsor-seeking strategies. Sponsorship is the first of many opportunities for a legislator to decide whether to support a given proposal. Given the large number and great variety of legislative proposals each session, a "part-time" legislator cannot be expected to possess the technical expertise necessary for making informed decisions on all issues. Consequently, decisions on bills outside a given legislator's immediate field of interest are frequently made after consultation with colleagues and trusted lobbyists who have access to relevant expertise. In this way, decisional cues are offered and exchanged in an environment of bargaining and reciprocity.

Standing Committees

At least one standing committee closely related to the topic must review and analyze every bill proposal. The committee is charged with investigation into the merits of, and objections to, the proposal. The influence of committee chairs on public policy decisions can be decisive. A chair can inhibit or accelerate passage of a bill with a large variety of maneuvers related to control of the committee's agenda, limits on public testimony and hearings, consideration of amendments, and scheduling of meetings and debates. A chair may, for example, simply "pocket" a bill by refusing to include it in the committee's agenda or not bringing it up for a vote. Legislators seeking release of the disfavored bill risk the committee chair's ire, together with a loss of cooperation on other issues. Such a flagrant exercise of power is unusual, however, since loss of reciprocity cuts both ways and could seriously disadvantage any legislator in representing his or her constituents. Nevertheless, the initial referral of a bill to a standing committee may sometimes reflect deliberate avoidance of legislators hostile to the bill under consideration.

Testimony is received, arguments are made, and the committee vote eventually taken on whether to recommend the bill to the full house or senate. Among many options available are the following: (a) report out with "do-pass" recommendation; (b) propose amendments; (c) return the bill to its sponsors for redrafting; (d) take no action, allowing the bill to die in committee; or (e) report out with a recommendation plus a minority report. It is not uncommon for a major new bill to emerge from committee in a form much different from its content at introduction. This is particularly true when opposing parties hammer out compromises in the effort to reach an acceptable position.

Bills reported out of committee for a second or third floor reading must first be referred to the chamber's Rules Committee for assignment on the daily floor calendar. This "gatekeeping" function means that the Rules Committee can delay or constrain a bill's progress. While this committee does not amend or hear further testimony on a bill's content, it frequently consults in public meetings with sponsors and/or committee chairs to discuss timing and limitations, i. e., the "rules," of floor debate for a particular bill. These committee decisions are crucial for the survival of controversial legislation.

Chamber Actions

At its first floor appearance a bill is read by title only for routine assignment to committee. Not until the second reading do legislators as a body make decisions. At this point, upon recommendations from the standing committee(s), substantive debate begins between a bill's supporters and opponents. Amendments may be proposed and voted on by the full membership only on second reading. At the conclusion of debate the bill, with any approved amendments, is returned to the Rules Committee for calendar placement for third reading. This final appearance allows for debate, but no further changes in a bill's substance. The discussion may include recommendations concerning implementing the bill into public policy, but the actual choice, after third reading and debate, comes down to a "yes" or "no" vote.

While a legislator's voting options appear to be a simple dichotomy, a great deal of group strategy may operate at this stage. Approval must be by a constitutional majority (i. e., of the entire membership of the body, not merely a simple majority of those in attendance). Hence, a bill's fate may depend upon the scheduling of a vote or whether there are motions to delay the vote, to table, or to reconsider. There is one significant difference between the two chambers. A bill may be "bumped" from second to third and final reading, omitting a second referral to the Rules Committee. However, this abridgment is likely only in the senate, and only if a bill includes no amendments. In fact, a significant number of bills are narrow in scope and not controversial. Passage of these is facilitated by inclusion on a "consent calendar," approved routinely as a group, without debate, at the beginning of each session.

The simplest examples of the legislative process are the bills passed without amendments by each chamber. Bills must be approved in identical versions before they can be forwarded for the governor's consideration. Consequently, a bill amended in one house must be (a) passed with identical wording by the other; (b) returned for reconsideration by the amending house;

or (c) assigned to a conference committee for reconciliation. Ultimately, each chamber must process and pass each bill if it is to become Washington law. Passage can occur in sequence, with a bill passing completely through its house of origin before introduction in the opposite house. Alternatively, companion bills may be introduced in both chambers simultaneously. In either case, introducing a bill includes a first reading (of three) in abbreviated form and referral to a standing committee by the presiding chamber officer. Most bills, however, die quietly in committee. The final version of a bill passed in each chamber is signed by the presiding officers in the house and senate and forwarded to the governor.

Executive Actions

Bills that survive legislative procedures must still face consideration by the governor, who has several options. Indeed, many state governors, including Washington's, are granted greater discretion than the U. S. President in dealing with legislative actions. The governor may choose to (a) sign the bill into law; (b) allow a bill to become law without signing it; (c) sign the bill into law, but veto one or more sections (the "item veto" is especially useful in appropriation measures); or (d) veto the entire bill. The legislature, to be sure, may override gubernatorial vetoes by a two-thirds vote in each chamber. It is rare, however, that the legislature overturns executive vetoes (see Table Two).

The executive branch interacts with the legislative both as source and subject of a large proportion of statutory law. As discussed in chapters seven and ten, one of the governor's chief responsibilities is to assemble all requests for state funding together with revenue projections. The state budget proposal is submitted through the Office of Financial Management (OFM) to the legislature for committee hearings, debate, and adoption. More than simply transmitting funding requests, the budget constitutes public policy choices for the State of Washington for a two-year period. Even in the best of times these choices inevitably present sources of controversy. When the legislature is dominated by a political perspective different from that of the governor, or when the state's economy is under stress, adopting the state budget can become a major dilemma. Legislative actions concerning the governor's proposals can modify or even reverse program emphases by increasing, decreasing, or eliminating agency requests altogether. The executive branch is not without battle resources, however. Threatened with legislative disapproval, the governor can use his or her ready access to press coverage to rally public support. In the final analysis, the veto powers—veto threat, veto in part, or veto in entirety—are the governor's ultimate weapons.

State executive agencies with whom lobbying interests are closely associated may become virtually invulnerable to legislative cuts, especially insofar as their programs are understood and supported by standing committee members who share comparable professional backgrounds. Such support networks among interest groups, executive agencies, and legislative committees can considerably impact related legislation.

Executive branch agencies also find themselves working with legislators on casework involving specific constituent complaints. Given a difficult time by a state agency, a constituent may contact his or her state legislator to help solve the problem. Usually, a staff member determines the nature of the problem and then calls the appropriate state official requesting, on behalf of the legislator, that specific attention be focused on the constituent's situation. Ideas for new legislation have, on occasion, resulted from casework directing attention to a troublesome aspect of Washington public policy.

Bill proposals modify the status quo. The participants and processes described above allow multiple opportunities to delay, dilute, and defeat each new proposal. As a result, there is a built-in procedural advantage for status quo defenders. On the other hand, there are few rules limiting the political strategy or frequency with which one may seek policy objectives. Strategic compromises in wording and timing can dramatically improve a bill's chances. Moreover, new participants enter the system each session. The climate of opinion changes as more information is added to the public agenda. And the interrelationships among levels, branches, and units of government may serve to transform yesterday's radical departures into tomorrow's status quo.

Laws by the Voters

Although analyzed thoroughly in chapter six, any discussion of lawmaking must include references to the initiative and referendum processes by which the voters can bypass the legislature and make their own laws. At least some individuals and groups are likely from time to time to feel that legislators have failed to be representative. For such occasions the Washington Constitution provides the electorate a means to take matters into their own hands. Initiatives and referenda often generate heated political campaigns. Enormous amounts of money can be spent to pass or defeat such measures. These processes by which the voters can bypass legislative bodies constitute the few remaining examples of direct democracy in American state and national government.

The Legislature as Institution

At the middle of the twentieth century, state legislatures were not known for their competence, efficiency, or democratic representation. Legislatures may have been the first United States branches of government to institutionalize the concept of representative democracy, but into the 1960s many deserved ridicule as "inefficient and corrupt."[25] Writing that legislative institutions are now "transformed and at risk," Alan Rosenthal summarized the earlier critique widely shared of state legislatures:

> They were unrepresentative, malapportioned, and dominated by rural areas of the states. The legislative process was, in many instances, a sham; power within the institution was narrowly held, and not democratically exercised. Major issues were sidestepped, and initiatives for state policy were left to the governor. The legislature's role in the most important business of government, that of allocating funds, was minimal. Whatever the positive outcomes and however well served the people of a state might be, relatively little could be attributed to the performance of the legislature.[26]

Encouraged by U. S. Supreme Court reapportionment cases, many legislatures, including Washington's, moved into a new phase during the late 1960s and 1970s. Rosenthal characterized the decade 1965 to 1975 as "the rise of the legislative institution."[27] Modernization and professionalization became more common. Urban dwellers began to take their legislative places in proportion to their population following the 1970 census, though not without difficulty. In Washington, apportionment from the 1970 census had to be completed by the U. S. District Court.

Throughout the 1960s and 1970s the federal government sidestepped legislative control and accountability by allocating grant funds directly to local and state bureaucracies struggling to exist on regressive state revenues from sales and property taxes. Gubernatorial powers grew steadily by virtue of longer terms, permissibility of succession, and consolidation of budgeting authority.[28] Meanwhile, federal categorical grants flowing into state programs left legislators with "a feeling of impotence when trying to control spending."[29]

The administration of Ronald Reagan in the 1980s brought a new federal/state relationship, one that provided state legislatures with room to engage in their own modernization movement. It also brought a new set of challenges. The Reagan economic recovery program simplified and then cut federal aid to state agencies. The program also began to require legislative accountability for funds in the form of audits and annual reports.[30] As a result, legislative responsibility increased, as did the need for well-balanced sources of state revenue.

With the encouragement of its electorate, the Washington legislature responded to the challenges of the 1980s by moving to professionalize. It expanded legislative facilities, affiliated with the National Conference of State Legislatures, and computerized bill and budget information in an effort to improve time management, increase efficiency, and provide the bases for comprehensive planning for the future of Washington's government. Two major projects demonstrate commitment by the membership to institutional development of the Washington legislature. The Washington 2000 Project describes

Table Three

Legislative Expenditures for the State of Washington
as a Proportion of Total State Expenditures

Biennium	Proportion of General Fund Expenditures (%)	Proportion of All Funds— Operating and Capital (%)
1975-77	.60	.40
1977-79	.54	.36
1979-81	.54	.36
1981-83	.54	.36
1983-85	.57	.40
1985-87	.56	.38
1987-89	.61	.41
1989-91	.62	.42

Calculated from data in "Washington State Expenditures—General Fund" and "Washington State Expenditures—All Funds, Operating and Capital," *State of Washington Data Book 1989* (Olympia: Office of Financial Management, 1989), pp. 38-39.

legislative procedures that "set long-range goals and objectives, and provides a mechanism for future implementation. . . primarily proactive instead of only reactive, with a focus always ten to fifteen years into the future." Standing committees are now able to draft long-range "futures" bills and prepare forecasts of fiscal impacts.[31] A second example of institutional foresight is the leadership provided by the Washington legislature in the development of the Pacific Northwest Economic Region. In cooperation with Alaska, Oregon, Idaho, Montana, British Columbia, and Alberta, bipartisan leaders from the Washington legislature have joined their policy-making counterparts to create an alliance for growth and economic development—an approach unique in its cross-national linkage and integrated collaboration.[32]

Despite the professionalization, legislative expenses as a proportion of state expenditures have remained surprisingly constant at less than 1 percent over the 16-year period from 1975 to 1991 (see Table Three).

The future did not look bright in 1991 for those seeking to demonstrate the viability of democratic representation at the state level. With as many as 36 states facing serious fiscal problems, even the wealthiest states had reason to worry. Connecticut was reported "on the verge of political chaos" as the legislature failed to approve an income tax to remedy its $2.7 billion budget deficit. The tormented state entered its 1992 fiscal year with a shutdown in state services and facilities and a multilevel stalemate among its four legislative caucuses and independent governor.[33] States in such distress can no longer look to the national government for help. Republican federalism, an enormous budget deficit, military ventures, and crisis in the thrift industry reveal very empty pockets for the foreseeable future. Washington legislators have understood the need for an institutional sense of purpose in a state represented by a complex diversity of interests. The 1990s present an unavoidable test of their competence, efficiency, and democratic commitment.

Governance by democratic principles and legislative process is no easy task. Deciding the extent to which the legislature, or a legislator, fulfills a representative responsibility is no less a chore. The following questions may help us think about legislative processes, democratic representation, and constituent responsibility.

To which constituency should a legislator respond? Should it be the political party under whose banner he or she was elected, residents of the geographic district, the most important local economic interest, or perhaps a demographic group with whom he or she closely identifies?

How much should the legislator resemble the constituents in order to represent them well? Should race, gender, income, religion, education, or other characteristics be considered in deciding the extent to which the legislator is representative?

Are legislative processes well enough understood by most citizens? How would you make the work of the legislature more widely understood? How would you change legislative procedures if you could?

Notes

1. The quotation is from *The Twelve Labors of Hercules*, an undated, unattributed pamphlet describing the murals painted by Michael C. Spafford on the north and south gallery walls of the Washington State House of Representatives.

2. Alan Rosenthal, "The Legislative Institution: Transformed and at Risk," in Carl E. Van Horn, ed., *The State of the States* (Washington, D. C.: Congressional Quarterly Press, 1989), p. 69.

3. The state of Nebraska stands alone among the states as the only nonpartisan, unicameral legislature.

4. Washington State Constitution, original text Article II, Section 3, repeated by Amendment 74, 1983 Substitute Senate Joint Resolution No. 103, approved by Washington voters 8 Nov. 1983.

5. See "History of Redistricting and Reapportionment in Washington State," in Sidney Snyder and Dennis Heck, eds., *Members of the State Legislature by District* (Olympia: Washington State Legislature, 1987).

6. United States Supreme Court cases *Baker v. Carr* (1962) and *Reynolds v. Sims* (1965).

7. It is because of this advantage that national party organizations have seen fit in census years to provide campaign assistance to state legislative candidates in selected districts where parties are in competition for control of the legislature.

8. This and the following information on the redistricting commission is taken from the booklet entitled *Joint Legislative Redistricting Brochure* (Olympia: Washington State Legislature, 1990).

9. The commission was plagued at the outset by traditional cross-state rivalries when no commission member was selected from the east side of the state.

10. Average district population based on 1989 estimates was projected to be 97,163.

11. John M. McGehee, "Reapportionment Commissions: The Reform We Don't Need," 5 *State Legislatures* 11-15 (Dec. 1979).

12. Edward D. Seeberger, *SINE DIE: A Guide to the Washington State Legislative Process* (Seattle: University of Washington Press, 1989), pp. 3-5.

13. In comparison, the U. S. Congress gender distribution was as follows: senate—2 percent women, 98 percent men; house—6.4 percent women, 93.6 percent men. Of all state legislative seats, approximately 17 percent were held by women, 83 percent by men. Washington Senator Jeannette Hayner's position as majority leader was comparable to only three women contemporaries who were elected by legislative colleagues to the position of house speaker in Arizona, Oregon, and Minnesota. Information from the Center for the American Woman and Politics, CAWP News & Notes (New Brunswick, N.J.: Eagleton Institute of Politics, Rutgers University, 1990).

14. Seeberger, *SINE DIE*, pp. 12-13.

15. Rosenthal, "Legislative Institution," p. 73.

16. See, for example, the editorial analysis by Shelby Scates, "State Legislature Opens to Strains of Dueling Agendas," *Seattle Post-Intelligencer*, 22 Jan. 1991.

17. Walfred Peterson, "Interest Groups and Lobbies in Washington State Government," in Thor Swanson, William Mullen, John Pierce, and Charles Sheldon, eds., *Political Life in Washington: Governing the Evergreen State* (Pullman: Washington State University Press, 1985).

18. Information on legislative standing committees is taken from the *1989-90 Legislative Manual, State of Washington* (Olympia: Washington State Legislature, 1989-1990).

19. The Public Disclosure Commission reported 1,090 lobbyist registrations for January-September 1989, and total lobbying expenditures of $10,982,245. "If an individual lobbyist registers for more than one employer in a category each is counted as a separate registration. Likewise, if an employing organization has more than one registered lobbyist, each one counts in the number of registrations" (p. 44). Consequently, the number of lobbyist registrations is an overestimate of the actual number of persons lobbying. *Political Spending by Major Interest Groups in Washington State, 1988-89* (Olympia: Washington State Public Disclosure Commission, 1990).

20. Ulcer gulch is the slang term for an area between the two chambers where lobbyists hang out, do business, and listen for useful gossip. It is furnished with seats, ashtrays, coffee machines, and many telephone booths—with doors for privacy.

21. Washington State Constitution, Amendment 68.

22. The exceptions are initiatives (from the people) to the legislature, messages pertaining to amendments, differences between the houses, conference reports, and matters incident to interim meetings between sessions and to closing the business of the legislature.

23. W. F. Mullen and K. G. Wolsborn, "The Effects of the Tie in the Washington State Legislature in 1979." Paper prepared for the 1980 annual meeting of the Western Social Science Association, Albuquerque, New Mexico.

24. Sid Snyder, *Enacting a Law in Washington State: The Major Stages* (Olympia: Washington State Legislature, n. d.).

25. Terry Sanford, *Storm Over the States* (New York: McGraw-Hill, 1967), p. 39.

26. Rosenthal, "Legislative Institution," p. 69.

27. *Ibid.*, p. 70.

28. Carl E. Van Horn, "The Quiet Revolution," in Van Horn, *The State of the States,* pp. 1-13.

29. James Skok, "Federal Funds and State Legislatures: Executive-Legislative Conflict in State Government," in Marilyn Gittell, ed., *State Politics and the New Federalism* (New York: Longman, 1986), p. 269.

30. Gittell, "New Federalism: A Challenge to the States," in Gittell, ed., *State Politics and the New Federalism,* pp. 516-522.

31. *Washington 2000 Project Description* (Olympia: Washington State Institute for Public Policy, n. d.), p. 11.

32. Alan Bluechel, "Reaping Profit from a New World Order," 64 *Journal of State Government* 18-21 (Jan./Mar. 1991).

33. Michael Specter, "Dragging Connecticut Toward an Income Tax," *Washington Post National Weekly Edition,* 22 Jy. 1991.

Members of the 40 Mil Tax Commission deliver signed petitions for state initiative #129 to the Secretary of State's office in the capitol building, 1938. Vibert Jeffers photo. *Susan Parish Collection*©

Chapter Six

Direct Democracy in Washington

Hugh A. Bone and Herman D. Lujan

Introduction

IN HIS INSIGHTFUL account of America written in the 1850s, Alexis de Tocqueville observed that Americans saw themselves as the masters of a responsive government.[1] As the franchise spread, the numbers of people taking part in the selection of their leaders increased, even though it took years from Tocqueville's time for women, blacks, and those as young as eighteen years of age to finally and completely obtain the right to vote for public officials. Still, the idea of permitting the electorate to vote on constitutions and constitutional amendments dated from the beginnings of state government. Referenda on *bond issues* (that is, selling state or local government bonds to finance public projects) were also established at an early date.

The post-Civil War period was marked by widespread corruption of state legislatures and abuses of lobbyist influences. Political machines corrupted some cities. This led reformers to propose that, at the state and local levels, ballots be used not only to select leaders but also to recall public officials before the ends of their terms. This reform movement advanced the concept of direct legislation, where voters could initiate a law or require a law passed by a legislative body to be submitted to voters for their approval before going into effect.

As Congressman John Baker observed, the various forms of direct democracy are logically related. When representatives fail to act (nonfeasance), the initiative is available to the people. If the legislature enacts unwanted laws (misfeasance), the people can use the referendum to repeal those laws. If officials abuse their public trust (malfeasance), they can be recalled.[2]

By the end of the Progressive era in the 1920s, over one-third of the states had adopted the initiative and referendum. Interest waned but was revived during the protests of the 1960s, leading a number of other states to adopt the devices. By 1990 only six states had no initiatives or referenda on the ballot. In that election, of the 207 initiatives or referenda voted upon, 104 passed.

Fifty-seven were direct initiatives, of which 20 passed. It is also worth noting that a few states even permit their constitutions to be amended through the initiative process.

Although Washington does not allow the constitutional initiative, it provides extraordinary opportunity to place propositions on the ballot—some four different types of mechanisms in all. The most widely used is the direct initiative, whereby 8 percent of the electorate who voted in the last gubernatorial campaign may sign a petition for a proposed law. If the secretary of state validates the requisite number of signatures, the proposition appears on the next general election ballot. For a measure to be adopted, a majority of those voting on the proposition must vote affirmatively.

The same procedure is used to draw up an indirect initiative. In this case, the validated initiative first goes to the legislature. That body may adopt it and, if so, it becomes law without further action. The state's renowned blanket primary was adopted this way in 1934. But if the legislature amends or rejects the initiative, it, along with the legislative alternative, if there is one, goes before the voters in the next election. In 1972, for example, the legislature decided to offer its own proposals for litter control and shorelines management and the electorate chose the legislature's alternative in both cases. Over the years, the legislature has seen about 75 percent of its referrals accepted. In 1991, the legislature chose neither to adopt nor submit its own abortion rights and death-with-dignity policies and the measures went directly to the voters.

There are two types of referenda. In the first case, the legislature may decide to refer a passed bill, often because of political reasons, to voters. A majority vote is then required for adoption. In 1972, voters acted on eight measures which the legislature referred to them. Six were money measures which amounted to large sums, so the legislature wanted to obtain voter responsibility for future debt.

Four percent of the voters who participated in the last gubernatorial race must sign a petition to have a legislative enactment placed on the ballot for the voters' approval before it becomes effective—usually referred to as a demanded or petition referendum. This process has been used much less frequently than direct initiatives, but with devastating effect, so far as the legislature is concerned. Through 1984, the people upheld the legislature on only two such measures out of 30!

In briefest compass, the initiative process is a method of enacting policies on which the legislature, for whatever reason, has failed to act. By contrast, the demanded referendum is a method of preventing "bad" or dubious legislation from going into effect.

It is worth mentioning that constitutional amendments also require voter approval. The legislature has submitted many amendments during the first century of the state's constitution, with proposed amendments appearing on nearly every election ballot, adding to the voter's burden. In what seems to be the record, voters in 1972 were asked to decide the fate of 26 direct and indirect initiatives, referred and demanded referenda, and constitutional amendments.

Another mechanism available to voters is the recall of those in office, except for judges of courts of record. No major Washington state officer has been recalled. In contrast, a number of local officials have been removed, or have survived by thin margins.

Extent of Use

Traditionally, Washington, along with Oregon, California, North Dakota, and Colorado, has heavily used the initiative over the years. In 1990, Arizona (with nine initiatives), Nevada (five), Massachusetts (four), Nebraska (three), and Montana (two) joined the group of states making frequent use of the initiative. Like Washington, the high use states are Western, more recent entries to the union, and likely to have strong interest groups. They are *dominant/complementary* to *complementary* in the Ronald Hrebenar/Clive Thomas typology of states. *Complementary* states are those in which interest groups are constrained by other parts of the political system and must work with them to achieve success, while the *dominant/complementary* are those states where interest groups are less constrained, but cannot act unilaterally, needing the support of at least some other political forces to be effective.[3] It would appear that the initiative is an additional tool for groups in their competition with other political elements, especially political parties and the legislature, for influencing political decisions and public policy.

Table One presents a summary comparison of the origin and disposition of the four types of proposed laws in Washington state. Among initiatives, there are many more starts than finishes. Previously, about three-fourths of the direct initiatives filed failed to get the number of signatures needed in order to reach the ballot. That proportion has declined since 1974 to 11 percent. Many more direct initiatives appear on the ballot than those of the other three means.

The use of initiatives nationwide has varied a great deal. In Washington, initiative use increased substantially after 1932. In the last two decades, conservatives have resorted to initiatives more than in earlier years, particularly in states other than Washington. One study of the first 60 years' experience in Washington found employment of the direct initiative between 1914-1943

Table One

Initiatives and Referenda in Washington: Starts and Dispensation by Time Periods
1914-1990

Type of Proposition	Filed	On Ballot	Passed	Failed
A. 1914-1942				
Direct Initiatives to Voters	154	32	15	17
Indirect Initiatives to Legislature	12	3	2	1
Referred by Petition to Voters	24	18	17	1
Measures Referred by Legislature	6	6	3	3
Total	196	59	37	22
B. 1944-1973				
Direct Initiatives to Voters	128	35	17	18
Indirect Initiatives to Legislature	34	8	4	4
Referred by Petition to Voters	12	10	9	1
Measures Referred by Legislature	27	27	23	4
Total	201	80		
C. 1974-1990				
Direct Initiatives to Voters	245	19	10	9
Indirect Initiatives to Legislature	71	7	5	2
Referred by Petition to Voters	9	2	0	2
Measures Referred by Legislature	8	8	5	3
Total	333	36	20	16
D. Composite 1914-1990				
Direct Initiatives to Voters	527	86	42	44
Indirect Initiatives to Legislature	117	18	11	7
Referred by Petition to Voters	45	30	26	4
Measures Referred by Legislature	41	41	31	10
Total	730	175	110	65

and 1947-1973 about the same, but with greater use of the referendum during the second period.[4] Table One demonstrates that the use of the direct initiative in Washington has increased 91% (from 128 to 245) since 1974. Indirect initiatives have also increased. By contrast, the use of the demanded referendum was substantially greater before 1942. At the time, it was used to "correct" what many groups regarded as "reactionary" legislation. It may be noted that a larger proportion of referenda filed reached the ballot than did initiatives. This may be due in part to the 4 percent signature requirement for referenda in contrast to 8 percent for initiatives.

The pattern of use in previous periods holds true to the present. Direct initiatives remain a major form of policy access for voters. Controversial issues, where political costs of support or opposition are high, are the most likely candidates for some form of initiative action. Initiatives allow interest groups to avoid the mediation of partisanship in bringing the uncompromised issue

Figure One

Comparison of Voter Turnout and Voting on State Measures*, 1976-1990

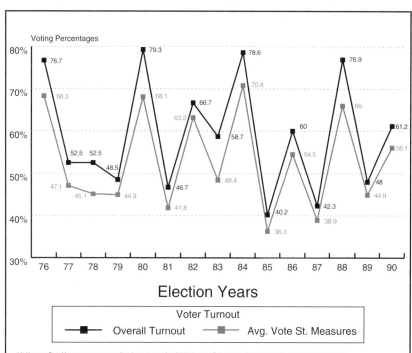

* % Votes on State Measures are averages of total voter turnout for all Initiatives and Referendums (by petition and legislature) placed on ballot.

directly before the voters. It allows the partisan legislature to defer responsibility by direct referral to the voters, as exemplified by the example of 1972.

Washington has a higher approval rate of initiatives than California or Oregon—nearly fifty percent to only about one-third for its southern neighbors. Approval of indirect initiatives is slightly higher. Measures referred by the legislature show a greater acceptance rate than is the case for initiatives. But when demanded by the voters, referrals result in an overwhelming veto of legislative actions.

Voter Participation

Critics of direct legislation have argued that voter response to ballot propositions often falls far short of the ideal "voice of the people." They claim that propositions do not elicit the voter turnout obtained by candidate-driven elections. This, they believe, is due to disinterest, lack of information, or the complexity of propositions. Further, they allege that those initiatives which secure

Table Two

A Comparison of Fall-Off Percentages in Washington Contested Races, 1984 and 1988

	1984	1988
Overall Turnout	78.6%	76.9%
President	1.9%	2.3%
Governor	1.7%	1.9%
Attorney General	5.5%	5.3%
Commissioner of Public Lands	9.9%	7.9%
Supt. of Public Instruction	11.9%	11.1%
Initiatives		
Fishing Rights	8.4%	xxxx
Sales Tax Trade-In	9.2%	xxxx
Abortion Funding	5.8%	xxxx
Increase Minimum Wage	xxxx	6.1%

a place in the ballot and stand a chance of approval get to that position because of large spending. These critics argue that groups with sizable financial resources are most likely to win passage of their initiatives while those with meager funds are unable to obtain signatures on petitions or conduct successful campaigns once the measures make the ballot.

Figure One addresses these contentions. Careful analysis of voting history on propositions shows that turnout for initiatives is always below the overall turnout in each election. As one might expect, overall turnout and the average vote on statewide measures (initiatives and referenda) are highest in presidential election years. Since initiatives and petition referenda require the mounting of a campaign to obtain signatures, they increase public awareness long before the election and this helps to counter the effects of ballot drop-off.

So-called ballot fatigue occurs both for voting on candidates and propositions. It is generally agreed that more people vote for persons at the top of the ballot, with a decline as voters proceed down the ballot. Propositions appear last on the ballot and amendments are the last of the propositions. Table Two offers a comparison of fall-off percentages by position on the ballot for 1984 and 1988.

Voting typically falls off rapidly when one gets below the top candidates, especially the president and governor. While ballot order is an imperfect guide to fall-off, it is not unusual for fall-off for such offices as public land commissioner or superintendent of public instruction to be greater than for initiatives. Table Two reflects this, with fall-off being greater for superintendent of public instruction than for any initiative. This suggests that issue saliency is important. As shown in Table Two, abortion funding and increasing the minimum wage did better than the superintendent of public instruction and the commissioner of public lands. Controversial issues may lead more people to vote on them than do on low profile offices. Conversely, initiatives dealing with sewers, highway maintenance, and perceived technical questions are likely to see greater voter fall-off. Issue saliency, therefore, is an important factor in whether initiatives become major elements on a crowded ballot.

Who Uses the Initiative?

Those who are unenthusiastic about initiatives claim they are used mainly by affluent, highly organized groups capable of collecting signatures and waging campaigns. It is true that there have been numerous expensive initiative contests. But Table Three shows that a majority vote for an initiative is not the result of big spending. In fact, between 1985 and 1990, of the 11 initiatives and resolutions adopted, in only two did supporters spend more than $100,000. Of those defeated, only Initiative 547 on growth management involved more than one million dollars spent in opposition. Perhaps the most illustrative case involved Initiative 102, the so-called "Children's Initiative" to support education and children's services. In spite of nearly five-to-one spending by supporters, the initiative failed.

Initiatives 547 and 102 provide an interesting contrast. Initiative 102 proposed a tax increase to raise at least $360 million per year for children's services, public school programs, and welfare benefits for families. The proposal involved a sales tax increase of nine-tenths of a cent, unless the legislature found some other revenue source. Social service agencies, teachers, labor unions, major medical organizations, religious groups, and political leaders including the governor and speaker of the house of representatives backed the proposal. The Republican party central committee, Boeing Company, Weyerhaeuser Corporation, SAFECO Insurance, leading conservative politicians, and a group known as the Mothers' Campaign for Family all opposed it. Proponents spent more than opponents. The opposition made much of the initiative being a tax increase in sheep's clothing. The initiative lost in every county in the state.

Initiative 547 would have required all counties and cities to adopt comprehensive plans and would have established two appointed state panels to review and approve local plans, imposing sanctions on local units which did not comply. It would have banned development if adequate roads, schools, and other infrastructures were not in place and would have prohibited the conversion of forest land to other uses until comprehensive plans were approved. It also called for a wetland preservation system. Finally, it would have changed state law to allow government decisions on development applications to consider regulations adopted after these applications had been submitted. Its adoption would have also meant the repeal of a growth management act just passed by the legislature.

Table Three

Reported Spending on Statewide Ballot Issues
1985-1990

		$ For	$ Against
1985			
HJR 12*:	Investment of state industrial insurance funds	none	none
HJR 22:	Eliminating conditions to voter approval of school levies	72,666	42,736
HJR 23:	Permitting counties and cities to finance public improvements through taxes from increased values of benefit properties	302,080	none
HJR 42*:	Permitting promotional hosting by agricultural commodity commissions	21,941	none
1986			
Init. 90:	Funding comprehensive fish and wildlife conservation and recreation programs	165,325	none
Ref. 40*:	Finding of nuclear waste repositories	49,525	none
HJR 49*:	Setting of salaries for state elected officials	3,000	none
HJR 55*:	Permitting voters to approve excess levies, not exceeding six years for construction, modernization, or remodeling	none	none
SJR 136*:	Increase authority and membership of the commission reviewing judicial conduct and require public proceedings	none	none
SJR 138:	Modify the process, timing, and eligibility to fill vacancies in legislature and county offices	none	none
1987			
Init. 92:	Limiting physicians' charges for Medicare patients	215,443	736,463
Ref. 41:	Challenging the delegation of authority to money	150,238	none
HJR 4212:	Lengthening legislative terms	none	none
HJR 4220:	Additional tax for school construction	45,351	none
SJR 8207*:	Judges pro tempore revisions	none	none
SJR 8212:	Investment of Public Lands Permanent Fund	none	none
1988			
Init. 518*:	Increasing minimum wage	178,276	16,432
Init. 97*:	Taxing hazardous substances to finance waste	316,105	none
Init. 97B:	(legislature's alternative hazardous waste cleanup –.8% tax)	1,264,409	none
HJR 4223:	Assistance for residential energy conservation	9,496	none
1989			
Init. 102:	Children's initiative	531,079	134,575
SJR 8200*:	Crime Victim's rights	435	none
SJR 8202*:	Commission on judicial conduct	none	none

Table Three (Continued)

		$ For	$ Against
1990			
Init. 547:	Growth Management	311,186	1,674,757
HJR 4203:	Amending provisions for creation of new counties to alter requirements for county formation, annexation, and consolidation	none	none
HJR 4231:	Permit voters at elections to approve excess property taxes for up to six-year periods	none	none
SJR 8212:	Permitting the basing of tax value of low-income housing of five or more units upon current use	none	none

* Measure adopted by majority vote of the people

Environmentalists, neighborhood and youth organizations, and the state Democratic party strongly supported the initiative. The governor (a Democrat), most city and county officials, the Municipal League, housing authorities, planners, and farm and business groups opposed it. The opposition outspent the advocates by five-to-one advertising their theme "Let the recently passed law work before you try to change it; it was, after all, passed by a legislature in which Republicans ruled the senate and Democrats dominated the house." The opposition won. In both initiatives, the nature of the issue added to spending and partisan competition to bring about its defeat.

More important than money or partisanship is the fact that a wide range of interest groups have employed initiatives and referenda. An astonishing assortment of sporting groups, pensioners, consumers, chiropractors, temperance groups, public employees, environmentalists, and many others — including elected officials — have turned to the ballot to achieve policies when they felt the legislature had not adequately responded. In most cases, they spent relatively small sums of money. If there is any old-fashioned democracy left, it may be the initiative process, where money has not yet come to dominate.

In this light, the initiative appears to be a vehicle for popular reform and public morality. As reform, it has dealt with reapportionment, the blanket primary, authorization of permanent voter registration, repeal of the poll tax, and some civil service regulations. As morality, it was used when many people did not like the legislature's and the liquor board's tight regulations. Although efforts to return liquor retailing to private enterprise failed by small margins, voters repealed blue laws and provided for liquor-by-the-drink when the legislature would not so act. So the initiative as popular reform keeps the government in check through reapportionment, blanket primaries that reduce partisan control, and civil service regulations that increase constraints over bureaucrats. The initiative as public morality keeps the government from controlling some personal mores by letting the people determine appropriate behavior through repealing liquor and other blue laws. Through the initiative, old-fashioned democracy lets the people keep one eye on the government and the other on themselves.

Overview: Theory and Practice

Even though extensive criticisms of the initiative and demanded referendum have appeared over the years, no serious movement has ever been mounted to repeal them or restrict their uses. By using percentages of the preceding gubernatorial vote, the number of signatures for placing propositions on the ballot is automatically adjusted to the size of the electorate. In retrospect, the theory and practice of these devices show both strengths and weaknesses.

The direct initiative is criticized for bypassing the legislature, which serves as the people's representative. Laws are methods of responding to generally complex problems. Legislators, initiative critics claim, are knowledgeable and can work out compromises. Initiatives provide no such opportunity. People can only vote initiatives up or down, so voters must take the good with the bad. The indirect initiative has the advantage of bringing the legislature into the process and, one might argue, groups desiring change should consider it a better route than the direct one. However, the indirect method has the drawback of delaying adoption by a year.

Others argue that many propositions are too technical or too complicated for ordinary voters to understand and, therefore, are better left to the legislature. This, of course, applies primarily to technical constitutional amendments, yet few would argue for giving the legislature sole authority to amend the constitution. Besides, Washington does not provide for a constitutional initiative.

There is the view that the initiative favors well-organized groups who have ample resources to finance signature campaigns and elections. As observed earlier, cases can easily be found where money contributed to passage or defeat. At the same time, many useful policies have received voter approval with little being spent on their behalf. Money, therefore, often is less important than the salience of the issue and the strategy pursued in framing its presentation to the electorate. Washington voters can think for themselves and weigh the issues, and they are not easily bought.

Proponents of the initiative and demanded referendum note their theoretical and practical virtues. They are seen as ways of overcoming special interests that, at a particular time, prevailed in the legislature. They are "corrective" tools in the hands of the people, and are a necessary adjunct to popular control. They offer an avenue for action and needed reform in the presence of legislative neglect. They make it difficult for the legislature to shirk responsibility, for the threat of an initiative can prod the legislature to act. They can also keep government from meddling too much into matters of personal comportment and public morality.

Opponent's fears that initiatives will result in harmful laws detrimental to propertied interests, raise taxes, or lead to expensive programs have not been borne out. On those very few occasions where such a case could be made, there is recourse in the fact that the legislature can amend an initiative by a two-thirds vote in both houses. Although this was done only once, it remains a useful safeguard.

Many legislators sponsor initiatives and become activists on their behalf by writing supportive statements in the voters' pamphlet. Other legislators have written statements for the opposition. In short, the legislature is often an active participant in the process.

In these times of decline in political party influence, split-ticket voting, split-party government, and the rise of political action committees (PACs), the tension of checks and balances which democracy requires becomes increasingly important. As PACs drive elections, party influence declines, and party cohesion suffers in the halls of the legislature and between the executive and the legislature. Party resistance is further weakened by the blanket primary and when split-party government is the rule rather than the exception. This, of course, has been the case in Washington in the last decade.

Over time these conditions induce a situation in which legislators cumulatively may owe more to the special interests which elected them than they do to their party or their constituents. Legislators become contract agents working on behalf of their supporters, responding more to their interests than to those of the broader public.

This is where the initiative offers an opportunity to those outside the halls of government to place proposed policies on the public agenda and to pry open the increasingly closed process of contract relationships between lawmakers and entrenched lobby groups. In theory as well as in practice, direct democracy, old-fashioned or not, sets up a constructive tension with representative government. Americans tend to be pragmatic, and direct legislation becomes a means to keep the legislature responsive and responsible to the broader public interest.

In Washington and elsewhere, initiatives enjoy a high rating in public opinion polls for this very reason. They offer an avenue of access when the representative process breaks down. Moreover, they work for everybody, not just the rich and famous. If you do not like the propositions of the other side, you can vote against them. And if you support a proposition that loses, you can try again. To the pragmatic American voter, the initiative is handy, useful, and fair, and fair play is at the heart of old-fashioned American democracy.

Notes

1. Alexis de Tocqueville, *Democracy in America,* ed. Richard Heffner (New York: Mentor, 1956).
2. *Congressional Record,* 22 May 1911, Appendix, p. 7.
3. Clive Thomas and Ronald Hrebenar, "Interest Groups in the States," in Virginia Gray, Herbert Jacob, and Robert Albritton, eds., *Politics in the American States,* 5th ed. (Glenview, Il.: Scott, Foresman/Little, Brown, 1990), pp. 147-148.
4. Hugh Bone and Robert Benedict, "Perspectives on Direct Legislation: Washington State's Experiences, 1914-1973," 28 *Western Political Quarterly* 330-351 (June 1975).

Governor Clarence Martin signs a consumer protection bill into law in the 1930s with representatives of the American Institute of Meat Packers looking on—while holding a plate full of fatty steak. Vibert Jeffers photo. *Susan Parish Collection*©

Chapter Seven

The Office of Governor and Statewide Elected Officials

George W. Scott

The Governor

Evolution of the Office

To remain viable, governmental institutions must adjust to ever-changing environments. The Washington governorship is no exception. In confronting shifts in its political environment, the state's executive has passed through five phases, beginning with territorial days (1853-1889).

The 14 territorial governors before 1889 were short-tenured presidential appointees noted more for their partisan politics than their administrative acumen. The exception, New Englander Isaac Ingalls Stevens, graduated first in his class at West Point and served as superintendent of Indian affairs and surveyor for a transcontinental railroad route in addition to being Washington's first territorial governor. Territorial governors were extensions of the federal government as well as the army's partner in keeping law and order. They suppressed Indian uprisings in the 1850s and imposed taxes, but otherwise had few responsibilities. Public services such as justice and education remained primarily local functions.

In the second phase, beginning with statehood and lasting until the Second World War, governors assumed a dominant role in state politics. The post-Civil War corruption of legislatures by corporations was all too evident. The state constitution adopted in 1889 borrowed liberally from other Western states that had recently joined the union. It created a strong executive with substantial veto powers to check the legislature. Article III granted a four-year term of office and the option of calling extra legislative sessions. Legislators who lived far from Olympia faced the threat of a governor forcing them to remain in or return to Olympia, an intimidating prospect for citizen-legislators with salaries, as late as the 1950s, as low as $300 a year. The governor set the state's political agenda.

The third stage of the evolution began during World War II and lasted until the mid-1950s. It might be called the rationalizing or professionalization of the office. The loss of patronage and "pork"–the ability to award supporters jobs or to influence legislators with state-funded projects–ushered in this era. Legislative minorities siding with the opponents of change had delayed reform for decades, waiting until they became a majority so they could "grandfather" their own people into a rudimentary civil service system. But in 1943 Governor Arthur B. Langlie (1941-1945; 1949-1957) issued an executive order that began partial civil service protection in departments under his control. Governor Monrad C. Walgren (1945-1949), a believer in partisan prerogatives, reverted to the old spoils system. Upon his return to office for two more terms, Langlie reinstated and expanded civil service protections. His successor, Albert D. Rosellini (1957-1965), a nominal supporter of civil service as senate majority leader, proved less interested in reform as governor. However, the state employees union's successful 1960 initiative forced the issue, bringing the protections of a civil service system to more state employees.[1] Gubernatorial appointments based on merit and qualification have, since then, grown to over 650 a year, while patronage positions have dwindled to about four dozen.

Until the 1950s, governors regularly placed in their budgets money for roads, buildings, or higher education for a legislator's district in return for the legislator's cooperation on bills the executive supported. However, since then the state has allocated major expenditures, except for social and health services, according to fairly rigid formulas. The governor's capital budget (for construction and repair of buildings) is prioritized before being sent to the legislature for final approval. On occasion, influential legislators are still able to gain a building project for their districts. However, as the size of districts and the number of government programs grew, these benefactions became less visible and faded as a means of rewarding friendly lawmakers. In this third phase of the governorship, traditional political rewards disappeared, filling the expanded executive branch with professional personnel, selected and promoted on qualifications rather than politics.

A divided government–where one party controlled the legislature and the other the executive–characterized the fourth phase of the governorship, from the 1950s to the 1970s. Such division can nearly paralyze most governors and their agendas. Democrats have held the governorship for 32 of the last 60 years; Republicans have had nominal control over both houses of the legislature for 22 years, and over one of the houses for another 22. Despite the existence of weak political parties, policy has to be brokered within and between the parties and with the executive.

The governor's power to veto any legislative act unless overridden by a two-thirds vote in each house became crucial. Langlie, a Republican governor

Table 1

Party Representation in State Legislature and Governorship, 1949-1991

Year	Governor's Party	Senate		House of Representatives	
		Democrats	Republicans	Democrats	Republicans
1949*	Republican–Langlie	19	27	67	32
1951*	Republican–Langlie	25	21	54	45
1953	Republican–Langlie	21	25	41	58
1955*	Republican–Langlie	22	24	50	49
1957	Democrat–Rosellini	31	15	56	43
1959	Democrat–Rosellini	35	14	66	33
1961	Democrat–Rosellini	36	13	59	40
1963	Democrat–Rosellini	32	17	51	48
1965*	Republican–Evans	32	17	60	39
1967*	Republican–Evans	29	20	44	55
1969*	Republican–Evans	27	22	43	56
1971*	Republican–Evans	29	20	48	51
1973*	Republican–Evans	30	19	57	41
1975*	Republican–Evans	30	19	62	36
1977	Democrat–Ray	30	19	62	36
1979*	Democrat–Ray	30	19	49	49
1981	Republican–Spellman	24	25	43	55
1983*	Republican–Spellman	26	23	55	43
1985	Democrat–Gardner	27	22	53	45
1987*	Democrat–Gardner	24	25	61	37
1989	Democrat–Gardner	24	25	63	35
1991*	Democrat–Gardner	24	25	58	40

* Sessions with divided government.

in a Democratic age, went beyond the traditional uses of the veto, which had previously been used primarily to negate pork barreling, to delete obvious legislative mistakes and to void bills that were arguably unconstitutional. Governor Rosellini went further, using the "line item" veto to reverse the intent of several bills by deleting a single word, such as "not" after a "shall." Frustrated by a legislature controlled by the opposite party, Daniel J. Evans (1965-1977) turned to creative use of the veto. Nicknamed "Danny Veto" for his relentless use of a red pen, Evans also legislated with the veto. After Evans systematically deleted pieces of the Landlord-Tenant bill of 1973, tipping the balance in favor of tenants, outraged legislators reacted by proposing and gaining a constitutional amendment stating that the governor could excise no less than a full paragraph of legislation.[2] The governor's chief of staff called the limitation Evans's greatest political loss.[3]

Nonetheless, Evans had the skill, force of personality, public support, and willingness to spend political capital to seize the initiative and to set the political agenda for the state. The governor sent up to 70 "executive request" bills to each legislature, and briefed the media with daily press conferences during legislative sessions. Evans enjoyed considerable public support and provided political leadership to an often-divided government during most of his 12 years as governor. But for governors who ruled during years of divided government, he proved to be the exception.

In the fifth and present phase, which began in 1973, power in state government generally dispersed, and along with this dispersion, the governor's power waned. The legislature gained power parity when it acquired a full-time professional staff equal to the executive's. But simultaneously, the new public disclosure law (1971), extraordinarily long legislative sessions (extending to six months in 1977), frozen salaries, and the demoralizing effect of President Richard Nixon's Watergate scandal on public life, depleted the legislative leadership needed to enact programs. Legislators became more reliant on their staffs, which grew from 40 to 300 during legislative sessions. Moneyed professional lobbyists, who became in fact a "Third House," proliferated, creating their own chamber – called "ulcer gulch"– located between the two legislative chambers. Finally, major interest groups brought post-session class-action suits to the supreme court in an effort to gain through litigation what they had been unable to obtain from the governor or legislature.

A significant part of both the governor's and the legislature's authority is now shared by non-elected staff and lobbyists. It is harder for any to move an agenda, and easier for any one of the major players to kill a bill. The governor, with the first say on the budget, the final one with the veto, and a unique position for seizing the initiative, still holds center stage, but he or she is now at best only first among equals.

The Governor as Politician

In the first two decades of statehood, governors campaigned by horse and buggy – where there were roads – and later went by railroad to the larger cities. With completion of the first decent pass over the Cascades in the 'teens it became possible to tour eastern Washington by automobile. Personal appeals and endurance remained the aspirant's best assets; money was secondary. In 1940, Langlie spent just $5000 to win his first term as governor by 5,000 votes. He made "stump" speeches in every hamlet in the state. Initially, newspapers dominated the media, informing readers of candidates and campaign issues. By the 1920s, radio began to cover campaigns. Beginning in the 1950s, television started to dominate. For example, in 1956, Albert Rosellini, who had gained name familiarity as the aggressive chairman of a televised state senate crime investigating committee, used television to carry him to easy victory over his opponent.

Television exposure is critical in the two weeks before the election, and the advantage lies with the incumbent. The cost of gubernatorial campaigns has gone up astronomically. In 1988, the finalists spent $3 million. Making a dozen speeches a day is now subordinate to raising millions of dollars for the media. Televised debates are common. The margin of victory may turn as much on performance on the TV screen as in office, and the largest lobbies funnel daunting sums of money to the leading candidates to be used for this medium. (See chapter three.)

A legislator who has weathered the political storms of the house and senate is well prepared to understand the political demands of the governorship. State government, with 89,000 employees, is now, next to Boeing, Washington's second largest employer. It is more complex than the airplane manufacturer, with over 300 departments, agencies, boards, and commissions. A few years in the legislature, likely in positions of leadership, helps a governor deal with former legislative colleagues, understand the complexities of modern state government, and appreciate the need to coordinate programs. A former legislator is also familiar with the many lobbyists, whose largess is critical to modern money-driven campaigns.

Legislative experience may help one to successfully manage state government, but it is not needed to get elected. King County executive John Spellman (1981-1985) capitalized on name familiarity in the state's most populous region to win election. However, Spellman had a difficult time understanding the cacophony of two houses and the voices of two dozen legislative leaders. He proved unable to get the legislation passed that he needed in order to move his programs forward. Booth Gardner (1985-1993) was Pierce County executive and a former legislator. Even when confronted with a divided government, Gardner developed the necessary legislative relations to institute important parts of his agenda.

Dixy Lee Ray (1977-1981), a former marine biology professor, Science Center administrator, chairman of the Atomic Energy Commission, and political outsider, rode to victory on anti-government sentiment in 1976. She benefitted from the two major mechanical influences in a gubernatorial race: Washington's "blanket primary" allows crossover voting, and Ray clearly drew Republican voters. There was also a field of four significant Democratic primary contestants, who split the traditional party vote. Ray won the primary and the general election, but failed to find suitable staff or mount a legislative program. She was a secondary player two years into her term, and lost in the 1980 Democratic primary.

Pre-World War II governors came from a wider variety of occupations and often had little knowledge of the then-simpler government. Today, the skills needed to manage state government must be learned before becoming a candidate, not after being elected. Successful governors have been experienced politicians prior to moving into the governor's mansion.

Lifestyle

The governor's pay is $99,600 a year, perhaps half the salary of a corporate executive with fewer employees. The universities' football coaches and presidents are paid more. All may work six-day weeks, but the governor also regularly makes evening and weekend speeches, public appearances, and, as chief of state, attends numerous ceremonial events. Frank Mullen, an astute observer of Washington's executive branch, once wrote: "On one rather typical November day, the governor presented a medal of heroism to a member of the state patrol, congratulated the 'Airman of the Quarter' from a nearby Air Force base, received a bicentennial history book and posed for pictures with retiring governmental officials."[4]

The governor's workload would be unmanageable without the help of over 40 staffers who serve as the executive's eyes, ears, and hands. The governor's chief of staff coordinates them all. They work more closely with agencies and the governor than do the elected members of the executive branch. To a significant measure, any governor's success depends on the effectiveness of members of the immediate staff.

Despite the potentially overwhelming responsibilities, the governorship appeals to many interested in becoming the state's most powerful person.[5] Governors exercise their power primarily in four ways: setting the state's political agenda, threatening or using the veto, appointing supportive personnel to departments and staff, and using the budget process. The governor's Office of Financial Management must present a proposed biennial spending plan in December, three weeks before the legislature convenes. Supplemental budgets to correct oversights and underestimates began in the 1950s, and became annual events in the 1960s when Evans called the legislature into session in even-numbered years as well as odd. The Ray administration began the practice of offering a supplemental budget with every quarterly revenue estimate. The effect is the same: the governor has the first opportunity to propose how revenue is to be spent. The legislature finds it hard to deny the expectations set by his or her proposal. Legislative leaders press their viewpoints, and between April and June are forced to compromise among themselves and between themselves and the governor. The internal program configurations in the budget change, but—the 1981-1983 and 1991-1992 recessions excepted—in 20 years, net spending has never varied more than 2 percent from the governor's initial proposal! Nevertheless, the old saw "the governor proposes, the legislature disposes" still soothes solons' egos.

In the last half century governors have had to surrender some of their budgetary powers to new constitutional constraints, like the Fourteenth Amendment to the state constitution (1944), which dedicated all gas-tax dollars to highways and the ferry system. Public schools, the state's "paramount duty," take between 45 and 50 percent of the general fund. Several supreme court decisions since 1970 have underlined their right to first priority. Moreover, formulas now guide the construction of higher education budgets; only the grand totals remain open to policy decision. The state must meet matching requirements to receive federal funds for many programs and these requirements constrain state actions in many areas.

The economy keys the governor's fate. Good economic times bring higher revenue. One can spend and innovate without imposing new taxes, a luxury enjoyed by both Evans and, until the last year of his tenure, Gardner. Contrarily, the administrations of Clarence D. Martin (1933-1941) and Spellman testify to the debilitating effects of a depression or a recession, when the need to cut spending while taxing more made for tense, limited tenures. However, in good or bad times, it is with the "purse" that the executive becomes the legislator.

The Governor as Legislator

The legislature is the governor's first priority when it is in session. He or she holds breakfasts at the executive mansion, where the most junior legislator of either party can feel at the center of events. The wise governor leaves the door open for legislators who wish to visit the "second floor" of the capitol building – the governor's offices – and is most effective working first with legislative leadership and then dealing with individual senators and representatives when he or she needs crucial votes. Evans had "brown bag" lunches for senate and house Republican leadership; Ray hosted cocktail parties.

The governor's legislative liaison lobbies for and tracks the status of the executive's bills, and acts as a conduit between legislative leadership of both parties and the second floor. At critical times the governor may visit the parties' caucuses to argue for his or her budget or a bill. Evans was confident enough to testify before legislative committees. Ray once sent a staffer to chastise the house for not moving a favored piece of legislation – with negative results.[6] Governors may complain publicly when the legislature fails to act on prized bills, even if she or he knows the legislators' reaction will be negative. Later they might threaten a veto if the legislature's version is different or talk about calling legislators back to a special session. The governor's strength in shaping legislation often hinges on his or her public popularity.

The governor can set the legislative agenda by submitting well-chosen and well-crafted executive request bills. Interest groups, senior citizens, businessmen, or state employees press the governor to sponsor legislation. The executive reacts to initiatives, citizen movements, or popular sentiment. Ideas will emerge from a strong staff; suggestions for operational changes rise from the departments. Clearly, a firm feel for the legislative process is indispensable in maintaining the initiative. Evans's well-timed television speech in the winter of 1970 brought passage of five precedent-setting environmental bills instigated and brokered by the administration. He shared the credit by complimenting the legislature—"Never has a legislature done so much of consequence."[7]

The legislature, of course, ultimately enacts the laws. Nonetheless, without the governor's initiative through the budget proposal and executive request bills, without his or her prodding and cajoling, the legislature would have a difficult time generating and passing major policies.

The idea that a governor's agenda will be identified as that of his or her party is only partly true. Democrats Martin and Ray and Republicans Langlie and Evans, who held office for 36 of the last 60 years, were philosophically different from many in their respective parties. Even so, the executive's agenda tends to align with party sentiment, if only because legislators of the governor's party must supply most of the votes needed to pass the executive's program.

The Governor as Party Leader

Washington politics means "freestyle politics."[8] One major cause, of course, is the long tradition of weak parties forever divided into two wings—liberal and conservative. Governors and aspirants to that office are often at odds with many members of their own parties. The party's infrastructures are usually under the sway of the ideologically pure. Candidates for governor must struggle to satisfy party activists who may be much more conservative or liberal than the general electorate, which tends to be relatively moderate. Governors use their political parties to assist with campaigning, clearing appointments, and generating program ideas. However, neither political party attracts much money and, but for a few activists, their organizations are ineffective. Would-be governors must build personal campaign teams of friends and allies from prior associations, and draw in individual party activists inclined to their approach.

The governor may be the most visible party member, and its nominal head, but the title "Chief Democrat" or "Chief Republican" means little to in-house opponents. Many governors have drawn considerable criticism from members of their own parties, both publicly and privately.

The weakness of the state parties, endemic factionalism, and split-ticket voting make parties modestly helpful at best. To avoid losing independent voters, who are very numerous, the governor is likely to campaign for relatively few party candidates and behave as a partisan only at party gatherings.

Although it may appear as if governors can ignore their respective parties, as party leader they are expected to play a major role in party affairs and benefit from their party work. The legislature is organized around the parties—e.g., committee chairs, caucuses, speaker, and floor leaders—forcing the governor to give some attention to partisanship. At the national and regional level, governors, as heads of their parties, assume leading roles in national party events and exercise influence over federal appointments and the granting of federal projects. National recognition for the state often depends upon the governors' political party leadership. Despite the weakness of Washington's Republican and Democrat organizations, governors or would-be governors ignore them at their own political peril.

The Governor as Administrator

The governor-elect's first challenge is likely the most difficult. The rigors of a campaign of up to two years have left him or her exhausted. Now, in a mercilessly short 60 days, the future chief executive must find two dozen cabinet officers and personal aides who are both competent and conversant with the state bureaucracy. Those who assemble an administrative team and run it are the governor's eyes, ears, alter egos, and a large part of his or her profile. The fate of the administration turns on the resourcefulness of the recruitment team. Whether key individuals are on station by January is the first measure of the governor's strength.

The governor's administrative role has grown. State government recently has tackled social problems that only a generation ago were outside its ambit. It has financed a $200 million convention center to boost the economy and supervises the building and running of nuclear plants and their waste. It is in the gaming business (the lottery) and it is a mortgage banker (the State Housing Authority). Administering the state's many responsibilities requires a vast bureaucratic organization. The executive's central staff has grown from 10 to 40 in 50 years. There is a chief of staff, legal counsel, legislative liaison, administrative assistants who handle correspondence, and special assistants for energy, natural resources, education, human resources, and general government. These assistants have close proximity to the executive and serve as conduits to the governor's power. In contrast, members of the cabinet, dispersed about the capitol campus, have become operational managers who see the boss infrequently. The exceptions are the director of the Office of Financial Management and the heads of the Department of Revenue and the Department of Social and Health Services, the former because of their critical fiscal role and the latter because of its size (one-fourth of all state employees).

Governors regularly draft legislators for key cabinet and commission appointments because of their knowledge of state government. Some observers argue that governors have used the prospect of a gubernatorial appointment, with a significant increase in pension, to gain favorable votes on key issues from legislators. Certainly, such gubernatorial appointments are recognition for significant service and signify confidence in a person's ability to implement administration policy. Astute governors find ways to use the brightest and best without regard to party. The most versatile administrators reappear. A governor's ability can be measured in the competence of aides, who must anticipate problems and quickly and adroitly advise the governor on how to address them. Spellman fired his revenue director ostensibly for uttering the politically sensitive words "income tax."[9]

One of the most important gubernatorial aides in recent years has been the press secretary. The media is a major source of anxiety for governors. The regular capitol press corps, about 15 reporters, can triple during a legislative session. Any gubernatorial act or lack thereof can be news, and media presentation of that act can be crucial. Ray sealed her fate by being combative with journalists, who returned the favor. Spellman's press secretary Paul O'Connor distrusted the media and became a liability. Effective press secretaries are hard to find. Being in a most sensitive position, they often serve short terms.

A natural rivalry exists between the governor's central staff and agency directors. The first operate with more ready access to the governor. Department heads are spread across Olympia and cabinet meetings are rare. The chief of staff's prime task is to ensure that the governor is not isolated, nor surrounded by sycophants. The chief must balance the advice of various advocates, raise questions and objections, and offer program alternatives to meet both practical and political needs. The governor's assistant for legislative affairs plans strategies, promotes executive request bills as they progress through the two houses, meets legislative leaders, and briefs individual legislators. It is a delicate role, particularly when members of the executive's own party disagree with the path being taken.

Handling mail absorbs a fifth of the central staff's time. The governor's office receives 2,000 to 4,000 letters a month, depending upon whether the legislature is in session. Most are requests for appointments or state services, bills, pleas to untangle a bureaucratic snarl, or seek a pardon or parole. The governor cannot provide more assistance than the law allows, although he or she can route people to the proper agencies and cut the paper snarl. When the governor's office forwards a letter with a request to investigate, a response to the initial letter is ready for the governor's signature within a short time. To many citizens, the governor, like the president, is a court of last resort.

Statewide Officials

Washington also has eight other statewide elected officials, whose power is collectively less than the governor's. The state constitution established all but the

Insurance Commissioner. It would take a constitutional amendment to abolish the offices. The statewide officials, in order of importance are:

The *Attorney General* (AG) who runs one of the state's largest law firms, with 300 assistants attached to agencies. Since 1970 the AG has fought a dozen cases in the United States Supreme Court on salmon fishing rights, taxation on Indian reservations, and equal pay for women. It is this law enforcement role that makes the AG's office the best platform for campaigning for higher office – the governorship or the United States Senate. In the last half century, AG's Don Eastvold (R) and John O'Connell (D) failed in their bids to be governor. Slade Gorton (R) has twice been elected U. S. Senator.

The *Superintendent of Public Instruction* oversees the formula allocating half the state budget to public schools, enforces education laws, and plays a significant role in the creation of new laws. The *Insurance Commissioner* protects the holders of billions of dollars of coverage and helps prevent consumer scams. The *Commissioner of Public Lands* is charged with sustained use of hundreds of thousands of acres of public forest with profits going to build and repair schools. The *Lieutenant Governor's* job is full-time only when the senate is in session, over which he or she presides. Since 1981, when control of the senate has often hung on a single vote, the lieutenant governor has used his prerogative of casting the tie-breaking votes in key situations to aid his party. The *Secretary of State* does corporation filings, is chief of elections, and the state's archivist. The *Auditor* and *Treasurer* are responsible for checking the books of all state agencies and for keeping tabs on state investments and revenues, respectively. Several of these offices – e.g., *Auditor, Treasurer, Land Commissioner* – play only minor roles in partisan and policy decisions. Reformers have often suggested that the election ballot could be shortened by making them gubernatorial appointees or absorbing their functions into other departments. However, the need to amend the constitution, tradition, partisanship, and the fact that each office has its own political base prevents such drastic changes.

The Bureaus

The number of state employees doubled in the prosperous 1960s, briefly declined in the recession of 1981-83, and then rose by 20 percent. However, with the economic downturn of 1991-1992, it is anticipated that another slight decline will occur. Two-thirds of state workers are under the Department of Personnel and the civil service system begun by initiative in 1960. Recruiting, classification, and removal procedures are clearly defined. Initial selection is on merit, but the system is based on longevity and tends to favor insiders. Collective bargaining exists for over three-quarters of the employees under the Department of Personnel, but not those in higher education. State patrolmen, ferry system workers, and faculty and staff of the state colleges and universities have their own personnel boards and pension systems.

There are several kinds of state employees. In order of their numbers they are: those running the agencies in Olympia, along with those working in institutions outside the capitol; those in higher education; appointees to boards and commissions; and consultants.

Additionally, Article IX of the Washington Constitution ("It is the paramount duty of the state to make ample provision for the education of all children residing within its borders") has, as interpreted by the state supreme court (see chapter eight), indirectly added K through 12 public school teachers to the state rolls. Over 40 percent of "state employees," some 37,000 in 1992, are teachers paid primarily with state money, but working for over 280 local school districts.

The Department of Social and Health Services, the largest agency, has a staff of more than 14,000, from guards in the state prisons to psychiatrists to welfare administrators. They tend to the needs of the blind, disabled, aged, those on welfare, and children in foster homes. The departments of Employment Security (unemployment and industrial insurance claims), Ecology, Wildlife, Revenue, and General Administration (purchasing, state buildings and grounds), are next in size among the 22 agencies, with over 300 employees each.

The Department of Transportation (highways, the ferry system) is the most monolithic and unique. Amendment Fourteen precludes the legislature from allocating its biennial "dedicated fund" of more than $1 billion for anything except transportation programs. The department is under the Transportation Commission, a board the governor appoints but cannot fire. As Dan Evans found out after he appointed Charles Prahl in the 1960s, directors and commissioners do not necessarily cooperate with the governor once in office. Evans's four attempts to get a Department of Transportation under the governor's control failed. The department's allies are usually eastern Washington legislators fearful that all "road money" will go to west-side mass transit; highway builders; crafts unions; and those fearing that making the director a gubernatorial appointee would revert the department to the "pork barrel" days.

Task forces of citizens and public officials appointed by the executive have repeatedly asked that the governor be given the authority and responsibility to strengthen staff services, and to reduce the number of elective offices. The other prominent theme, efficiency through consolidation of like functions, is rarely heeded. A wave of public sentiment, such as the one that created the Department of Ecology in the 1970s, can sometimes succeed in moving the legislature to action. But the legislature rejected other recommendations to limit executive departments and allow the governor to reorganize the executive branch subject to a "veto" by either house of the legislature.

The power to name over 900 people a year to boards and commissions – people who are essentially unsupervised once confirmed – is the governor's most underrated power, and the only one with an impact after he or she leaves office: three-fourths of the appointments are for terms that exceed the four-year term of the appointing governor. The executive now appoints more judges at all levels of the state judiciary to fill vacancies than are elected.[10] The appointees guide 250 boards and commissions, most of which are small and single-function – some created by statute, some by executive order. They range from the regents of the two research universities to the Aeronautics Commission and include three dozen boards that license and discipline professions and occupations, such as dentistry and engineering.

Several boards and commissions have great authority. The Liquor Control Board prices and markets over $500 million worth of liquor every biennium. The Utilities and Transportation Commission regulates charges by private utility companies and common carriers. The Board of Industrial Insurance Appeals makes awards to injured workers. Positions on the 23 community college boards, or those on the five four-year institutions of higher education, go to gubernatorial supporters interested in the service and the honor. They are unpaid except for per diem and travel expenses.

A "Sunset Law" passed in the 1970s automatically phases out agencies not specifically reauthorized. Three-fifths of the small agencies on the initial list were eliminated. But every session the legislature creates as many agencies as it terminates.

Conclusion

Since the 1970s, the executive's power has been diluted by the rise of staff and the Third House – a sort of five-branch government. The governor can still be more powerful than the legislature, if he or she is a strong personality and is willing to seize the initiative and use the budget, media attention, and veto. Because of the complexity of state government a governor must have a grip, from the outset, on the state's structure, issues, options, and players. Former legislators often have an advantage here. However, during the last decade the legislative environment has deteriorated to where fewer experienced leaders are available for higher office. Voters must understand that the state governmental system is a pyramid; those now elected to local office and the legislature will provide many of the viable candidates for governor and Congress a decade from now.

The executive shares power with eight other state elected officials, each with a constituency and with boards and commissions that function independently once appointed. Civil service leaves the bureaucracy unaffected by the passing of administrations. The legislature still retains the final word on the budget. Not surprisingly, the abiding characteristic of the relationship between the governor, the bureaucracy, interest groups, and the legislature is tension, one born of checks and balances.

Notes

1. Norm Schut, interview by the author, 5 Dec. 1989, Washington State Legislative Oral History Project. See also Frank Anderson, *A History of Personnel Systems in Washington State* Olympia: Washington State Department of Personnel, 1989).
2. Amendment 62 to Article II, Section 12 of the state constitution was approved by the people 5 Nov. 1974.
3. Justice James Dolliver, interview by the author, 25 Jan. 1990, Washington State Legislative Oral History Project.
4. Frank Mullen, "The Executives and the Administration," in Thor Swanson, Frank Mullen, John C. Pierce, and Charles Sheldon, *Political Life in Washington: Governing the Evergreen State* (Pullman: Washington State University Press, 1985) pp. 75-93.
5. Except when senior and talented United States Senators hold office, e.g., Warren G. Magnuson (1944-1980), or Henry M. Jackson, (1953-1983).
6. Governor Dixy Lee Ray, Address to the 48th Legislature, 12 Jan. 1977; *The Daily Olympian,* 23 Feb. 77.
7. Governor Daniel J. Evans, news conferences, 23 Jan. 1970, 9 Feb. 1970.
8. See Daniel M. Ogden and Hugh A. Bone, *Washington Politics* (New York: New York University Press, 1960).
9. Governor John D. Spellman, interview by the author, 20 Dec. 1991, Washington State Legislative Oral History Project.
10. For general discussion on the evolution and status of the governorship, see Larry Sabato, *Goodbye to Goodtime Charlie: The American Governorship Transformed,* 2nd ed. (Washington, D.C.: The CQ Press, 1983), and Coleman B. Ransome, Jr., *The American Governorship* (Westport, Ct: Greenwood Press, 1982), in particular chapters 1, 3, and 5.

The Washington State Supreme Court in 1989. Back row, left to right: Robert F. Utter, Charles Z. Smith, James A. Andersen, Robert Brachtenbach, James M. Dolliver. Front row, left to right: Keith M. Callow, Fred H. Dore, Barbara Durham, Vernon Pearson. *Courtesy Washington State Supreme Court.*

Chapter Eight

Politicians in Robes: Judges and the Washington Court System

Charles H. Sheldon

THE POPULAR VIEW of judges places them in the courtroom: attired in black robes, seated above the proceedings, ruling decisively on lawyers' objections, encouraging witnesses, and instructing jurors. Although a realistic view of the trial bench, this picture is incomplete. Judges are responsible for a number of obvious and not-so-obvious functions of which the courtroom drama is only a part.

The Judging Function

First and foremost, judges in Washington *resolve disputes* between private parties (civil disputes) and between the state and individual (criminal cases). Such settlements are made according to standards found in federal and state laws, constitutions, or previous court decisions. This particular function most commonly identifies courts. But judges can exercise considerable discretion within their traditional role of dispute resolution. In many areas of the law, judges, through their *common law powers,* establish the standards by which disputes are resolved. Instead of turning to a statute or the constitution, judges rely on what predecessors on the bench have decided. *Stare decisis* means like cases are to be decided alike. That is, courts should follow precedent and decide today as courts have ruled in similar cases in the past. The common law tradition in areas such as torts, liability, and contracts is still decisive today. Statements like "in the public interest" or "inimical to sound public policy" often guide the outcome of such cases.[1] What courts decide as good or bad public policy remains until the legislature replaces, changes, or revokes a ruling.

Judges perform a second function as they go about settling disputes. They occasionally affirm or *establish public policy.* State courts have the power of judicial review whereby they consider the constitutionality of legislative enactments. If laws are not consistent with state or federal constitutions, they are declared null and void. Of course, only about one-fourth of the cases before the Washington Supreme Court involve a constitutional question, and opportunities for judicial review by lower courts are even less common. Nonetheless, if the law under constitutional scrutiny impacts the public in some way, and most do, judges are involved in policy making. For example, in 1978 in *Seattle School District v. State* (90 Wn. 2d 772, 1978), the state's high court ruled that the Washington Constitution required the state to fully fund basic public education from kindergarten through the twelfth grade, thereby relieving school districts from reliance on special property levies. The court ordered the legislature to define "basic education" and to come up with the necessary funds. The court here performed a lawmaking or policy function.

While exercising judicial review, which is a powerful policy-making weapon, the Washington Supreme Court is able to change, if not defy, U. S. Supreme Court rulings about provisions of the U. S. Constitution. By relying on "adequate and independent state grounds" and by providing more protections for the individual, state judges can ignore the nation's high court constitutional interpretations.[2] For example, the Washington Supreme Court in *State v. Boland* (115 Wn. 2d 571, 1990) read Article I, Section 7 of the state constitution to be more protective of privacy rights than is the Fourth Amendment of the U. S. Constitution.[3] The Washington court ruled that when a person's trash is in a garbage can on the curb waiting for collection, it is protected from unwarranted search and seizure by the police—even though the U. S. Supreme Court had read the Fourth Amendment to allow such search and seizure. Because the court interpreted Article I, Section 7 to be more protective of privacy than the Fourth Amendment, and since the state court in Boland limited its decision to the state constitution, the police in Washington must obtain a warrant from a judge before they can search a person's trash for evidence.

Judges are often reluctant to admit to a policy-making function, such as in the *Seattle District* and *Boland* cases. But some have recognized their policy role:

> Policymaking is indisputably a part of the functions of judging to the extent that judging involves law making to fill the interstices of authority found in constitutions, statutes, and precedents... Moreover, the substantial interest identified by the phrase "on the policy making level" is closely aligned with an interest referred to by phrases such as "exercise of discretion" and "exercise of judgment," which are indisputably descriptive of most of the performance of those persons within the judicial branch who serve as judges.[4]

Judges are both policy makers and resolvers of disputes, and a successful and respected judiciary balances these two functions.

Third, judges perform the function of *administering* the judicial system. Judges set rules of procedure on how to settle disputes. For example, the 1991 *Court Rules,* published by the State Law Reports Office in Olympia, contains over 800 pages and includes such categories as "Code of Judicial Conduct," "Juvenile Court Rules," and "Rules of Evidence." The justices of the state supreme court, after consulting with those affected, approve these codified rules. By having much to say about how things are done throughout the judicial system, judges have something to say about the law.

Fourth, judges oversee another important segment of the legal and political world: the state supreme court serves the function of *supervising the legal profession.* The court is responsible for overseeing requirements for admission to the profession and defining and enforcing legal ethics. The justices approve the "Rules of Professional Conduct" and review the punishments to violators meted out by the Washington State Bar Association (disbarment, suspension, and censure). Indirectly, lawyers play important roles in state politics. They often dominate the legislature. They are instrumental in drafting laws for the legislature and pressure groups. They advise business people, citizens, and governments on the law and manage disputes brought to the courts. Those who regulate the ethics of these attorneys have a heavy responsibility. And the courts hold this responsibility.[5] The state's high bench also adjudicates the ethics of judges by deciding on appeals from the decisions of the Judicial Conduct Commission.

And judges perform a fifth and final function. Assuming that "a government of laws, not of men" means something, judges, more than any of the other political actors, symbolize this law. The ceremony, black robes, "Oyez, Oyez," and "Your Honor" reflect this *symbolic function* attached to judges. Judges represent the law, and by their decisions and behavior can contribute to or subtract from the respect citizens have for the law.

By simply settling disputes between contending parties, the courts in Washington, as elsewhere, can become policy makers. By exercising judicial review, judges make law. By filling gaps in the law, in precedents, and in constitutions, judges become crucial actors in the state political system. Not all judges view themselves as policy makers, but all recognize that their decisions are more important than simply resolving a dispute between two parties. Although not as obvious as legislators, governors, or county commissioners, judges throughout the judicial system in Washington are public servants making decisions that affect the public. They symbolize the law. It is not "out of order" nor a sign of disrespect to call judges "politicians in robes."

The Judicial Dilemma

The phrase "politicians in robes" illustrates the dilemma confronting judges. On the one hand they must remain objective, aloof, and uninvolved to fairly settle a dispute brought before them. Judges cannot favor one side or the other.

They must be independent of the interests represented by the litigants and if they cannot be, they should withdraw from the case. *Judicial independence* is the very essence of judging. If the "rule of law" means anything, it means that those who apply it—judges—must be independent of the pressures of politics, public opinion, and special interests. Such independence is necessary to their law-interpreting function.

However, if judges are policy makers, another pressure demands their attention. In a democratic society, those who make policies are to be held accountable for them. Majoritarian democracy means *public accountability.* The fundamental question confronting all judges is how to balance the demands of accountability with the needs of independence. Actually, how judges balance the two contending demands determines whether those functions attributed to the state's benches are performed, and performed well. The fate of the balance between accountability and independence is in the hands of judges. But how those judges are selected can determine who they are and how they view their roles.

Judicial Selection: Elections and Appointments

Judges in Washington are selected through a nonpartisan election system with the governor, county commissioners, or mayors appointing persons to fill vacancies that may occur through death, resignation, or removal. However, those appointed must stand for voter approval at the next general election. Judicial reformers thought they could achieve a balance between accountability and independence by keeping political parties out of the selection process and allowing voters to select those sitting on state benches.[6] They viewed the appointment provision as only a stop-gap means of filling a vacancy until voters could have their say. Actually, nearly two-thirds of judges at all levels of the state benches are initially appointed to a vacancy.

To some extent, the nonpartisan system has worked to redress the imbalance between accountability and independence. However, informal activities and participants determine the degree of balance, rather than the formal provisions of judicial selection. If qualified lawyers (only those who are licensed attorneys in the state can become judges) have equal opportunity to become judges, if those appointed or elected are representative of the public, and if all interested parties can participate in the recruitment, the ideal balance can be achieved (see Figure One).[7]

Access refers to the degree of opportunity lawyers have to become judges. Ideally, except for some technical requirements, all lawyers have an equal chance to be chosen. Elitism has no place in a democratic system. Women and minorities should not be at a disadvantage. In this state, all persons who have passed

Figure One

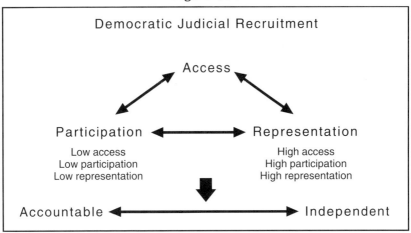

a bar exam after three years of law school or four years of study under the supervision of a licensed attorney and have practiced law for five years have met the technical requirements.

Because of the formal and informal prerequisites for a judgeship, state courts are not *representative* of the population. The composition of the state benches fails to constitute a cross-section of the population. For example, in 1990 minorities accounted for 11.5 percent of the state's population and women 51 percent. However, the technical requirements of access narrow opportunities. Admissions to law school, the high costs of a legal education, and prospects for a job after graduation limit access. For example, approximately 7 percent of the 15,000 active attorneys were minorities and only 28 percent were women. Certainly the politics of judicial selection limits further the representativeness of the state benches. Of the 371 judges on the bench in 1990 only 16 (4.3 percent) were minorities. In 1991, 59 women, out of the 383 judges (15.4 percent), sat on state benches.

It is possible for courts to achieve another kind of representativeness without mirroring the racial, ethnic, and gender aspects of the state or jurisdiction. If judges and court personnel are sensitive to cultural and gender issues, representativeness is enhanced. Despite some recent improvements, Washington needs to work toward greater representativeness.[8]

A constitutional democracy rests upon popular consent. As a reminder, Article I, Section 1 of the Washington Constitution reads: "All political power is inherent in the people and governments derive their power from the consent of the governed." Although people approved the Washington Constitution in 1889, periodic renewal of consent enhances the authority of public servants. In other words, public officials are allowed only relatively short tenures, to be renewed periodically through the election process. This also applies to judges. District, municipal, and superior court judges are elected for four-year terms[9] and court of appeals and supreme court judges for six years.

In some counties, *participation* in the selection and retention of judges is intense. For example, before the mayor appoints a municipal judge in Seattle, the candidate must be screened by the mayor's ad hoc judicial appointments committee, and in both elections and appointments he or she usually seeks the endorsement of a number of legal and political groups (e. g., Washington Women's Political Caucus, Asian-American Bar Association, the Loren Miller Bar, Washington Women Lawyers, Municipal League, Seattle-King County Bar Association, and likely the state and county labor councils, the *Seattle Times* and *Post-Intelligencer,* and a number of business and political leaders). In elections, highly spirited contests between candidates sometimes characterize judicial races. Interested voters, although fewer in number, are drawn as much to judicial ballots as to races for other local public offices.[10] With a fair amount of participation by diverse groups, qualified candidates, individuals, and interested voters in both elections and appointments, the judicial selection system in King County and Seattle tends to balance accountability and independence. But in Spokane and most other counties, few groups are involved in recommending or rating candidates for appointment to the county commissioners, the mayor, or the governor. Only a few interested voters in most counties bother to cast their ballots for judges in primary elections. As a result, those selected tend to be more independent.

As portrayed by Figure One, to balance public accountability with judicial independence there must be equilibrium among access, representativeness, and participation. Easy access, exact representativeness, and high participation will lean the judicial system toward accountability. Difficult access, poor representation, and low participation tend to leave the judges independent, free to ignore public demands. In order to perform those often-conflicting functions assigned to them, judges must be products of a selection system that neither holds them completely accountable nor gives them complete independence. Whether Washington utilizes nonpartisan elections, the merit plan, or gubernatorial appointments matters less than what transpires within these formal selection systems.[11]

In Washington three major actors dominate the recruitment process and determine to a great extent whether a balance exists among access, participation, and representation and thus between accountability and independence. These three are: the legal profession, the governor, and the electorate.

The Legal Profession and Judicial Recruitment

The Washington State Bar Association and its county counterparts (especially the Seattle-King County Bar Association) play significant roles in recruiting judges to all levels of the court system. For vacancies on the supreme court and the court of appeals, a special standing committee of the state bar, the Judicial Recommendation Committee, investigates the background of potential judges, interviews the candidates, then recommends to the board of governors of the bar association those whom the committee members feel are "well qualified" for appellate appointments. The board then submits those recommendations to the governor. County and city bar groups recommend appointees for superior and other court vacancies to the governor and county councils.

The governor is obligated by the state constitution to fill a vacancy on the high bench, but he or she is not required to follow the bar's recommendations. The governor's choice, however, usually coincides with the bar's recommendation.

Prior to elections, a committee of the Seattle-King County Bar Association interviews, investigates, and rates candidates in contested races for the supreme court, court of appeals (Division One), and King County Superior Court. Other county bar groups conduct preferential polls of their membership, releasing the results to the media shortly before elections, hoping, of course, to influence voters.

Gubernatorial Appointments

The informal appointment process varies with each governor and with each appointment. Nonetheless, a general process has characterized the important appointments, and variations are usually a matter of degree. The legal community usually anticipates a vacancy, with the governor's office receiving numerous inquiries from prospective candidates and their friends. The candidates submit resumes and the governor or an administrative assistant interviews them. Background information is collected, even though the governor may know the candidate personally. The chief executive's close assistants assume most of the responsibilities for screening and accumulating data. Upon request of the governor's office, state or county bars submit their recommendations. The bar associations, of course, are under some pressure to weigh heavily the governor's preferred candidate, simply because it is at the pleasure of the chief executive that they are consulted at all. Without a receptive governor, the bar's recommendations would be futile.

The executive may consult the bar office to assure that candidates have had no problems with conflicts of interest or violations of professional ethics. Before making the final selection, the governor consults with his or her immediate staff, a few respected lawyers, bar leaders, and judges.

Recent experiences of supreme court appointments indicate three clear requisites for a successful appointee: friendship and a close working relationship with the governor in the past or, lacking this close relationship, involvement of a wide variety of persons in the recruitment process. A "well qualified" rating from the bar, some previous partisan activities, endorsements from leading groups, and the ability to get elected are also necessary for appointment to the state supreme court. One or two of these attributes would be needed for appointment to lower benches.

The Judicial Electorate

Judicial elections rarely rise to the level of excitement associated with most political contests. The *Canons of Judicial Ethics* require that campaigning judges refrain from discussing matters that eventually may be the subject of litigation. Technically, then, judges should discuss nothing of legal substance. The dignity of the judiciary and the dictates of judicial ethics assure that personal attacks on a candidate are most rare. Also, lawyers challenging an incumbent cannot help but think of the possibility, however remote, that they are running a risk because they might be arguing their client's cause before that same judge should their challenge fail. The nonpartisan nature of the judicial office also eliminates the traditional identity found in partisan campaigns: the political party label. Thus, from the viewpoint of the voter, judicial contests appear dull and unenlightening. Stands on issues are replaced with name familiarity. Endorsement by prominent lawyers, interest groups (legal, police, civic), and public figures substitutes for the political party label. Incumbency usually supplants a need for a public record upon which to run.

Nonetheless, the *judicial* voter is not entirely ignorant of the names and qualifications of judicial candidates. Despite the lack of excitement in most judicial races, the voters who eventually cast their ballots for judicial candidates have often made valiant attempts to educate themselves on the qualifications of judicial aspirants. Roll-off (the percentage of voters in an election who do not cast their ballots for judicial candidates) usually varies between 75 and 66 percent. In other words, only about 66 to 75 percent of all voters in a given election bother to vote for judicial candidates. In uncontested races, roll-off often drops to more than 50 percent. But voters who do make choices among judicial contenders usually consult a number of sources, are fairly knowledgeable, and appear to understand the special requirements of judicial office.

Those who cast a ballot in a judicial contest rely heavily on the *Voters' Pamphlet,* which is published only for general elections. Since most nonpartisan judicial races are decided in the September primary elections, voters consult other sources. Newspaper editorials, discussions with family and friends, bar polls, recommendations from law enforcement groups, mailings from candidates, lawn signs and billboards, and newspaper ads are available and voters use them.[12]

Over the years, few judicial candidates have been challenged. The primary election, held in September, is the crucial election for the few candidates who face opposition. Due to the nonpartisan nature of judicial elections, a candidate receiving more than 50 percent of the primary vote is elected, for his or her name appears alone on the final general election ballot. Superior court candidates achieving a majority vote in the primary and having a single-county jurisdiction are duly elected. Their names do not even appear on the general election ballot. Should three or more candidates split the vote sufficiently to prevent one from garnering an absolute majority, the top two names appear on the November ballot.

Despite the low participation of voters in judicial elections, despite the lack of readily available information on candidates, and despite the lack of contested races, the judicial electorate brings a balance to judicial recruitment. A study of Spokane voters concluded that:

> Popular elections should not be seen as infrequent gatherings of the great unwashed, wherein rational outcomes are a matter largely of chance occurrence. Rather the judicial electorate involves a rather self-selected group of voter participants. These participants are likely to be atypical of the general public with regard to their uncommon interest in public affairs, their years of experience following local affairs in their own area and their level of knowledge about local government.[13]

Major participants in the recruitment process of judges in Washington play complementary roles. The bar, through its selection committee and polls, provides the expert legal appraisal of candidates. Interest groups and newspapers tend to provide needed clues to voters as to the general sympathies of the candidates. The governor adds the political considerations that are a necessary ingredient in the recruitment process simply because of the political nature of judges and their decisions. Finally, the voters add the "legitimating" element so necessary for any political position in a democracy, and certainly essential for judges. Judicial selection in Washington is a complex blend of the concerns of a variety of participants, which tends over time to balance the demands of public accountability with the needs of judicial independence.

Structures and Business of State Courts

The state judiciary comprises four levels of courts (see Figure Two). Courts of limited jurisdiction are found at the bottom of the structure, although they hear nearly nine out of ten of all cases and are the courts with which most people come into direct contact. Next come district and municipal courts.

Figure Two

Washington Court System, 1990

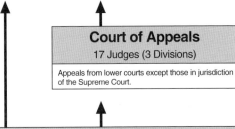

Supreme Court
9 Justices

Appeals from the Court of Appeals

Direct appeals when actions of state officers are involved, the constitutionality of a statute is questioned, there are conflicting statutes or rules of law, or when the issue is of broad public interest.

Court of Appeals
17 Judges (3 Divisions)

Appeals from lower courts except those in jurisdiction of the Supreme Court.

Superior Court
147 Judges (30 Judicial Districts)

Exclusive original jurisdiction in all civil matters involving a dollar amount over $10,000; title or possession of real property; legality of a tax, assessment or toll; probate and domestic matters.

Original jurisdiction in all criminal cases amounting to felony.

Original jurisdiction in all criminal cases when jurisdiction is not otherwise provided by law.

Exclusive original jurisdiction over juvenile matters.

Orders for protection from domestic violence and antiharassment orders.

Appeals from courts of limited jurisdiction heard *de novo* or appealed on the record for error of law.

Route of Appeal

Courts of Limited Jurisdiction
203 Judges (94 full-time attorney; 89 part-time attorney; 20 part-time non-attorney)
(107 district court; 96 municipal)

District Courts	Municiple Courts
(60 courts established by 39 counties in 67 locations; 96 municipalities contract for services from district courts, and 37 violations bureaus are maintained.)	(134 courts established by cities)

Concurrent jurisdiction with superior courts in all misdemeanor and gross misdemeanor actions with a maximum fine of $5000 or less and/or jail sentence of one year or less committed in violation of state/county statutes or county/municipal ordinances.

Jurisdiction in all matters involving traffic, non-traffic, and parking infractions.

Temporary orders for protection from domestic violence.

Concurrent jurisdiction with superior courts over civil actions involving $25,000 or less*

Small Claims of up to $2500*

Preliminary hearings of felonies.*

*District Court Only

Superior courts are the trial courts of general jurisdiction. Appeals are most often taken to the intermediate court of appeals, and the supreme court is the court of last resort.

The trial courts in Washington share responsibility for hearing civil and criminal cases. The 60 district courts throughout the state, with 107 judges, settle civil disputes involving $10,000 or less, small claims, traffic violations, domestic violence, driving while intoxicated, parking, and misdemeanors with a maximum of a $5,000 fine or jail sentences of one year, or both. They also hold preliminary hearings for those accused of serious crimes (felonies). Municipal courts, of which there are 134 presided over by 96 judges, share responsibilities with district courts and also decide violations of municipal ordinances. In some cities, district courts act as municipal courts. All of these courts in Washington had a total of 2,196,993 matters filed with them in 1990. Only 58,719 of these ever made it to the trial stage. In the other cases, guilty pleas were entered, settlements were made out of court, charges were dropped, or bails were forfeited, making trials unnecessary.

District court judges are elected on nonpartisan ballots for a four-year term by the registered voters in the jurisdiction of the court. Or they are appointed by county commissioners to fill a vacancy until the next general election. Depending upon the law that established the court, some municipal court judges are elected, like their district court counterparts, and some are appointed.

Superior courts handle fewer matters than the courts of limited jurisdiction, but are responsible for resolving more serious disputes. A total of 198,672 filings were recorded with superior courts in 1990. Of these, 8,738 resulted in a formal trial (2,648 being before a jury and 6,090 before a judge when the right to a jury trial had been waived or a juvenile hearing was involved), resolving issues varying from the guilt or innocence of one accused of murder to an award of a small amount of money in a civil trial.

The 147 superior court judges are elected on nonpartisan ballots for four-year terms, or are appointed by the governor to fill a vacancy until the next general election, and must be licensed to practice law in the state to be eligible for the office.

The 17 judges on the court of appeals are elected for six-year terms. Vacancies are filled by gubernatorial appointees serving until the next general election. These judges sit in three divisions located throughout the state. Nine judges, sitting in three-judge panels, hear cases in Division One in Seattle, four judges are in Division Two in Tacoma, and four judges in Division Three in Spokane. All appeals from the superior courts ordinarily go to the court of appeals, with the exception of those serious cases (e. g., constitutionality of laws and the death penalty) which can be appealed directly to the supreme court. In 1990, a total of 4,004 filings were made with the various divisions of the court of appeals and the judges disposed of 3,440 of these, leaving a backlog of unresolved cases. Actually, the intermediate court of appeals is slowly falling behind on clearing its docket as filings increase over the years. By 1990 the backlog had reached crisis proportions, with 4,011 filings still pending at the end of the year. A variety of remedial reforms were instituted to deal with the crisis, but as yet no lasting solution seems evident. For example, in 1977 four new judges joined the court and in the late 1980s supreme court justices joined their appeals colleagues to hear cases. The new judges, with the help of the high court justices, increased their output and accompanied fewer decisions with a written opinion, but the docket pressures remained. Court rules and statutes will likely be changed in the near future in order to lighten the court's work load. The problem, of course, is that in making access to the court more difficult, many deserving appeals will go unheard. On the other hand, without some reform, judges simply cannot give full attention to each appeal brought to them.

Nine justices elected for six-year terms, or appointed by the governor to fill a vacancy until the next general election, sit on the state's court of last resort, the supreme court, to which all final appeals on state issues can be made. The published opinions of the justices, *Washington Reports,* provide precedent followed by lower courts, attorneys, other public officials, courts in other states, and the supreme court itself. Because of this final authority, the supreme court is at the apex of the state court structure, even though other courts handle more cases and probably have a more direct and immediate impact on the average litigant.

The jurisdiction of the supreme court, as defined in the state constitution and in statutes, involves original jurisdiction when cases are heard for the first time by the high court. However, very few filings in original jurisdiction are made with the court. More commonly, the supreme court has the authority to review in its appellate jurisdiction all decisions of other state courts if more than $200 is involved. Direct appeal may come from superior court decisions and from the court of appeals. However, the high court exercises discretionary review in virtually all cases sent to it.

In 1990, 1,036 filings were made with the high bench and 1,022 matters were disposed of by the justices. They wrote 119 opinions, and either dismissed, denied review, transferred to the court of appeals, or settled out-of-court the remaining cases. Of course, the written opinions involved disputes that the court regarded as requiring its greatest attention.

The justices of the supreme court are also responsible for promulgating rules of procedure for courts, for exercising some administrative responsibilities pertaining to the state legal system, for reviewing the few disciplinary actions taken by the bar association against lawyers charged with unprofessional conduct, and for supervising rulings of the commission on judicial conduct.

Judicial Administration

To coordinate a system that includes nearly 400 judges, more than 3,000 support personnel, innumerable attorneys who argue cases, and thousands of citizens whose causes are brought to the courts or who are involved in jury duty, requires a considerable number of administrative entities and support agencies. Court administration in Washington provides a number of needed and useful services for the judiciary. Research, study, and recommendations on such problems as court congestion must be conducted and reforms instituted. Involved in such efforts are institutions like the Board for Judicial Administration, Judicial Information System, Court Congestion and Delay Task Force, Task Force on Indigent Fees, Administrator for the Courts, and State Law Library. Coordination and communication among the many groups involved in the Washington justice system require considerable effort. Involved are the Board of Judiciary Education, Administrator for the Courts, Board of Judicial Administration, Judicial Information System, Bench-bar-press Committee, and judges, clerks, and administrators' conferences. Court calendars must be formed and records and documents catalogued and filed (court clerks, county clerks, court administrators, reporter of decisions, court reporters, bailiffs, and law librarians). Special attention must be given to the impact of the court system on women and minorities (Commission on Gender and Justice and Commission on Minorities and Justice).

Judges at all levels need assistance in various aspects of their decision-making, and receive that help from law clerks, court commissioners, *pro tempore* and visiting judges, the Board of Judiciary Education, law librarians, administrative assistants, and legal interns. Finally, the public needs to be assured that sufficient judicial independence is maintained and that ethical standards are observed. Providing this assurance are the Task Force on Canons of Judicial Ethics and the Commission on Judicial Conduct.

The Commission on Judicial Conduct, established by constitutional amendment in 1980, provides a means of supervising the ethical behavior of judges without utilizing the cumbersome and drastic measures of impeachment or without obtaining a joint resolution of the legislature to remove a judge from office. The commission investigates complaints and recommends to the supreme court the censure, suspension, or dismissal of judges. The commission can also recommend the removal of a judge for serious disabilities that prevent him or her from performing the duties of office. The mere existence of the commission likely prevents many judges from succumbing to unethical and dishonest temptations.

Differences Between Trial and Appellate Courts

One can view each level of the state judiciary as a separate court system where different participants interact within special procedures. To understand the judiciary, one must understand the internal workings of trial and appellate courts.

The trial and appellate levels of the Washington court system perform different functions, are regulated by different procedures, involve different personnel, and represent different authority. Trial courts try fact. In other words, they ascertain what actually happened and determine the issues involved in the litigation. Appellate judges only review information placed on the record at the trial. The facts, as established in the lower court, are assumed to be correct and complete. Appellate courts determine if all participants in the lower court case observed due process and appropriate legal procedures, and if the judge applied the correct law in the acceptable manner. The appellate courts do not call juries, contemplate evidence, inquire of witnesses, or cross-examine. Two advocates file written briefs and argue before courts consisting of from three to nine judges. Written opinions are usually required when decisions are rendered, although in unimportant cases at the court of appeals level a written opinion is not mandated. Should some aspect of the trial appear questionable, the appellate court simply reverses the lower court's decision and dismisses the case or returns (remands) it to the trial court for further consideration. Thus, the functions and procedures of trial and appellate courts are different.

Appellate courts are collegial bodies requiring conferences, cooperative efforts, and collective decisions. Their decisions are rendered in isolated courtrooms within a cloistered atmosphere quite unlike the excitement of a trial court. Indeed, many would argue that the two levels of the court require two kinds of judges. Trial judges must have a better understanding of human nature, for they deal directly with the public. Trial work requires quick decisions on procedural questions while maintaining a dignified courtroom demeanor. On the other hand, appellate judges must develop a love of legal research often resulting in lengthy and complicated written legal opinions. They must be experienced in persuading, cajoling, and compromising with their colleagues in order to reach a ruling supported by a majority of the judges.

Finally, as a decision of trial judges or jury is appealed up to the court of appeals and possibly to the supreme court, the authority of the decision deepens. Whether affirmed or revised, a decision of an appellate court, and especially the state's court of last resort, constitutes a precedent future courts will follow.

Trial Court Procedures: Criminal Cases

The preliminary appearance is the first step in the criminal justice process. The persons arrested are brought before a district or municipal court judge to be informed of why they are being held in jail. The amount of bail, if any, is determined and the date set for the next appearance, when a formal criminal charge is made. If charges are filed, the accused are arraigned before a court; at this time they are informed of the charges and asked whether they will enter a plea of guilty or not guilty. A guilty plea puts the convicted into the hands of a sentencing judge.

If the crime is a misdemeanor and the accused enter a plea of not guilty, their next appearance before a district court judge will be at the trial itself. These cases may involve juries of less than six people. Superior courts usually base the appeals from district courts on electronic tape recordings of the original trial, although a new trial (*de nova*) is held.

In a felony charge, the accused next appears before a district judge for a preliminary hearing. At that time the prosecutor presents evidence and a list of witnesses to the judge, who decides whether the evidence is sufficient to bind the accused over to superior court for trial. If there is insufficient evidence to support the charge, the judge dismisses the case.

Plea bargaining between the prosecuting attorney and the defense lawyer can begin immediately following the preliminary hearing. In cases filed directly in superior court, negotiations between counsel can begin immediately after the arraignment. Most felonies in Washington involve some plea bargaining.

Should a plea be refused and negotiations break down, a trial date, no later than 60 days following the preliminary hearing, is set, and both sides begin preparations. An omnibus hearing precedes the trial by about two weeks, at which the judge is assured that the defense has all the information that is available to the prosecutor and that all procedural questions, such as admissibility of evidence or confessions, are resolved. Following the omnibus hearing, jury selection begins and the trial date is set.

The defendant is tried either before a jury or, should the right to a jury trial be waived, before a judge. Sixty percent of all criminal trials in superior courts in 1990 involved juries. The jury or the judge is the trier of fact. The weight of the evidence is established, and should the evidence indicate that the prosecutor's charge is proven "beyond a reasonable doubt," the defendant is found guilty. If some doubt persists, the jury or judge must find the defendant not guilty. A guilty decision leads the defendant to the sentencing process.

Prior to 1984, Washington trial courts employed an "indeterminate sentencing" system. Those convicted of crimes were sentenced within a broad range of years defined by law; the Board of Prison Terms and Parole determined the actual time of incarceration. However, the judges now follow carefully drawn guidelines in order to *maintain uniformity* in the process by sentencing the convicted to a defined term, which the person must complete before release. The Board of Prison Terms and Parole is being phased out. This "determinate sentencing" now has replaced the old system.

A guilty plea, either at the initial arraignment or up until trial, prevents the accused from appealing the case to the court of appeals or the supreme court. However, an appeal can be made if the jury or the judge finds the accused guilty after a trial. A total of 1,575 appeals were made from the 2,317 criminal trials held in 1990.

Trial Court Procedures: Civil Cases

Criminal cases involve crimes that have been perpetrated against society. In contrast, civil cases involve one citizen suing another over such non-criminal matters as breach of contract, damages to person or property because of negligence, or domestic conflicts like divorce and child custody. In some circumstances the state may also be involved in a civil suit such as a *habeas corpus* filing with a federal district court. The process judges follow is distinct from the criminal process. Actions are commenced by one person (a plaintiff) filing a complaint against another, or having a sheriff serve a summons requiring the person (the defendant) against whom the complaint was filed to appear in court and defend him or herself. At the pleadings and motions stage of the civil process, the parties to the dispute file with the court and exchange written assertions, claims, cross-claims, and counter-complaints. Pleadings and motions define the issues, answer assertions, and exchange claims so that all are aware of the suit's content. A pretrial discovery hearing may be held before a judge, in which the parties isolate and agree upon facts, simplify the issues, amend the pleadings, and limit the number of expert witnesses to be called. Counsel prepare for trial by taking depositions (sworn statements collected outside of court) and gathering testimony and evidence. Rules of discovery require that the parties exchange the information they have gathered as they prepare for trial.

Next comes a trial before a judge, and sometimes before a jury of 12 or less, a process that resembles a criminal trial to a significant degree. In contrast with the need for a jury or judge to be convinced "beyond a reasonable doubt" as in the criminal trial, a civil suit is decided if the "preponderance of the evidence" dictates a verdict and only a majority jury vote, in contrast with unanimity, is required. At any time during the process the parties can settle out of court. They simply agree and move that the matter be removed from the court's jurisdiction, which results in dismissal. Also, the judge can terminate the litigation any time throughout the process by dismissing upon motion or by a summary judgment. If the suit appears frivolous, ill-conceived, or fraudulent, the judge can order dismissal. If the outcome is obvious, the judge can hold a brief hearing or mini-trial and summarily decide the case. In 1990 the superior courts had 116,608 civil filings. Of these, they held 778 jury and 3,971 non-jury trials. Thus, the vast majority of civil suits were dismissed, won by default, decided through summary judgment, or settled out of court.

Civil cases dominate the dockets of trial judges, but criminal matters take priority. Because of the constitutional requirement at both the federal and state levels of a speedy trial, the accused in a criminal case must be brought to trial within 60 days, 90 days if bail has been posted – or be released. Thus, many civil suits must be postponed when criminal cases crowd the dockets of superior and district courts.

As in criminal cases, losers in civil suits are entitled to at least one appeal should they feel the outcome unjust. The court of appeals had 1,533 civil appeals filed in 1990 and the supreme court received 114 civil filings for review in the same year.

The Appellate Judicial System

The court of appeals and the supreme court share appellate jurisdiction. The supreme court can transfer cases up from the court of appeals for the justices' direct consideration and can also transfer them down to the lower court if they regard them as less important. The court of appeals can also certify cases from its dockets up to the high court. In 1990, the supreme court transferred 81 cases to the court of appeals while the court of appeals certified 52 to the supreme court, or transferred them to another division. The question in the decision to transfer cases is often whether "fundamental and urgent issues of broad public import requiring prompt and ultimate determination" are involved.

The docket of the high court is largely a product of judicial discretion. The supreme court hears most cases simply because the justices choose to hear them. A majority vote of a panel of five of the justices determines whether to transfer, retain, or review a case. If agreement is lacking in the question of whether to hear an appeal, the full court (*en banc*) decides by a majority vote decision. Of the 1,036 filings in 1990, the justices accepted only 128 for full consideration, while only 119 qualified for full review with written opinion.

Except for the number of judges involved in each decision (three in the court of appeals and nine in the court of last resort), the number and nature of the cases heard, and the finality of the decisions, the decisional sequences of the two appellate courts are similar. The following describes the supreme court deliberative process, although it applies as well to the intermediate court of appeals. Supreme court justices render a final decision only after having exposed a case to four separate deliberative stages. All cases must experience preparatory, hearing, conference, and opinion stages.

Table One

Decisional Stages and Sources

Preparatory stage
       Written briefs (attorneys)
       Prehearing memos (reporting judge and law clerks)
       Trial court record (law clerk)
       Petitions for review (court commissioner)

Hearing stage
       Oral arguments (attorneys)
       Queries from bench (justices)

Conference stage (justices)
       Reporting judge's presentation
       Discussion and debate
       Chief justice's summary
       Tentative vote

Opinion stage (justices and law clerks)
       Assigned justice's draft opinion
       Concurring drafts
       Dissenting drafts
       Intra-court memos
       Informal discussions and persuasion
       Final signatures on opinions

Source: Adapted from Charles Sheldon, *A Century of Judging: A Political History of the Washington Supreme Court* (Seattle: University of Washington Press, 1988), p. 309.

The justices turn to a variety of sources as they contemplate and deliberate over the four stages. Table One outlines the important sources the justices use in each of the four stages in the appellate process.

Preparatory Stage

In preparing to review an appeal on its merits, the high court follows a two-step process. First, the justices must decide whether to hear the case. Next, they must prepare for the hearing. The court assigns, by lot, each of the filed disputes to a justice responsible for reviewing the requests. A recommendation on the request from the court commissioner's staff becomes part of the assigned judge's considerations. Whether to review the case or not is recommended to a panel of five judges by the responsible judge. The panel takes a vote following that presentation.

Upon acceptance of jurisdiction, the court chooses a reporting judge, again by lot. With assistance from his or her law clerk, the justice's personal assistant, the reporting judge reviews the trial court record, researches the issues and law, and prepares a prehearing memo that is circulated to the other justices prior to oral arguments. Questions during the oral arguments and discussions during the conference deliberations depend upon the reporting judge's prehearing memos, the written briefs that lawyers on both sides have filed with the court, law clerks' research, court commissioners' recommendations, and the justice's research and recollections.

Hearing Stage

The oral argument stage performs three major functions. First, and perhaps foremost, it presents the democratic image of the court, for no other aspect of the court's decisional process is subject to public scrutiny. The arguments before the supreme court take place in the high-ceilinged, oak-panelled courtroom of the Temple of Justice in Olympia. The robed justices sit in high-backed chairs across the front of the chamber, elevated above the lawyers' tables and spectators' area. The chief justice in the center is flanked by his or her most senior colleagues, with the most recently elected or appointed judge sitting on the chief's extreme left and the next most junior on the extreme right. Although few attend the morning and afternoon arguments, the broad heavy oak doors of the chamber are likely ajar. Government in a democracy must be visible and open. Judges, no less than legislators or civil servants, must appear to be accessible. Oral arguments allow the court to give at least a symbolic gesture toward public accountability.

Second, the justices must weigh the arguments presented by attorneys. Each side in a case is usually allotted 20 to 30 minutes to present its case and to answer questions the justices pose. Thus, the system provides an opportunity for jurists to receive answers to questions which may have troubled them after their reading of the briefs or the prehearing memos, or from listening to the oral presentations. Generally, each justice can interrupt counsel. While some cases stimulate little questioning, in others counsel's time may be largely consumed by inquiries. Attorneys practicing before appellate courts are encouraged by the questioning, simply because it indicates that judges are alert to their concerns. However, attorneys must be prepared to provide the right answers. The questions are almost evenly divided between inquiries on points of law and quests for clarification of facts which may be obscure in the lower court record.

Third and finally, oral arguments furnish a forum for an adversarial confrontation between attorneys for parties to the dispute. Each side is allowed to present its version of the proper resolution of the issue and to challenge the opposition's assertions.

Oral arguments are indeed useful to the justices. But again, the justices seek particular types of information from the attorneys presenting their arguments. Table Two reports a ranking of how the hearing stage helps the jurists.

Table Two

Justices' Views of the Functions of Oral Arguments

Rank	Function
1	To force attorneys to focus on most important matters
2	To prepare for conference deliberations
3	To legitimate the decisional process
4	To clarify facts
5	To persuade colleagues
6	To communicate with colleagues
7	To reinforce prehearing memos
8	To show that briefs have been carefully read

Source: Sheldon, *A Century of Judging*, p. 312

Conference Stage

Immediately following oral arguments the justices retire to their conference room for a discussion and preliminary vote on the cases just heard, usually four. Although conference decisions are tentative, this is the most crucial phase in the decisional process. All deliberations are secret, with no persons other than the justices allowed in the conference room. Each case is called, and the reporting judge on that particular case summarizes his or her view of the case and recommends disposition: affirm, reverse, or affirm in part and reverse in part the lower courts' decision. The style of reporting varies with each justice and each case so that the reporting judge may expend from 10 minutes to an hour in this phase. The reporting judge's summary may be complete, with full reasons for his or her conclusion, or it may be brief. Then each justice, beginning with the one to the right of the reporting judge and continuing counter-clockwise around the table, discusses the case and recommends a tentative disposition. The chief justice comments and votes on the case last. The time spent on these conference deliberations may vary from a few seconds for a single "I agree," to three-quarters of an hour for each justice. No strict time schedule is imposed, but rarely are discussions on a particular case carried over to the next conference. If the view of the reporting judge prevails, he or she is assigned the task of writing the majority opinion. Other justices may indicate they plan to write concurring (agreeing on outcome but for different reasons) or dissenting (disagreeing on both outcome and reasons) opinions.

Opinion Stage

If the reporting judge's view prevailed in conference, the conference discussion will indicate what he or she needs to do in the written draft to convince a wavering judge or to win over a potential dissenter. Perhaps some justice has reserved his or her vote until the drafts are reviewed. The opinion writer could develop a draft that may well answer what has troubled one or several of the other jurists. What has transpired in conference, although regarded by all as tentative, fashions the direction and thrust of the opinion-writing and circulating stage of the decisional process. Rarely is the conference vote reversed, although certainly that opportunity is available.

Article IV, Section 2 of the Washington Constitution reads in part: "In the determination of causes all decisions of the court shall be given in writing and the grounds of the decision shall be stated." While these published opinions provide compelling reading, their most important function is to hold the justices accountable. They provide lawyers, law professors, law students, journalists, politicians, and the public with information to "judge the judges."

The circulation of drafts of the written opinions which explain the reasons the justices decided as they did represents an important aspect of the high court's decisional process. The end result of the circulation of written opinions is, of course, precedent for future cases. No decision is final until all nine justices have signed one or another of the written opinions. The chief justice is responsible for monitoring the writing process by keeping tabs on the justice doing the writing, determining if someone is having difficulty completing an opinion, and keeping track of who has signed the various drafts. Each justice receives a copy of the draft opinion. Upon reading the draft he or she can: (1) agree and sign; (2) write a concurring opinion; 3) draft a dissent; or (4) express tentative agreement but urge some changes. When everyone has had an opportunity to review the final versions and has signed one or another of the opinions, the chief justice files them with the clerk of the supreme court, and they become official and final. The losing litigant may request a rehearing, but the court rarely grants them.

The importance of this opinion-circulating stage is seen when it is understood that the outcomes of some important cases are changed as a result of the exchange of drafts. For example, the majority may fail to hold the five or more votes it received in the preliminary conference vote and a convincing dissenting opinion may pick up the necessary numbers of signatures to become the new majority. More likely, however, is that the justices stick with their votes in conference and, at most, the opinion-writer makes some changes in the majority draft to accommodate views of the other justices. The final results often contain a number of compromises.

The writing of a dissenting opinion may be motivated by several reasons and either enhance the work of the court (collective) or a particular judge's position (individual). Table Three ranks—in order of importance to the justices—these dissenting motivations.

Table Three

Motivations for Dissent from the Perspectives of the Justices

Rank	Motivations	Collective or Individual
1	To win over the majority or to win more "votes"	Collective
2	To point out the impact of the majority's opinion on society	Collective
3	To lay groundwork for the future	Individual
4	To keep the majority "honest"	Collective
5	To "write it as I see it," despite the majority or concurrences	Individual
6	To provide a forum for minorities, the discouraged and ignored	Individual
7	To improve the majority opinion	Collective
8	To participate in freedom and democracy requires occasional dissent	Individual

Source: Sheldon, *A Century of Judging,* p. 317.

Although the supreme court is the court of last resort in the state, some appeals can be made directly to the United States Supreme Court when questions of federal law or the federal constitution are involved. Rarely are such appeals made, and rarer still are they accepted by the nation's highest court. If the decisions rest on adequate and independent state grounds, the rulings remain unreviewable by the nation's high court. Thus, for all practical purposes, the Washington Supreme Court's decisions are final.

Conclusion

For at least appellate judges, the deliberative process is largely a personal affair where the judges, although not totally free from constraints, are guided by their own views of the law and their role in the state political system. Thus, judicial selection is a crucial aspect of the state's court system. The selection process must be carefully scrutinized by those involved, who must exercise care that those winners of the election and appointment contests are of high caliber, deserving of a position on the state's benches. Once they are in office, judges are only as accountable as they feel compelled to be, although on occasion they may be replaced by a challenger in an election.

This returns us to the original issue posed at the start of this chapter. Judges must, on the one hand, remain aloof from politics and the interests of the litigants in order to assure fairness in the adversarial struggle between attorneys and in order to render unbiased decisions. On the other hand, in settling these disputes, judges often affirm, change, or make public policy and must, therefore, be accountable to the public. A balance between these two potentially antithetical demands must be reached. To a great extent, whether a balance is reached depends upon the values, experiences, and views of the judges. But the judicial electorate, bar associations, the governor, and those interest groups attempting to influence the selection of judges are also responsible for affecting the balance. None may take that responsibility lightly.

Notes

1. See Justice Robert Brachtenbach, "Public Policy in Judicial Decisions," 21 *Gonzaga Law Review* (1985/86).
2. The movement to rely more heavily upon state constitutions is referred to as "new federalism." See, for example, "Symposium: The Washington Constitution," 8 *University of Puget Sound Law Review* 157-194 (Winter 1985). Justice Robert Utter's article in the collection, "The Right to Speak, Write and Publish Freely: State Constitutional Protection against Private Abridgment," is especially relevant.
3. 115 Wn. 2d (1990). Article I, Section 7 was interpreted to be more protective ("No person shall be disturbed in his private affairs, or his home invaded, without authority of law") than the Fourth Amendment ("The right of the people to be secure in their persons, houses, papers and effects, against unreasonable search and seizures"), permitting the state bench to ignore Fourth Amendment rulings of the nation's high court.
4. *E. E. O. C. v. Massachusetts*, 858 F. 2d 52 (1st Cir. 1988).
5. See James Dolliver, "Law as a Profession: Will it Survive?" 26 *Gonzaga Law Review* 267-275 (1990/1991).
6. Before 1907, Washington judges were nominated by political party conventions and ran in elections under their party label. For a discussion of the history of the Washington judiciary see Charles Sheldon, *A Century of Judging: A Political History of the Washington Supreme Court* (Seattle: University of Washington Press, 1988).
7. Sheldon and Nicholas Lovrich, "State Judicial Selection," in John Gates and Charles Johnson, *The American Courts: A Critical Assessment* (Washington, D.C.: Congressional Quarterly Press, 1991), pp. 161-188.
8. For reports on the representativeness of courts see *Minorities and Justice Task Force, Final Report* (Olympia: State of Washington, 1991), and *Gender and Justice in the Courts* (Olympia: State of Washington, 1989).
9. Some municipal judges are appointed, depending upon city ordinances. Some district judges serve under contract as municipal judges.
10. In nonpartisan races the candidate who wins a majority of the votes in the primaries in September is designated the winner, except in some municipal races that must be decided in the November general elections. In statewide contests for the supreme court and in court of appeals multi-county districts, the roll-off may exceed 30 to 40 percent of those who vote for leading offices. In the 38 contested judicial races in 1990, only 21 incumbents were retained in office. Seventeen new judges out of the 90 candidates for the 38 positions were elected. The races were often close. One district court race was decided by four votes. A municipal court judge in Seattle mounted a successful write-in campaign, and a relatively unknown attorney from Tacoma defeated an incumbent chief justice on the supreme court.
11. Several formal methods are used by states for selecting judges: partisan and nonpartisan elections, gubernatorial appointments, legislative election, and the merit plan. The merit plan involves nominations by a blue-ribbon commission, appointment from the commission's list by the governor, and, after a period of probation, an election by registered voters in which the judge runs on his or her record.

12. See Sheldon and Lovrich, "Knowledge and Judicial Voting: The Oregon and Washington Experience," 67 *Judicature* 234-245 (November 1983); and Lovrich and Sheldon, "Voters in Contested Non-partisan Judicial Elections: A Responsible Electorate or a Problematic Public," 36 *Western Political Quarterly* 241-256 (June 1983).
13. Lovrich, John Pierce, and Sheldon, "Citizens Knowledge and Voting in Judicial Elections," 73 *Judicature* 33 (1989).

The Little Hollywood district in Olympia in the late 1930s. Vibert Jeffers photo. *Susan Parish Collection*©

Chapter Nine

Local Government Then and Now: The Growth Management Challenge in the 1990s

Greg Andranovich and Nicholas P. Lovrich, Jr.

Introduction

WHETHER IT IS IN YOUR daily newspaper or on television, more likely than not the news stories receiving most media prominence involve our national government. While events in Washington, D. C.—in Congress, at the supreme court, and in the executive office of the president—do affect your life in many ways, locally made decisions "touch you" every day. Municipalities, counties, and special districts make many decisions that directly affect the quality of your life. The air you breathe, the water you drink, the roads over which you drive, the methods employed to provide for the recycling and/or disposal of your garbage, the schools you and your children attend, and the health care to which you have access are all governed locally. Local government is also the place where a citizen can have the greatest influence on public decision-making. You can easily attend and participate in a city council, county commission, or special school district meeting. But attending and participating in national government policy-making is extremely difficult and prohibitively costly for most citizens.

At the same time, notwithstanding their importance, local governments are, in Judge Dillon's words, "legal creatures of the state." State law establishes local governments and delegates rights and duties derived from those that the U. S. Constitution reserves to the several states, requiring (or mandating) certain activities and prohibiting others. Indeed, state law can alter local government authority at any time. In this chapter, we discuss the structural characteristics of the local government environment in the State of Washington,[1] as well as the implications of growth management at the local government level. Growth management—planning for the ever-expanding responsibilities and environmental interventions of local government—is likely to be an overarching issue in the public affairs of Washington, significantly affecting local government well through the year 2000.

Local Governments

Role of the State

The role of American state governments has evolved to include the administrative management of regional and local affairs within their respective boundaries. The contemporary environment of intergovernmental relations among national, state, and local governments tends to be functionally grounded, with overlapping responsibilities in specific policy areas such as health care services, criminal justice, environmental protection, education, and economic development. In each policy arena, however, several state agencies often oversee policy development, resulting in a sometimes frustrating and seemingly contradictory pattern of public decision-making—especially in quality-of-life issues such as environmental protection or growth management, which cut across several policy areas. In Washington, two state agencies have principal authority to influence local decision-making across the full spectrum of local government responsibility: the Department of Community Development and the state auditor's office.

The Department of Community Development (formerly the Planning and Community Affairs Agency) participates in the distribution of targeted federal funds by means of grants-in-aid to local government jurisdictions. It also provides technical assistance to local jurisdictions on a broad range of issues and recommends suitable legislation on local government issues to the state legislature and governor. The auditor's office, more specifically its municipal corporations division, establishes budget and accounting procedures for all local governments in the state. The division also conducts post-audits on all local government financial transactions in order to assure correct budgeting procedures and expenditures.

Cities and Towns

Findings from the 1990 census indicate that Washington continues to be an "urban state" with over half of the population residing in its 268 municipalities. Most Washingtonians live in the state's 25 largest cities.[2] The number of municipalities in Washington has remained relatively stable over the last 25 years, although several rural communities have lost their legal status as towns by disincorporating. At the same time, a number of municipal consolidations have come to pass and a few new suburban areas have incorporated.

This relative stability is due in large part to state legislation intended to forestall the growth of small municipalities within Washington's urban areas. For example, one statute prevents a city of less than 3,000 from incorporating and gaining separate legal status if it is within five miles of an established city of 15,000 or more. Before a new municipality can incorporate, a boundary review board – existing in about half of Washington's counties[3] – must give its approval. Such approval is contingent upon a showing that the new entity will be economically viable and will not greatly affect the fiscal well-being of either the county government or municipal governments in the surrounding area. The most recent incorporations have taken place in the state's rapidly growing Puget Sound area at Mill Creek in Snohomish County in 1983 and at Federal Way and SeaTac in south King County in 1990.

Incorporation brings certain advantages and responsibilities. For example, incorporation gives residents zoning powers to preserve existing land use patterns, allows control over service delivery (e. g., police, fire), provides greater access to federal and state funds, or even allows a community to gain a local post office. Perhaps the most important advantage comes with control over land use, particularly as areas on the fringes of municipalities grow.

Annexation is a tool for controlling land use. Most annexations take in small parcels of land, usually including a high revenue-producing facility such as a shopping mall or a clean or "high-tech" industrial location. Other cases of annexation are developer-initiated and occur by petition. In recent years, a small number of cities – Bellevue, Everett, and West Richland being the most prominent – have accounted for most of the state's annexation activity.[4] Kirkland's 1987 annexation by election of areas with more than 14,000 residents represents a most unusual case today. In any event, in counties where they have been established, boundary review boards must review and pass judgment on all but the smallest additions.

Structure of Municipal Governments

As noted, laws governing the basic structure and powers of a municipality, county, or special district can be found in the state constitution, in legislative enactments, and, in a few cases, in home-rule charters. Such charters provide substantial autonomy from the state legislature for the organization and management of city affairs, so long as the home-rule charter is consistent with the constitution and laws of the state. Charter options, which permit considerable flexibility in the organization of municipal government, depend upon the population size classification of the municipality. Voters in all but the largest and smallest Washington cities can select from a sizeable list of packages of municipal powers and structures. This combination of related issues pertaining to structural options and concerns regarding the proper classification of municipalities based on size of population has dominated the political discussion surrounding the chartering of Washington cities. As things currently stand, cities of more than 10,000 residents may adopt home-rule charters by petitioning the state.

Compared to other states, Washington has tended to be rather restrictive in the powers granted to home-rule cities. State courts have ruled in a number of cases involving local government powers, generally tending to reinforce the principle that home-rule is a matter of legislative grace. Such grace can be withdrawn at the full discretion of the state. There are 10 cities (all first class, with population greater than 20,000) in Washington that have adopted home-rule charters, with the most recent being Richland, which incorporated as a first class city in 1958.

The issue of local autonomy in institutional design was bolstered in 1967 when the state enacted the optional municipal code. The code permits cities or towns to drop their existing classification to become a "code city." Becoming a code city means that a municipality has the broadest powers of self government allowed to any city, excepting only the ability to design local revenue sources. This also is called statutory home-rule.[5] This option provides an alternative to the cumbersome adoption process required under the home-rule option, greatly simplifying the public participation aspects of code status adoption. Today there are 130 "code cities" in the state.[6]

Washington municipalities may adopt any of three principal types of city government—the mayor-council, council-manager, or commission form. The organization of local government authority differs markedly under each of the three forms (see Figure One).

Mayor-Council

The mayor-council form of government is the most widely used framework in the state; Seattle, our largest city, uses this form, as do some of the state's smallest municipalities, such as Colfax and Grand Coulee, which have fewer than 5,000 people. How can the mayor-council form of government be used in the largest and smallest cities alike? The term mayor-council represents a rather generic classification of cities entailing the clear separation of executive and legislative powers and featuring separately elected mayors and council members. In larger cities, mayors tend to have considerable public visibility, employ a professional staff, and exercise at least nominal control over the city bureaucracy. In larger cities the office of the mayor is relatively highly developed and tends to be more fully oriented toward executive managerial responsibilities than is the case in the typical smaller jurisdiction.

Historically, the mayor-council form of government has been the most widely used, both in the State of Washington and across the nation. The state's optional municipal code of 1967 required municipalities of fewer than 2,000 persons to operate as mayor-council governments. In these smaller jurisdictions, mayoral duties tend to be more ceremonial than executive in nature, acting in a way local government textbooks would describe as "weak mayor-council" governments.

Figure One

Cities by Classification/Code and Forms of Government

Classes,[1] per RCW 35.22	Mayor-Council	Council-Manager	Commission	Total
1st Class (over 20,000 pop.)	5	5	0	10
2nd Class (10-20,000 pop.)	0	0	0	0
3rd Class (1500-10,000 pop.)	27	3	0	30
4th Class (less than 1500 pop.)	99	0	0	99
Code Cities[2]	96	28	3	127
Unclassified[3] (Territorial Charters)	2	0	0	2
TOTALS	229 (85.5%)	36 (13.4%)	3 (1.1%)	268 (100%)

[1] Classification by population is established by the legislature as a means of allocating powers, responsibilities, and salaries of municipal officers according to a city's population. When population increases beyond the threshold of the next higher class, a city may, by majority vote, enter that higher classification.

[2] "Code" cities are those organized under the optional municipal code of 1967 (Title 35A RCW), which grants broader powers to all cities without classification. They may adopt their own charter if population is 10,000 or more, though none have.

[3] The "unclassified" cities are Waitsburg and Union Gap, which never reorganized under general laws and are governed under charters granted by the territorial legislature.

Source: Adapted from Local Government Study Commission, *A History of Washington's Local Governments*, Vol. 1 (Olympia: Department of Community Development, 1988), p. 70; and *Officials of Washington Cities, 1990-1991* (Kirkland: Municipal Research and Services Center, 1990), p. 94.

Council-Manager

The second most widely used form of municipal government in Washington is the council-manager system. The council-manager system is a direct outcome of the Progressive reform era of American history from 1900-1920, a movement which sought to cleanse American politics of corruption by professionalizing administration in government. At the local level, professional city administrators—or "city managers"—are appointed by and responsible to the city council and serve at the council's pleasure. Council members are typically elected at-large on a city-wide basis. The non-tenured city manager in this system is the municipality's chief executive and has direct control over the city bureaucracy. The mayor's role, where it survives at all, tends to be that of first-among equals (*primus inter pares*) with the rest of the council.

Sunnyside, in 1948, became the first city to adopt the council-manager form of government in Washington, some five years after the state legislature made it possible for non home-rule cities to use this governmental format. Of the 36 cities now operating the council-manager system, all but five have populations of greater than 5,000. The council-manager form is currently most popular among cities with more than 10,000 persons (that is, in class one or class two cities). As elsewhere across the nation, the appeal of the council-manager form of government has been greatest among middle-sized, economically middle-class, growing municipalities and suburban communities. For example, Spokane and Tacoma, Washington's second and third largest cities, have adopted a council-manager system; the smallest municipality with a city manager is Fircrest (population 5,440) in Pierce county.

The idea of a full-time manager of city administration has not been lost on other cities. Without formally changing their form of government, many of the state's middle-sized mayor-council and commission governments have added appointed administrative coordinators – supervisors, superintendents, administrators, or administrative assistants – who function in a capacity similar to that of city managers. Almost one-third of the mayor-council and code cities employ these coordinators of administration.[7]

Commission

The commission form of government combines responsibility for both policy-making and administration. It concentrates legislative and executive power in a small commission elected at-large. In Washington, elective commissions are composed of three persons. Considered collectively, commissioners constitute the local legislative body; individually, each commissioner is viewed as an administrator who oversees specific municipal functions, such as personnel, public works, or recreation. One commissioner serves as the mayor, typically on a fixed rotational basis.

Fifteen Washington cities, including Spokane and Tacoma, have experimented with the commission form of government. However, no municipality has adopted this form in more than three decades, and the number of commission cities continues to dwindle. After residents in Olympia and Bremerton voted to abandon commission government in 1982, only three commission cities remain: Raymond and Shelton, which have administrative coordinators, and Wenatchee.[8]

The track record of commission governments has not been particularly impressive. Dissatisfactions with the commission form of government in Washington reflect a number of complaints, including the tendency of commissioners to become chief lobbyists for the functional area in which they perform assigned administrative responsibilities. Difficulty in attracting and then electing people with adequate administrative abilities to positions that are typically low paying has also proven to be a problem, as has intracommission conflict, which tends to polarize commissions and make constructive teamwork and mutual support unlikely.

Counties

Counties were the first units of local government established in Washington; some counties were created when the area still enjoyed territorial status. Although attempts are made from time to time to establish additional counties (most recently to create a new entity from the timbered western sections of Clallam and Jefferson counties), their number has remained constant at 39 since Pend Oreille became a county in 1911.

Washington counties, like those in other Western states, tend to be significantly larger than counties in the East. Within the state, however, a variety of county sizes exists. Okanogan, with more than 5,000 square miles, is larger than the State of Connecticut, while San Juan has less than 200 square miles (see Figure Two). Great population differences are also evident. King has more than 500 times the population of Garfield County, for example. Most Washington counties, however, are rural and feature small population bases; 60 percent of the state's counties individually serve fewer than 50,000 residents. This fact underlies the slow rate of change in county governance. At the same time, Washington's counties face some of the most dramatic challenges to governance in managing growth in the 1990s.

Traditionally, counties in Washington and elsewhere across the country have functioned as general service providers, more or less in the manner of quasi-municipal corporations administering state policy at the local level. Building and maintaining roads, enforcing laws outside of municipalities, supervising elections, and assessing and collecting taxes have been standard county government tasks. More recently, though, counties have become increasingly responsible for managing area-wide municipal-type problems that cannot be handled by a single municipality. In this regard, since the late 1960s the state legislature has enacted statutes that authorize – and often direct – counties to take the lead in developing open spaces, constructing parks and recreation facilities, operating water and sewer systems, and developing solid waste collection and disposal systems.

This growth has led counties away from their general core functions and toward more responsibility for quality-of-life services. It is part of a national phenomenon. The growth in county responsibility derives from political, economic, and population growth, as well as social changes that have followed the advent of post-industrial society over the past 25 years. The national government, through a variety of categorical grant programs reflecting the decentralist preference of American federalism, mightily influenced state political agendas and resulted in the initiation of a variety of new programs implemented primarily at the county level. In addition, the growing affluence and level of education of our population, the increased mobility of the work force, and the fast-paced technological advances in electronics and communications have resulted in the advent of many new demands on local government – particularly county governments.

The formal structure of county government in Washington has not changed greatly since the late 1800s. With few exceptions, counties are governed by a three-person governing board, known as the board of county commissioners.[9] Although the responsibilities of county commissioners have increased with the addition of new programs, commissioners continue to lack the authority to coordinate county functions. There are a variety of other elected offices at the county level, including the sheriff, auditor, assessor, clerk, prosecuting attorney, superior and district court judges, and treasurer. Some of the more populous counties elect coroners as well. In smaller counties, the coroner's office is combined with the prosecutor's.

The home-rule movement in the Puget Sound area marked a significant change in the organization of Washington counties. The state constitution was amended in 1948 to permit counties to adopt home-rule charters in much the same manner as cities (see Figure Two). For three decades thereafter, however, only King County successfully broke away from the traditional county structure. Its 1948 home-rule charter replaced the traditional county structure with what is essentially a mayor-council system. It established a nine-member county council elected by districts, with a separately elected chief executive. The political visibility of the position of chief executive provided the office's first incumbent, John Spellman, with the political capital to win the state's governorship in 1980. Under the King County charter, the prosecuting attorney, assessor, and judges have remained elected offices, but the other executive positions have been transformed into appointed administrators accountable to the county executive.

Since 1978, four other counties – Clallam, Pierce, Snohomish, and Whatcom – have also adopted home-rule charters. Pierce, Snohomish, and Whatcom followed the King County model for the most part, while retaining more elective offices than did King. In Clallam, the charter retains virtually the same structure as the old government, with the exception that there is now an appointed county administrator. There also have been a number of unsuccessful charter movements. In 1990, for example, Thurston County voters rejected a charter after elected freeholders (resident property owners) had proposed a new form of local government arrangement for the area's county and city governments.

Figure Two
Home Rule Charter Counties

Other Local Entities

Townships

Washington's constitution, unique among the western states, allows counties to establish township governments. These jurisdictions are permitted to provide minor services outside of municipal service areas. Only two counties, Whatcom and Spokane, took advantage of this constitutional authority. Over the years, however, the state legislature acted to severely trim the power of townships to tax and provide services. By the 1950s the primary function of the few townships existing was to provide garbage deposit sites in rural areas. As a consequence of these developments, all Washington's townships have been abolished; none has existed since 1975.[10]

Figure Three

Special Purpose Districts by Date of Enabling Legislation

Date	District
1890	Irrigation Districts
1895	Diking Districts
1895	Drainage Districts
1895	Townships
1903	River & Harbor Improvement Districts
1907	Metropolitan Park Districts
1909	Intercounty Diking & Drainage Districts
1911	Port Districts
1911	Public Waterway Districts
1913	Water Districts (domestic)
1915	Diking, Drainage, Sewerage Improvement Districts
1917	Ferry Districts
1919	Agricultural Pest Districts
1921	Weed Districts
1927	Reclamation Districts
1931	Public Utility Districts
1933	Sanitary Districts
1933	Cemetery Districts
1937	Flood Control Districts
1939	Fire Protection Districts
1939	Industrial Development Districts (Ports)
1939	Housing Authorities
1939	Soil Conservation Districts
1941	Sewer Districts
1941	County Rural Library Districts
1945	Health Districts
1945	Public Hospital Districts
1945	County Airport Districts
1947	Intercounty Rural Library Districts
1957	Park & Recreation Districts
1957	Air Pollution Control Districts
1957	Metropolitan Municipal Corporations
1959	Intercounty Regular Weed Districts
1961	Flood Control Zone Districts
1961	Irrigation & Rehabilitation Districts
1963	County Park & Recreation Service Areas
1969	Education Service Districts
1971	Solid Waste Collection Districts
1971	TV Reception Improvement Districts
1974	County Transportation Authority Districts
1975	Public Transit Benefit Area Districts
1975	Unioncorp. Transportation Benefit Area Districts
1979	Emergency Medical Districts
1982	Cultural Arts Districts

Figure Three (Continued)

Date	District
1983	Legal Authority Districts (Hydro)
1983	Roads & Bridges Service Districts
1985	Aquifer Protection Districts
1986	Lake Management Districts

Source: Local Government Study Commission, *A History of Washington's Local Governments*, Vol. 1 (Olympia: Department of Community Development, 1988), pp. 71-72.

Special Districts

The most numerous and least understood of local government entities is the special district (see Figure Three). Special districts are established to provide one type of specified service. Considered collectively, special districts can meet regional needs for a wide variety of specialized services. Under Washington state law, special districts can meet regional needs for a wide variety of designated services. Under Washington statutes, special districts are independent entities, possessing many of the same characteristics of corporate power that municipalities exhibit, including substantial public responsibility and considerable fiscal and administrative independence. Most special districts in Washington have popularly elected nonpartisan governing bodies. The major exception to this pattern of operation is the library district, which is governed by a county library board appointed by county commissioners.

School Districts

The school district is the most significant special district. School districts have the largest budgets and most employees of any special districts, and are the only type of special district uniformly found throughout the state. In Washington, school districts are the exclusive vehicle for providing public primary and secondary education. The school consolidation movement, pursued with vigor after World War II, has halved the number of school districts to approximately 300 since the 1960s.

The council-manager model—a small elected board and a professional executive (the school superintendent)—dominates the organization of Washington's school districts. School boards have had relatively limited discretion, with the state retaining most aspects of control over educational policy and school finances. The 1991 legislature, taking its lead from the reform-minded Governor Booth Gardner and the supportive Superintendent of Public Instruction Judith Billings, came close to enacting a significant departure from this pattern of operation by greatly reducing state directives and allowing considerable authority over curriculum and finances at the local school board level. As chair of the National Governors' Association in 1990 and head of the Education

Commission of the States in 1991, Washington's governor took the lead in bringing greater autonomy in school operations to the level of school boards and individual school principals and their teachers and parent groups.

In the area of school financing, Washington is among a few states with constitutions that recognize the obligation to provide "basic education" (K through 12). As a consequence, the state supreme court held in 1977 (*Seattle School District No. 1 v. State*) that because basic education was a "primary responsibility" of the state, all other state programs must give way to funding education programs in periods of tight fiscal conditions.

Other Special Districts

The number of special districts and the functions they perform have both proliferated greatly in recent decades. Most of this growth in non-school special districts has reflected population growth in unincorporated county areas across the state. This has led to greater demand for "urban" services, and the proliferation of fire protection, hospital, cemetery, sewer, transportation, health, aquifer protection, and park and recreation districts reflects this demand. It should be noted that several types of special districts are often authorized by statute to provide the same service; for example, at least 10 different types of special districts provide potable water in different areas of the state.

The use of special districts to provide services rather than empowering general purpose governments (i. e., municipalities or counties) to do so can be explained by a number of factors. Existing local government may be either too large or small to perform needed services. Their staffs may not have the necessary experience or training to address the additional tasks required, or financial resources and taxing authority might be lacking. Many people also believe that special districts provide greater accountability for certain types of local government expenditures. For example, the wide use of Public Utility Districts (PUDs) bears testimony to a strong sense among Washingtonians that the public wishes to exercise great choice in how power is developed and how it is marketed in their respective areas. Although it is recognized that a special district may satisfy certain immediate needs and provide for a form of public accountability, its general utility is also criticized because special districts serve to fragment local political responsibility for overall policy development, financing, and administration. Despite such criticisms, however, special districts continue to enjoy wide use and command strong popular support in the State of Washington.

Indian Tribal Governments

Indian tribal governments represent a special case in local affairs in Washington. Tribal lands encompass nearly two million acres (see Figure Four).

Figure Four
Washington State Indian Reservations

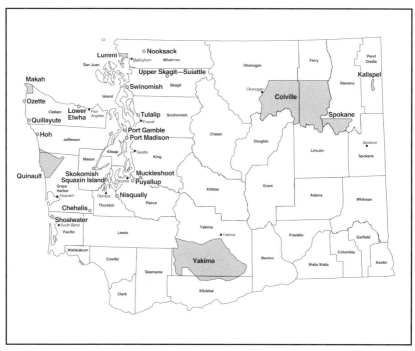

Authority over these lands stems from treaties made between the Indian tribes as sovereign nations and the federal government in the mid-nineteenth century. Treaty tribes exercise limited local autonomy from general state statutes relating to taxation and the exercise of police powers within tribal lands. There are 26 recognized tribal communities in Washington; the largest concentrations of Native Americans are found on the Yakima, Colville, Quinault, and Spokane reservations. The imprecise language of the treaties negotiated with the northwest tribes has yielded widely varying interpretations of powers and rights over resources, and jurisdictional conflicts (and a steady stream of litigation) have been and continue to be a part of the local political landscape in all parts of Washington. The Boldt decision of 1974 (*U. S. v. Washington*) was a landmark decision that recognized the responsibilities of the tribes in fisheries management. Taken together with the Orrick decision of 1979 (*U. S. v. Washington* [Phase II]), it has linked fisheries management with environmental protection.

Tribes are empowered to review and make formal commentary upon environmental impact statements of proposed projects and activities which significantly affect their lands, air, and watersheds. Despite the Boldt decision, this process has often led to conflict over which regulations take precedence – i. e., whether federal, tribal, state, or county powers apply. In 1987, an agreement of understanding between the Swinomish Tribal Community and Skagit County officials concerning jurisdictional roles in the regulation of land use went into effect after more than three years of negotiations. Other important agreements between the tribes and Washington state include the Timber/Fish/Wildlife Agreement (1987), the Centennial Accord (1989) and the Chelan Agreement (1990), all of which have refined government-to-government relations and respective roles in managing natural resources.[11] These agreements, and the processes behind them, may provide a framework for future collaboration.

The Growth Management Challenge for Local Governments

What will we say about the turn of the new century in Washington, looking back from New Year's eve, 1999? Will growth be concentrated in existing cities or spread in a crazy-quilt pattern throughout the state? Will economic development be shared throughout the state or continue to be concentrated in our "urban" counties? Will our air and watersheds be closed to recreational uses, become polluted, or remain part of a vibrant ecosystem? At present, about 60 percent of our lakes and rivers do not meet clean water standards; 80,000 acres of forest land have been lost to urban development in the last 10 years; 50 percent of our wetlands have been destroyed; and 3.1 million tons of garbage and 500,000 tons of hazardous wastes are generated in the state each year.[12]

The growth management challenge in Washington brings these and other related considerations to the forefront of local policy agendas. For example, control of land use is one of the primary responsibilities of local government, but as states experience unusual rates of growth they often act to preempt local authority in this area. In this section we provide an overview of the growth management issue, offering a brief review of traditional growth management mechanisms, a summary of recent suggestions for enhanced growth management efforts, and a closing discussion of some policy gaps and challenges which remain to be addressed in this area.

What is Growth Management?

Growth management refers to a process of deciding how to grow. Growth in itself is neither "good" nor "bad," but rather a fact of life for the State of Washington in the late twentieth century. For policy makers, both in the governmental and private sectors, the question is how to best take advantage of the benefits of growth while minimizing its inevitable costs. After all, as Barry Commoner and others made us aware in the 1970s, growth leads to interdependence and there is no such thing as a "free lunch" in an interdependent world.[13]

In Washington, the effects of growth can be felt locally, regionally, and statewide. Catalysts for growth more often than not occur beyond the boundaries of local communities. Many of the problems associated with growth come in the arenas of the environment, transportation, housing, public health, and land use. Another characteristic of these issues is their transboundary nature – each crosses jurisdictional boundaries. Just think about driving on Interstate 5 from north Seattle south toward Tacoma, or consider field burning for grass seed production on Idaho's Rathdrum Prairie near the Washington border, or consider the sources of pollution in Puget Sound, or ponder the sad fate of the Snake River Sockeye salmon. In each instance, addressing the issue (to say nothing about defining the problem for the design of appropriate remedies) requires bringing together many jurisdictions (tribes, federal agencies, states, counties, municipalities, special districts) representing different economic and, particularly when tribes are involved, cultural interests.

Finally, it should be noted that the effects of growth tend to be quite uneven across the several primary regions of the state. While some areas must cope with the resource strain resulting from more of everything (people, jobs, pollution), other areas must learn to cope with less of everything. A significant challenge to state and local government decision-makers is that of providing for a more equitable distribution of growth throughout the state, particularly with respect to those communities affected by the loss of jobs and fiscal capacity resulting from the decline of the forest products industry. The efforts made to protect the spotted owl are but one of many serious blows to an industry that once provided the backbone to the state's economy.

Traditional Growth Management Mechanisms

As Washington's population continues to grow, the complexity of local governance increases. In metropolitan areas there is a growing need for local jurisdictions and agencies to cooperate and coordinate their policy efforts. While metropolitan areas are typically not organized as single political units, they are nonetheless recognized by the federal government for its reporting of economic and social characteristics (see Figure Five). Metropolitan areas present the primary challenge of regional policy making, of meeting the increasingly difficult problems of more complex forms of interdependence with higher levels of cooperation and coordinated policy responses.

Washington has many regional councils of government (COGs), a favorite mechanism of national and state governments for coping with problems that cross traditional jurisdictional lines. The Puget Sound Council of Governments (PSCOG), created in 1957, was one of the first multi-jurisdictional planning agencies in the United States; moreover, it represents one of the rare COGs that came into being through local initiative rather than in response to national

Figure Five
Metropolitan Washington

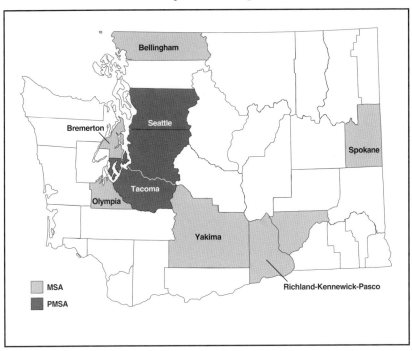

legislation.[14] In time, larger cities around the Sound joined its four original county members (King, Pierce, Snohomish, and Kitsap), and by the mid-1980s, PSCOG had 50 member jurisdictions, including three Indian tribes. In 1990, PSCOG faced dissolution, but several spin-off regional agencies (the largest is the state-authorized Municipality of Metropolitan Seattle, or METRO) have evolved as front-runners in the expanding arena of comprehensive, multipurpose regional/metropolitan governments.

The state legislature brought METRO into existence in 1958 in order to address the problem of advanced levels of pollution in Lake Washington. For the next 15 years METRO functioned as a special district, collecting and treating sewage from the many cities and sewer districts surrounding the lake. The agency's success in cleaning up the lake for recreational and aesthetic enjoyment attracted national attention. As a result, METRO broadened its role to include transportation planning. There have been recurring efforts to integrate METRO and King County into a regional authority, the most recent taking place in the fall of 1990. One of the primary obstacles to integration is the

Figure Six
Growth Management Counties

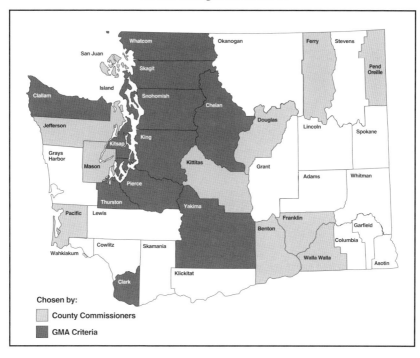

Chosen by:

County Commissioners

GMA Criteria

issue of representation, since special districts are often perceived as not offering representation on the one-person, one-vote principle.

Other forms of metropolitan governance include metropolitan (or area-wide)
special districts and "urban" counties. Metropolitan special districts such as
the port districts of Seattle and Tacoma, which shape the shoreline of the Puget
Sound within their jurisdictions, also have a far-reaching effect on local and
regional economies. For example, the Port of Seattle operates extensive marine terminal facilities as well as SeaTac International Airport, and has a billion dollar capital plant. The Port of Tacoma is considered the most modern
and technologically sophisticated seaport in the world, with state of the art
technology for containerized transshipment, grain loading, and timber product movement.

Urban counties, such as King, provide core services such as roads and
streets, police protection, and the regulation of land use, as well as quality-of-
life services—such as the Kingdome—to all county residents. This broader capacity of King County, along with Pierce and Snohomish, to function as

metropolitan governments is facilitated by their home-rule charters, which separate legislative from executive functions and provide for a level of executive coordination of most county activities far better than that achieved under the traditional form of county government employed in most Washington counties.

ESHB 2929 and Beyond

The use of traditional mechanisms to manage growth has brought some success, but not without overcoming many organizational and administrative obstacles. The issue most often underlying these obstacles is local control and autonomy. Who should make decisions that affect communities, local government, or a regional or state agency? The most recent and comprehensive attempt to manage growth in Washington has been state-initiated, but strongly focused on local needs. Governor Booth Gardner created a Growth Strategies Commission in August 1989 to recommend ways to preserve Washington's environmental resources and quality-of-life while maintaining economic growth in all of its regions.[15]

In 1990, the legislature enacted the Growth Management Act (GMA) to guide Washington's growth from the perspective of how citizens and residents of the state want to grow into the future.[16] That legislation required the state's fastest growing counties, and cities within those counties, to devise new comprehensive plans (most existing plans are quite dated) that include inventories of agricultural, forest, and environmentally sensitive lands. The cities and counties must then make zoning regulations consistent with these new plans. Such plans must designate urban growth areas, they must be coordinated with surrounding counties and cities, and they must provide for public participation in the planning process. Figure Six lists those counties required to plan and those counties that have opted into the planning process; comparing this list with Figure Five shows the anticipated trajectory of growth in the state for the coming decade.

The Engrossed Substitute House Bill (ESHB 2929) represents phase two of the GMA and can be viewed as a first attempt to provide directions and tools for implementing growth management. The bill elaborated eight principles of growth management (see Figure Seven) that place a high premium on coordination between jurisdictions. Under ESHB 2929, significant new roles would be authorized for local governments and the state.

For local governments, ESHB 2929 touches all regions of the state. For example, those local governments not planning under GMA are required to protect natural resource lands and sensitive environmental areas (such as wetlands, aquifer recharge areas, frequently flooded land, geologically hazardous areas, and significant fish and wildlife habitat) by September 1992. For all local governments, a variety of new planning goals and elements have been added

Figure Seven

Eight Growth Management Principles

- Growth management should be driven by local decision-making.
- Elected officials should have primary responsibility for planning decisions.
- State agencies and local governments, including special districts, should follow the same rules and goals governing land use planning.
- The state should ensure that local growth management efforts are effective.
- Special efforts should be taken to protect forest lands, farm lands, and critical areas in the interim before new local comprehensive plans and development regulations are developed.
- Disputes over plans should be resolved outside the court system, when possible, using methods that respect the needs of all parties to the disputes.
- Necessary regional public facilities should be provided on a fair share basis.
- The state should encourage strong regional economies and should establish a framework for actions to strengthen them.

Source: Washington State Department of Community Development, *Implementation Briefs,* Feb. 1991, p. 2.

to the comprehensive planning process, including water resources and the siting of public facilities. Special districts are required to conform to local comprehensive plans and developmental regulations, and to submit revised capital facilities plans to local governments within one year after local government plans are adopted.

At the state level, state agencies must conform with the planning goals of local comprehensive plans. The state Department of Community Development has received new responsibilities for developing guidelines, providing technical assistance, and reviewing and commenting on local plans. It is intended that challenges to the comprehensive plans be mediated by alternative dispute resolution techniques rather than through the courts, a hoped-for outcome that will require considerable state assistance. In addition, the state will develop an open space plan by the end of 1992 that identifies open space protected by either local or state agencies.

Policy Gaps and the Future of Local Government

The complexity of local government in Washington—from the sheer numbers of local governments, to the transboundary nature of quality-of-life and infrastructural issues, to coping with growth—has led to the realization that the state needs a more consistent, comprehensive approach to local governance. Can Washington successfully define the roles of local governance so as to bring about collaborative and cooperative relations rather than elevating competition among jurisdictions for increasingly scarce resources? Such is the challenge addressed in the state's Growth Management Act, and such is the task laid before local government officials across the state.

The next area of greatest concentration of effort in Washington will likely occur at the regional government level, an area that has traditionally been seen in zero-sum terms—that is, if my community wins, your community loses. When transboundary problems related to land use, transportation, economic development, air and water pollution, and the protection of natural resources become too large for any local government to resolve on its own, regional authorities may likely become the preferred next step for providing some measure of local self-determination. Including all local interests in such a regional authority is a formidable challenge. If this proves impossible to accomplish, the state will most likely exercise its constitutional discretion and establish a vision of the future that local officials will have little hand in drafting. In some sense, the grand American experiment in federalism and local self-determination is being played out in contemporary Washington politics, as it has across the breadth of the land historically. At present the ball can be said to lie in local government's court, with the state standing by to observe how local governments put their own wits to work to solve shared problems. At this writing it can be said that Washington's local government officials are off to a good start in this tough game of political leadership.

Notes

1. The authors owe a debt of gratitude to Thor Swanson, author of the local government chapter in the 1985 edition of this book. We have followed the general outline in section one of this chapter, and updated Thor Swanson's discussion with coverage of growth management in section two of this chapter. Thanks to Mary Welsh Jordan and WSU Press designers for the excellent maps, and to the editors for their comments on earlier drafts of this chapter.
2. See chapter one; also see "Exceptional Growth and the Return of Population Concentration in Washington," in Annabel Kirschner Cook, ed., *Washington Counts* (Pullman: Washington State University Cooperative Extension, 29 Apr. 1991).
3. Local Government Study Commission, *A History of Washington's Local Governments*, vol. 1 (Olympia: Department of Community Development, 1988), p. 39.
4. Local Government Study Commission, *The Quiet Crisis of Local Governance in Washington*, vol. 2 (Olympia: Department of Community Development 1988), p. 7.
5. *History of Washington's Local Governments*, p. 39.
6. *Washington State Yearbook* (Eugene, Or.: Information Press, 1989), p. 118.
7. *Officials of Washington Cities, 1990-1991* (Kirkland: Municipal Research and Services Center, 1990), p. 94.
8. *Ibid.*
9. In 1990, the legislature enacted a bill granting Spokane County the power to elect five commissioners, beginning in 1993.
10. *History of Washington's Local Governments*, p. 40.
11. *An Innovative Approach to Intergovernmental Coordination: Swinomish Tribe and Skagit County Cooperation* (Seattle: Northwest Renewable Resources Center, n. d.); *The Chelan Agreement: A Partnership of Responsibilities* (Olympia: Northwest Indian Fisheries Commission, n. d.). Also see Roy G. Metzgar, "Washington State Water Resource Planning: A Collaborative Attempt at Revision"; Peter D. Beaulieu, "The Chelan Agreement: Co-Responsibility in Water Resources Management"; and Terry Williams, "Cooperation: A Pacific Northwest Indian Perspective," papers presented at the 33rd annual conference of the Western Social Science Association, Reno, Nevada, Apr. 1991.
12. Data from *A Citizen's Guide to Washington's Environment*, Environment 2010 (Olympia: Department of Ecology, 1990), p. 1.
13. Barry Commoner, *The Closing Circle* (New York: Bantam Books, 1972).
14. The information on PSCOG and METRO comes from *Quiet Crisis of Local Governance in Washington*, pp. 33-36.
15. Washington State Growth Strategies Commission, *A Growth Strategy for Washington State* (Olympia: Department of Community Development, 1990), p. 2.
16. The politics of growth management are highly contentious. In the November 1990 election, Initiative 547, the "Balanced Growth Initiative," was placed on the ballot by the group Citizens for Balanced Growth. Although voters resoundingly rejected the initiative, there are likely to be other growth management initiatives brought before the voters of Washington state in the 1990s.

Elisa P. Ferry's inauguration as Washington state's first governor in Olympia, November 18, 1889. *Courtesy Washington State University Libraries.*

Chapter Ten

Public Finances of Washington State

Debra L. Sanders

M ONEY. IT IS THE LIFEBLOOD of all governments. Without money there would be no social programs, no public education—in essence, no government. A state's financial position determines what it can achieve for its residents now and in the future. State finances are becoming big business. The 1989-1991 Washington budget is over $24 billion. Where does this money come from and where does it go? Who decides how state funds will be spent? Do the residents of Washington get what they pay for? Are Washington's residents undertaxed or overtaxed?

Expenditures

Through expenditures, state and local governments provide a variety of public goods and services, such as education, and construct capital assets, such as public buildings, for state and local use. In addition, governments expend sizable amounts for which residents directly receive no services or products in return. A major portion of the latter expenditures provide assistance to needy individuals and subsidies to political subdivisions or institutions. How a state allocates its resources among these various public programs indicates some of the relative priorities within that state. To some significant degree, programs receiving public funds are viewed as more effective than those that do not.

The cost of furnishing public goods and services to Washington's residents has steadily risen over the past years. Table One provides a comparison of the 1975-1977 biennial expenditures with the 1989-1991 budget. The state budget has grown approximately four-fold over this 15 year period, from just over $6.4 billion to roughly $24.5 billion. Although state expenditure amounts have steadily increased, the pattern of spending for the major expenditure categories has remained relatively stable. The percentage of the budget allocated to human resources and natural resources and recreation (the preservation, utilization, and development of agriculture and natural resources) has increased slightly

Table One

State of Washington Biennium Expenditures 1975-1977 & 1989-1991
(Dollars in Millions)

	1975-1977	1975-77 Percent	1989-1991	1989-91 Percent
Education*	$2,874.8	44.7	$10,369.7	42.3
Human Resources	1,728.4	26.9	7,360.8	30.1
Government	916.0	14.2	3,228.5	13.2
Transportation	618.3	9.6	2,207.6	9.0
Natural Resources & Recreation	290.2	4.5	1,314.2	5.3
Other	4.9	.1	31.3	.1
Total	$6,432.6	100.0%	$24,512.1	100.0%

* Includes teacher's retirement plans
Source: *State of Washington Data Book, 1989* (Olympia: Office of Financial Management, 1989).

over the years, whereas expenditure percentages for education, transportation, and the cost of government itself have marginally declined.

Such predictable factors as inflation and population growth, as well as the state's continued urbanization, have brought about the steady rise in Washington's budget. The move from an agrarian society to a high-tech, industrial economy has created a migration in the labor force from the country to cities. This change in the composition of Washington's population has altered the wealth distribution of residents and caused shifts in demands for governmental services. A more urban society generates a host of problems, from crime to traffic, that produce demands for governmental action. The aging of the population as a whole has also increased demands for governmental services.

Table Two presents the per capita amounts of Washington's public expenditures for 1989. (Percentages shown on Table Two for Washington differ from those given in Table One because the tables cover different time periods and categorize expenditures differently.) To put the expenditures into perspective, Table Two also provides the per capita national average (all state governments combined) for each functional category. The table reveals that Washington's expenditures are greater than the national average in total, and are also more for each individual category, with the exception of human resources. The majority of Washington's expenditures are made for education, human resources, and general government. The amount expended for these three categories in total is approximately the same percentage as the national average. However, Washington's allocation of resources among these categories differs from the national average.

Table Two

Washington State and National Average Per Capita Yearly Expenditures, 1989

	Washington State Dollar Amounts	Washington State Percent*	National Average Dollar Amounts	National Average Percent
General Expenditures				
Education	$ 934.77	38.2	$ 702.02	33.1
Human Resources	598.16	24.4	636.37	30.1
Government	347.07*	14.2	301.19	14.2
Transportation	224.51	9.2	188.67	8.8
Environment & Housing	68.06	2.8	66.67	3.1
Other Expenditures				
Insurance Trust†	232.88	9.5	189.77	9.0
Liquor Stores	39.15	1.6	9.71	.5
Other	2.45	.1	25.88	1.2
Total	$2,447.05	100.0%	$2,120.37	100.0%

* Includes state employee retirement plans
† Includes unemployment and worker's compensation
Source: *State Government Finances in 1989* (Washington, D. C.: Bureau of the Census, 1990).

Education

As with many states, the largest portion of Washington's budget is spent on education. The budget category of education includes: 1) the public school systems (grades K to 12); 2) higher education (universities, colleges, and community colleges); and 3) other state/local educational institutions (vocational and technical training). Of the funds allocated to education, the majority (63 percent) is used for the public school systems. Higher education receives about 36 percent of the education budget, while less than 2 percent goes towards the support of all other education.[1] Even though the costs of higher education have grown at a prodigious rate, Washington has maintained fairly constant allocation ratios for the three education subcategories. The stable allocation ratios emphasize the importance placed on public school systems in Washington and the educational balance that the state desires to maintain.

Table Two shows that Washington allocated a greater percentage of its 1989 budget to education than did the rest of the nation; specifically, Washington spent about $200 more per person per year on education than the average state spends. Due to the state's commitment to quality education, Washington ranks within the top five states in per capita expenditures for all education and within the top ten for higher education support.[2]

The monetary support for education, perhaps more than any other budgetary category, relies on an intergovernmental flows of funds. Federal programs transfer funds to the state. These in turn are channeled to the universities and to local governments for public school systems. The lion's share of support for the public school systems is provided by the state (78 percent), with localities second (15 percent), and federal support third (7 percent). A state supreme court ruling that, according to the state constitution, the state is required to provide full funding for basic education spurred this substantial state role in educational financing. The state also provides most of the support for community colleges and state regional universities. The state's two research institutions (University of Washington and Washington State University), however, receive more of their support from federal and private funding than from Washington.[3]

Human Resources

The second most costly program for Washington state is human resources. This budgetary category includes programs for social services, public assistance, public health services, corrections, and public safety services. Washington budgeted almost $7.4 billion for these programs in the 1989-1991 biennium. This is just over 30 percent of the budget, up from about 27 percent in the 1975-1977 budget. There are two main reasons for the proportionately faster growth of human resources expenditures: the changing composition of the population brought about by increasing urbanization, with its accompanying social problems; and the aging of the population, with its rising health care costs.

Although human resource programs appear to be a tremendous financial burden for Washington, the federal government, in fact, foots a substantial portion of the bill. For example, of the total $5.5 billion budgeted for social and health services, the federal government funds more than $2.5 billion. In other areas, such as aid to families with dependent children and refugee assistance, the federal government pays as much as 80 percent of such programs' cost.[4]

The amount that Washington spent in 1989 on a per capita basis for social programs is less than the national average by about $40 per person. Spending less than the national average should not necessarily be taken as signifying that the services provided in Washington are inadequate or of lesser quality. The amount needed for this service is a function of the composition of the population and Washington's economy, and expenditures must be evaluated with that in mind. Note, too, that the large federal role in funding social services, with accompanying federal regulations, limits state discretion to some degree. Finally, by some measures, social programs in Washington are comparatively generous: benefits for recipients of aid to families with dependent children are larger than the national average.[5]

Table Three

State of Washington Biennium Revenues 1975-1977 & 1989-1991
(Dollars in Millions)

	1975-1977	Percent	1989-1991	Percent
Taxes	$3,678.9	54.6	$13,604.6	56.2
Federal Funds	1,641.8	24.4	4,935.2	20.4
State Charges	982.4	14.6	4,639.2	19.2
Licenses, Permits & Fees	220.3	3.3	695.7	2.9
Liquor Profits	121.5	1.8	177.4	.7
Other	84.8	1.3	154.9	.6
Total	$6,729.7	100.0%	$24,207.0	100.0%

Source: *State of Washington Data Book, 1989.*

Government

The state spent about 14 percent of its 1989 budget for governmental functions, comparable with the national average. This category includes not only the costs of running government, but also payments to political subdivisions and the costs for servicing and retiring bonds. These latter two outlays account for more than 50 percent of the governmental expenditures category. It is interesting to note that the cost of retiring bonds is included in the budget as an expenditure, but receipts from the sale of bonds are not considered as part of a state's revenues. That practice effectively exaggerates the cost of borrowing relative to the funds made available by borrowing.

Typically, the executive branch expends the most funds, followed by the judicial, and then the legislative branch. The executive branch generally incorporates the administrative portion of government and this accounts for its greater expenditures. For Washington, the executive branch is by far the most costly division of government. However, unlike most states, legislative branch expenditures are slightly more than the judicial branch.[6]

Washington ranks 14th among the 50 states for its level of expenditures per capita.[7] How can Washington afford to spend more per capita than most of the other states? The answer lies in the revenues it generates.

Revenues

Revenues provide the wherewithal for governments to purchase the public goods and services their citizens desire. As with everything else, the cost of providing these goods and services has escalated at a rapid rate. Accordingly, states have had to cultivate a variety of revenue-generating sources. Regardless of how revenue is generated, the ultimate providers of money are, for the most part, the state's residents.

Table Three shows the increase in the revenue budgets from 1975-1977 to 1989-1991. Notice that the proportion of funding Washington receives from the federal government has substantially decreased. To make up for this loss, the state has resorted to relying more heavily on taxes and state charges. Consequently, it has transferred to Washington residents more of the burden for funding public services.

A comparison of the data in Table One and Table Three indicates that expenditures have grown more rapidly than revenues and that the expenditures budgeted for the 1989-1991 biennium are greater than the projected income for that period. Given that statutes require the governor to submit a balanced budget,[8] how could the legislature have passed this budget? The answer is that the sources of revenue listed in Table Three do not represent all of the money available to the state. Washington finances much of its capital outlay for construction, which is contained in the expenditure budget, by debt. Yet the budget does not show these receipts from borrowing as revenues. Thus, the relationship between totals of revenue and expenditures, as shown in Tables One and Three, cannot be used as a direct measure of the degree of budgetary "balance."

The principal sources of current revenues (1989-1991 biennium) for Washington are given in Table Three. As the table indicates, over one-half of Washington's revenues come from taxes. The next two important revenue sources are federal funds and state charges. These three sources together provide more than 95 percent of the state's revenues.

Taxes

Justice Oliver Wendell Holmes described taxes as the price that we pay for a civilized society.[9] They can also be defined as compulsory transfers from residents to political jurisdictions in order to support some of government's objectives. Taxes differ from fees or charges in that taxpayers are generally not given a specific benefit in return for the payment. A fee or charge, by contrast, entitles the payer to some benefit, such as admission to a park or a driver's license. The tax structure of any government, and Washington is no exception, is constantly evolving. Changes in the state's economy, increases and shifts in the demand for public goods and services, and national and state political factors are just some of the causes of tax evolution within Washington.

Washington Tax History

From territorial days to the 1930s, Washington financed itself primarily through property taxes. Property was a common tax base used by most states because it was identifiable, its fair market value determinable, and people thought it to be a good measure of ability to pay. Also, the state oriented many of its governmental services during this time period towards property owners. However, by the 1920s citizens throughout the nation grew dissatisfied with the ever-increasing burden of property taxes. Because the property tax system was already in place, governments used it to finance the rapid growth of state expenditures. Property values, upon which the tax is based, increased and the legislature kept raising the property tax rates. Within a 12-year period, the property tax rate nearly doubled, from 1.4 percent in 1910 to 2.4 percent in 1922.[10]

During the 1920s, two governor-appointed tax investigations recommended broadening Washington's tax system as a method of relieving the ever-growing property tax burdens of its citizens. Governor Louis Hart's committee recommended numerous refinements in the tax laws and procedures that would have improved the uniformity and administration of property taxes. Eight years later, Governor Roland Hartley's committee reiterated the need for property tax relief. This task force went so far as to recommend an income tax as a method of reducing the state's reliance on property taxes. The legislature, however, did not act upon the recommendation at that time.[11]

After the economic boom of the 1920s, the nation fell into the Great Depression of the 1930s. The need for public goods and services grew steadily as unemployment spread throughout the state. To finance the increased demand for governmental social services, the state turned once again to property taxes. Tax burdens became too much for many citizens to bear, particularly those standing in unemployment lines. Property tax delinquencies grew at a prodigious rate and accordingly, state revenues fell dramatically.[12]

Major changes in the tax structure proved essential if Washington hoped to support the social welfare and relief programs necessary during the Great Depression. As a first action, the state reduced the rate of property taxes and placed a ceiling on permissible rates. The ceiling became so popular that the state reenacted it every two years. In 1944 it became a permanent part of the constitution.[13]

The limitation on property taxes reduced the state's ability to generate revenues at a time when it urgently needed money due to the depression. The legislature had to find a new revenue source. In 1932 it tried to broaden the tax base by enacting—and asking voters to approve—individual and corporate income taxes. However, the state supreme court held both of these taxes to be unconstitutional in the 1933 landmark case of *Culliton vs. Chase* (174 Wash. 363). The Washington Constitution defines "property" to include all assets, whether tangible or intangible, subject to ownership. Therefore, the supreme court found that income taxes are technically taxes on the property "income." The Washington Constitution requires uniformity in all property taxes. Since the income taxes passed could not meet the uniformity requirement, the court held them to be unconstitutional.

In 1933, the legislature enacted a business activity tax (the predecessor to public utility and business and occupation taxes) which taxed the gross receipts of all businesses. Unlike income taxes, this variable-rate tax was an excise tax rather than a property tax. Thus, the tax did not run afoul of the property tax uniformity requirement.[14] The state at this time also turned to borrowing, through the issuing of bonds, as another method of financing the ever-growing demand for social welfare programs.

As the Great Depression deepened, the state confronted a severe financial crisis. In 1935 the legislature enacted 14 new taxes and reinstated two others.[15] As one of the new taxes, the legislature again enacted an income tax, but the courts again found it to be unconstitutional.[16] Of the taxes enacted in the Revenue Act of 1935, only six still remain: retail sales, public utilities, tobacco, alcohol, business and occupation, and use taxes.

There have been few new taxes since 1935. Real increases in state revenues (i. e., not those caused by inflation) have come from the broadening of bases in existing taxes, increasing their rates, and the state's economic growth. For example, Washington recently increased the selective tax rates on gasoline, tobacco products, and alcoholic beverages. The state and many cities and counties have moved away from property taxes and now rely on sales taxes as their major source of revenue. The 1970 authorization of local option sales taxes has facilitated this movement by permitting cities and counties to add their own sales tax on top of the state sales tax. Although sales taxes provide most of the total taxes collected in Washington, many special purpose local governments still remain dependent on property taxes for the majority of their tax revenue.[17]

Current Taxes

Table Four provides the current dollar amounts of each tax and a breakdown of the proportion of tax revenues derived from each source for Washington and the national average. In comparing Washington with the national averages, several differences can be noted.

First, Washington depends much more heavily on *sales taxes* than does the average state. Washington obtains more than 75 percent of its tax revenues from general sales taxes whereas the national average is under 50 percent. This difference comes about primarily because Washington relies on general sales taxes rather than income taxes. This heavy reliance on sales taxes earns Washington the dubious honor of having the second highest state sales tax rate in the nation and the second highest per capita sales tax collections (for 1989, Washington's is $822.27 and the national average is $377.23).[18] This dependence on sales tax is common among states without income taxes. For example, South Dakota and Nevada (both states without income taxes) receive about 81 percent and 87 percent, respectively, of their tax revenues from sales taxes.[19]

Table Four

Washington State Tax Distribution Based on 1989 Collections
(Dollars in Thousands)

	Amount	Percent	National Average
Sales Taxes:			
General Sales	3,914,815	60.1	32.9
Motor Fuels	454,144	7.0	6.3
Public Utilities	155,011	2.4	2.2
Tobacco	129,704	2.0	1.8
Alcohol	102,851	1.6	1.1
Insurance	90,673	1.4	2.6
Other	49,881	.7	1.8
Total Sales Taxes	4,897,079	75.2	48.7
Property Taxes	1,006,528	15.5	1.9
License Taxes:			
Motor Vehicle	181,110	2.8	3.5
Businesses & Occupational	119,225	1.8	2.1
Other	53,522	.8	.6
Total License Taxes	353,857	5.4	6.2
Other Taxes:			
Income	000	0.0	39.6
Real Estate Excise & Transfer	176,894	2.7	.9
Severance	58,916	.9	1.5
Inheritance	17,328	.3	1.2
Total Other Taxes	253,138	3.9	43.2
Total	$6,510,602	100.0%	100.0%

Source: *State Government Tax Collections: 1989* (Washington, D. C.: Bureau of the Census, 1990).

Second, the percentage of total tax revenues acquired from *property taxes* is substantially higher for Washington (15.5 percent) than the average state (1.9 percent). In fact, Washington receives proportionately more of its total tax revenues from property taxes than any other state. With the exception of Wyoming (14 percent), all other states receive less than 10 percent of their tax revenues from property taxes, and at least eight states do not have this type of tax.[20] The reason for Washington's and Wyoming's considerable reliance on property taxes is again because there is no income tax to generate needed revenues. As the table indicates, states, on average, collect approximately 40 percent of their tax revenues from income taxes. To generate a comparable amount of revenue, Washington collects more general sales taxes and property taxes than the average state. Other states without income taxes, such as Alaska and Texas, use *severance taxes* on natural resources rather than high property taxes to supplement state revenues. A severance tax is levied on an industry that extracts something of value from the state; the most common targets are oil and gas, minerals, timber, and fish. Washington only collects a very minor portion of its budget through severance taxes on mining and fishing.

Lastly, business and occupation (B & O) tax collection in Washington is less than the national average. The B & O tax is based on gross receipts from business conducted in Washington. Since it is based on *gross* receipts rather than *net* income, the rates can be lower than a net income tax. Sometimes this tax is criticized because businesses with low profit margins may be hit harder than businesses with high profit margins.[21] Part of this problem is solved by varying the rate of tax based on the type of business. Having lower-than-average B & O taxes that favor high-profit businesses, coupled with the lack of a corporate net income tax, helps attract high-profit, high-tech industries to Washington.

Federal Funds

Up to this point the discussion of revenues has concentrated on Washington state taxes. Yet Washington receives a significant portion of its revenue from the federal government. Virtually all state and local programs are aided in some manner by federal funding.

The evolution of federal grants to state and local governments has a long history. Although national grants to states began shortly after the Revolution, not until 1913 did the federal government have sufficient revenue to extensively aid state and local governments. Federal income taxes on individuals became constitutional in 1912. The ability to tax income became extremely important to the federal government. Income taxes produce the greatest amount of revenue for the federal government and make possible most federal aid to states.

The depression of the 1930s brought severe financial difficulties to state and local governments. As previously discussed, the depression increased the demand for social programs at a time when state revenues rapidly declined. The federal government developed a series of New Deal grant-in-aid programs to help states through this trying period. Many of these programs continue today. The most beneficial aspect of federal programs is that they allow states to provide public services at levels far above what a state itself could afford. Most federal assistance to Washington aids education, social programs, and highways. As Table Five demonstrates, Washington fares slightly better than the national average in attracting federal funds when measured on a per capita basis, and ranks within the top half of the states in federal aid.[22]

Many of the funds the federal government provides come in the form of matching grants. For these programs, Congress appropriates a specified amount of money and requires that recipients match a percentage of the grant received.

Table Five

Washington State and National Average Per Capita Yearly Revenues, 1989

	Washington State Dollar Amounts*	Washington State Percent	National Average Dollar Amounts	National Average Percent
General Revenues				
Taxes	$1,367.49	48.2	$1,147.02	48.4
Federal Grants	458.94	16.2	437.08	18.5
State Charges	316.48	11.2	333.33	14.1
Local Transfers	11.17	.4	30.41	1.2
Other Revenues				
Insurance Trust*	635.65	22.4	396.45	16.7
Liquor Sales	46.69	1.6	11.26	.5
Other	00.00	0.0	13.12	.6
Total	$2,836.96	100.0%	$2,368.65	100.0%

* Includes retirement contributions, unemployment, and worker's compensation taxes

Source: *State Government Finances in 1989.*

The state's required matching percentage can range from 10 to 90 percent of the grant. These funds must be committed by the state to the purpose specified in the grant, and must be spent according to federal guidelines. Consequently, state legislatures often have little control over how federal funds will be used in their state.

The ratio of federal funds in the Washington budget has declined in recent years. Beginning in the late 1970s the purchasing power of federal aid to states began falling, and in the early 1980s the Reagan administration enacted sharp reductions. The federal aid reductions have meant Washington has had less money available for social programs. Consequently, there has been increased pressure for the state to generate more revenue through taxes and state charges.

State Charges

The percentage of revenues obtained through state charges has risen since 1975 (see Table Three). As the amount of aid from the federal government has decreased, the state has compensated for the loss by charging for specific benefits accruing to individuals or businesses. In this respect the state is acting as a business by making citizens pay for the service they receive. The state charges for hospital care, sanitation, water, inspections, higher education, and other services. However, recipients are usually not charged the full cost of these services. For example, tuition fees of students attending Washington colleges and universities pay for only about 30 percent of higher education costs; state, federal, or private funding pays the remainder.

In 1983 Washington instituted a new source of revenue, the state lottery, which brought in more than $250 million in 1989. The state returned about half of this money as winnings; about 13 percent covered the cost of running the lottery; the remainder went into the state's general funds.[23]

Lotteries have become a popular way for state governments to raise revenues without increasing existing taxes. At least 33 states and local governments now operate lotteries.[24] Nevertheless, critics charge that lotteries encourage gambling and entice the poor to throw away their money on a slim chance of winning. On the other hand, some view lotteries as rather painless ways of raising revenue.

Public Benefits and Burdens

To this point, state expenditures and revenues have been discussed separately. The two are, however, closely intertwined. The state can offer public goods and services only to the extent that it can afford them. The state provides most programs to insure that these goods and services are available to the general public. The question is, how will the "public" finance these programs?

As previously discussed, Washington receives nearly all of its funds from federal aid, state taxes, and state charges. The latter two account for more than 75 percent of the 1989-1991 revenue budget and taxes alone account for over 50 percent of the revenues (see Table Three). Consequently, Washington residents are the major supporters of state programs. Each resident's contribution to the support of the state, however, is not equal. Controversies regarding who should pay the costs of government are a recurrent phenomenon in the political arena. Two of the most common approaches to resolving those controversies are the benefit-received doctrine and the ability-to-pay principle.

Certain taxes and state charges are payments for "benefits" received from the state. According to the *benefit-received* doctrine, the amounts paid to the government by an individual should be in proportion to the benefits received by that person. In some instances this is a fair way to distribute the burden for public programs. However, there are two problems with using the benefits-received doctrine as the basis for financing state government: 1) individuals directly benefitting from a program may not have the ability to pay for the service; and, 2) the true beneficiaries of some public goods and services cannot be determined with any accuracy.

Gasoline and diesel fuel taxes are often cited as good examples of the application of the benefit-received doctrine to taxes. The tax is paid by those individuals who drive vehicles, and revenues are used to construct and maintain roads and highways. Nevertheless, people who do not drive also benefit from roads and highways. The system of roads and highways allows food delivery to neighborhood grocery stores, facilitates mail delivery, and permits emergency care to reach people at their homes.

State charges might seem a clearer area for applying the benefits-received doctrine. Yet recipients of these services may also lack the ability to pay and the true beneficiary of the services may not be obvious. For example, few individuals who attend public colleges could actually afford to pay the full cost of their education. As previously noted, tuition covers only 30 percent of each student's education at state colleges and universities. A college education obviously benefits the student receiving it, but it also benefits society as a whole. The college graduate may find a cure for cancer, develop a more productive strain of grain, or in some other manner contribute knowledge to help other citizens of the state.

Since most benefits of public programs cannot be attributed to specific residents, the benefit-received doctrine is not used extensively to distribute the costs of government among the residents. Rather, the *ability-to-pay* concept is used to justify most assessments on the general population. While the ability to pay is widely accepted in the abstract as an equitable method for assessing taxes, there is considerable disagreement over what constitutes the best measure of ability to pay. The three most common measures of ability to pay are property ownership, purchases (sales taxes), and income. The ability-to-pay argument for property taxes is based on the assumption that the more valuable property is, the wealthier the owner must be. The wealthier owner has a greater ability to pay higher taxes. The rationale for sales taxes is that individuals who purchase more have more ability to pay. Lastly, income taxes consider an individual's net earnings as the best indication of ability to pay.

The potential defect in the ability-to-pay justification of property and sales taxes is the assumption that individuals spend the same proportion of their wealth on the taxable items. Property and sales taxes measure wealth only as it is spent. Money saved or invested in nontaxable properties (e.g., stocks and bonds) escapes this kind of taxation. It is a general rule of economic behavior that as wealth increases, the proportion of total wealth saved and invested increases. This is called the declining propensity to consume. Consequently, the wealthy may pay more in absolute terms in property and sales taxes, but the poor pay a higher percentage of their wealth in taxes because they spend proportionately more of their income for the necessities of life. Taxes that weigh disproportionately on the poor are considered to be regressive.

Washington relies almost exclusively on sales and property taxes for generating tax revenues (see Table Four). These are regressive taxes. It could be argued that while the poor pay proportionately more of their income in taxes, they also benefit proportionately more from state government expenditures. In other words, if Washington provided relatively high services for its low-income citizens, then the high tax load of such people might be justified on the basis of benefits-received. It is hard to determine whether Washington provides such high services since it spends less than the national average on human resource programs but more than the national average on education. At any rate, one estimate indicates that poor families in Washington pay almost twice as large a proportion of their incomes in state taxes as do wealthy families.[25]

It is apparent that the wealthy have tax advantages in Washington relative to lower income residents, but how does the tax burden of Washington residents rank in relation to other states? Several methods can be used to compare tax burdens across states. One approach is to contrast the absolute dollars collected by each state. Since states vary greatly in population, comparing dollars collected tells little about the tax burden of individual residents.

A second method simply takes the dollar amounts collected by a state and divides this amount by the state's population. The result is the amount of taxes collected on a per capita basis. In 1989 Washington's total per capita state taxes came to $1,367.49, of which the state collected $822.27 through general sales tax. The national average for 1989 was $1,147.02 for total taxes and $377.23 for general sales taxes. Washington's higher-than-average amounts caused it to rank ninth highest for overall state taxes and second for general sales taxes. The taxpayers of Idaho and Oregon fare much better with regard to tax burdens than their Washington neighbors. The per capita burden for total state taxes in Idaho is $966.96 (ranked 32nd) and for Oregon $917.11 (ranked 37th).

Since tax burdens are partly a function of wealth, a third method of comparing states takes into consideration the personal income of the state's taxpayers. For 1989, total Washington state taxes were $85.04 per $1,000 of personal income, which again made Washington the ninth highest taxed state. By comparison the national average came to $70.31 per $1,000 of personal income, and Idaho's was $79.61 (ranked 13th) and Oregon's $62.80 (ranked 39th). As in most states, the tax burden relative to personal income in Washington varies from person to person. Compared to most other states, Washington places an unusually large share of the state tax burden on the poor and an unusually small share on the wealthy. Overall, Washington has relatively high state taxes, although when state and local taxes are considered together, Washington is near the national average. It also has a regressive tax structure.[26]

Budgetary Process

The governor's office has responsibility for developing state revenue and expenditure budgets (see chapter seven). The director of the budget performs the task. Because the governor approves the budgets, both before and after passage by the legislature, he or she has a significant influence over what is—

and is not—included. Statutes require that the governor submit a balanced budget to the legislature. Upon receiving the budget, the legislature has the power to make any changes it deems necessary. These changes normally take the form of increasing or decreasing the dollar amounts requested, rather than changes in the overall budgetary plan.[27]

The senate and the house of representatives must each pass the budget by a majority vote. Neither the constitution nor state statutes require that the legislature pass a balanced budget. However, the state cannot carry over a deficit from one budget period to the next. After the legislature passes it, the budget returns to the governor for final approval. The governor can sign the bill, refuse to sign it, or veto all or any portion of it. Washington is one of many states that gives the governor line item vetoing power. To override a gubernatorial veto requires a two-thirds vote by the elected legislature. The governor also has the power to reduce the budget without prior legislative approval. This budget reduction power, however, is restricted, in that any reductions made must be made across the board.[28]

The director of the budget acts as comptroller by verifying all claims made against the state for any goods or services it received. This function at one time belonged to the state auditor. The change in responsibility came because the state constitution authorizes the governor's office to see that the laws passed by the legislature are properly executed; therefore, the governor's office should administer the expenditures the legislature approves.

The Legislative Budget Committee also reviews state finances. This permanent joint committee is composed of an equal number of members from the senate and house of representatives appointed by presiding officers and confirmed by their respective houses. The committee examines the current condition of state funds (i. e., are revenues available to meet authorized expenditures) and determines whether legislative intent is being achieved. As a result of this committee's activities, state revenues and expenditures receive continuous attention.[29]

Conclusion

Washington spent more than $24 billion in 1989-1991. The chief funding of these expenditures comes from the residents of Washington, primarily through taxes and, to a lesser extent, state charges. As the federal government decreases its financial support because of the huge national deficit, Washington must derive more of its revenue from within the state. Where will it obtain these needed revenues and from whom? Since the state has a history of refusing to turn to income taxes, it is likely that it will continue to rely on sales and property taxes to meet ever-growing demands. Washington's constant reliance on these two taxes has created sales and property tax rates among the highest in the nation. The regressive nature of these taxes will cause any rate increases to fall disproportionately on lower income residents, and thus, exacerbate the unbalanced nature of Washington state's tax structure.

Washington has high state taxes, ranking ninth in the nation, and high state revenues, ranking seventeenth. But it is also a high expenditure state, ranking sixteenth for state general expenses. The amounts that Washington spends are significantly above the national average, especially in the area of education, where it ranks fifth. Bear in mind, however, that when state and local governments are considered together, total taxes and spending in Washington are very close to national averages. State government in Washington carries a larger share of the state/local financial burden than do most other states, particularly for education. The result is a somewhat lighter burden for local officials.

Notes

1. *State of Washington Data Book, 1989* (Olympia: Office of Financial Management, 1989).
2. *State Government Finances in 1989,* Series GF-89-3 (Washington, D. C.: Bureau of the Census, 1990). Bear in mind that higher education includes a variety of institutions, from major state universities to community colleges.
3. *State of Washington Data Book,* 1989.
4. *State of Washington Data Book, 1989; Statistical Abstract of the U.S., 1990,* 110th ed. (Washington, D. C.: Bureau of the Census, 1990).
5. *World Almanac* (New York: Pharos Books, 1990), p. 562.
6. *State of Washington Data Book,* 1989.
7. *State Government Finances in 1989.*
8. *The Book of the States,* vol. 28, 1990-1991 ed. (Lexington, Ky.: Council of State Governments, 1990).
9. *Compania de Tobacos v. Collector,* 279 U.S. 306 (1927).
10. Donald R. Burrows, *Washington's Property Taxes* (Olympia: Department of Revenue, 1974).
11. Burrows and D. C. Taylor, "Public Finance in Washington: The Role of Taxation," in Thor Swanson, William Mullen, John Pierce, and Charles Sheldon, *Political Life in Washington: Governing the Evergreen State* (Pullman: Washington State University Press, 1985).
12. *Ibid.*
13. Washington State Constitution, Amendment 17, approved November 1944.
14. *State ex. rel. Stiner v. Yelle,* 174 Wash. 402.
15. Burrows and Taylor, "Public Finance in Washington."
16. *Jensen v. Henneford,* 185 Wash. 209 (1936).
17. Burrows and Taylor, "Public Finance in Washington."
18. *State Government Tax Collections: 1989,* Series GF-89-1 (Washington, D. C.: Bureau of the Census, 1990).
19. *Ibid.*
20. *Ibid.*
21. Burrows and Taylor, "Public Finance in Washington."
22. *State Government Finances in 1989.* For overviews of the federal grants system see George Break, *Financing Government in a Federal System* (Washington, D. C.: Brookings, 1980), chapters 1, 3, 4; and David Nice, Federalism (New York: St. Martin's, 1987), chapter 3.
23. *State of Washington Data Book, 1989.*
24. *State Government Finances in 1989.*
25. Susan Hansen, "The Politics of State Taxing and Spending," in Virginia Gray, Herbert Jacob, and Robert Albritton, eds., *Politics in the American States,* 5th ed. (Glenview, Il.: Scott, Foresman/Little, Brown, 1990), p. 347.
26. *State Government Tax Collections: 1989,* pp. 114-117.
27. Mary Avery, *Government of Washington State* (Seattle: University of Washington Press, 1967).
28. *The Book of the States,* vol. 28 (1990-1991 ed.).
29. *Legislative Handbook* (Olympia: Washington State Legislative Council, 1968).

A loyal Democrat displays his car's political stickers in 1952. Vibert Jeffers photo. *Susan Parish Collection*©

Chapter Eleven

Citizen Control in Washington State

Paul R. Hagner

AFTER ALL IS said and done, the question remains: "Is politics important?" A noted political scientist, Philip Converse, once observed that "for many people, politics does not compete in interest with sports, local gossip and television dramas."[1] To be sure, if a debate between the leading gubernatorial candidates preempted a popular television program, phone switchboards would light up from Port Angeles to Spokane. To most people, politics is both uninteresting and extremely complex. It is important to state that these two beliefs feed off one another. The more complex a topic, the less willing are we to come to grips with its intricacies. The less known about a subject, the less interesting it becomes: thus there is no great motivation to pay much attention to it. This pattern of disengagement from politics has some very troubling consequences which this chapter will explore.

It is one thing to say politics is uninteresting; quite another that it is unimportant. While the outcome of this year's Rose Bowl might occupy a lot of our attention and interest, the result will have little, if any, long-term impact on our personal lives. Politics, on the other hand, as complex as it may be, constantly affects our daily existence. Except for instances of war, no governmental entity affects us more than state government. This book has repeatedly shown how the various elements of state government influence our health, education, safety, and the environment in which we live, to name just a few areas. So the important question is not whether politics is important, but whether or not we want to have a voice in the way politics affects us.

As discussed previously in this book, the relationship between public desires and what government provides by the way of policy is termed *political linkage*. In a democratic system, one assumes that a close matching of citizen needs and governmental activities results because of the powers citizens have over their elected representatives. The notion of *constituency control* lies at the heart of democratic theory. Warren Miller and Donald Stokes identify two central conditions necessary for the existence and persistence of constituency control:

1) "the attitudes or perceptions governing the representative's acts must correspond, at least imperfectly, to the district's actual opinions"; and 2) "the constituency must in some measure take the policy views of candidates into account in choosing a representative."[2]

The first condition seems to hold in Washington state. Evidence suggests that state government actions conform to policy orientations shared by a majority of the electorate. But this fact does not answer the question as to whether the observed correspondence is due to citizen control. The second condition, then, must be addressed. The second condition states that the citizens do have the *procedural ability* to control their state government and that, in the presence of such an ability, they actually make use of it.

Citizen Control in Washington State

Chapter one introduced us to a state of great diversity. We see this represented in the lay of the land itself. Anyone who has driven from Seattle to Spokane can sense the impossibility of developing a profile of the "average" Washington state resident. But even within this diversity there are some interesting commonalties. For instance, while Boeing and Weyerhaeuser are involved in two very different economic pursuits, they are similar in that they both exert a considerable leverage on the state's economy and its politics. Similarly, the state's east/west diversity can be subsumed under the general recognition that our products and pursuits force us to adopt an internationalist perspective. Whether we are supplying aircraft to militaries of the world or wheat to Africa and the Far East, we cannot afford to be isolationist in our outlooks.

Chapter one also introduced us to the fact that there are many opportunities for group-related forms of citizen control in the state. These opportunities are important to keep in mind because the "textbook" form of citizen control—election—does not indicate a comprehensive path for citizen input into the political process. While state turnout in the general elections is higher than that of the nation as a whole, fully 45 percent of those eligible to vote chose not to in 1988. Figures for primary elections offer an even more pessimistic picture. In the last 14 primary elections, only twice did more than half the eligible electorate participate in decisions. Over the past 14 primaries, the average turnout was 39 percent. In the seven most recent primaries, since 1973, only one-third of voters participated in the primary election process.

As chapter two points out, since the power of state government could be all-consuming, state constitutions tend to structure and limit that power rather than grant it. State constitutions that have persisted relatively unchanged for a long period of time and respond to a changing environment primarily by means of amendment, such as Washington's, tend to have excessive detail and can stand as a practical obstacle to flexible modern government. The persistence of a century-old document also entails the possibility of the persistence of century-old ideas and attitudes. As the chapter observed, the original Washington Constitution was steeped in a strong skepticism concerning governmental power. This produced a document expressing strong distrust of government officials, especially legislators. Such a detailed document takes a wide range of policy authority *away* from officials who can be held accountable to the electorate. In other words, when policy is detailed as specifically as it is in the Washington Constitution, elected legislators and executives are not given the flexibility often needed to deal with current state problems. The constitution, in effect, "ties the hands" of people who should be expected to reflect citizen control. It is important to note that constitutions were *designed* to limit public officials so as to protect individual rights. As detailed by chapter two, however, such protections tend to become the stuff of judicial, rather than electoral, contestation. Citizen control of such debates is less likely to be directly exercised. As the chapter notes, the constitution may well be too restrictive. It is precisely because of this problem of detail that the Committee for Economic Development recommended that "state constitutional revision should have highest priority in restructuring state governments to meet modern needs. Stress should be placed on repealing limitations that prevent constructive legislative and executive action."[3]

The chance of such a revision process occurring in Washington state, chapter two points out, is unlikely. Although procedural mechanisms exist by which citizens can institute constitutional reform, they would be difficult. The rules governing the calling of a constitutional convention are quite formidable. Thus, the only two real attempts at sweeping constitutional reform, once in 1918 and the other in the 1970s, met with failure, in part due to widespread citizen disinterest in changing the wording, and by that one would surmise also the intention, of the original document.

As chapter three details, citizens of Washington state are given considerable electoral opportunities to propose, amend, and otherwise influence specific policy proposals. Direct and indirect initiatives can effectively force politicians to deal with controversial policy questions. Referred and demanded referenda provide citizens with the opportunity to directly influence the legislative agenda itself. In addition, the state's voters must approve any constitutional amendment. Finally, the voters are given the right to recall any elected state official, except members of the judiciary. All told, this is a remarkable toolkit for Washington's citizens, should they wish to tinker with the mechanisms of government.

The question is: do they indeed tinker and, if so, who does it? As the chapter points out, initiatives have introduced many important issues, and monied interests cannot always determine their outcome. The fact that less than a quarter of initiatives succeed in acquiring the number of signatures required for inclusion on the ballot is not necessarily negative because it is possible that the proposed measure is so unpopular it really does not deserve the electorate's attention. A possible cause for concern lies in the chapter's discussion of the drop-off in voting for ballot measures. It appears that a significant minority of voters decide not to vote for initiatives even though they go to the polls to vote for candidates. The fact that many voters do not vote raises the suspicion that many have not taken the time to inform themselves about ballot measures. This means that a smaller, and perhaps less representative, segment of the electorate significantly influences state policies. It should be noted, however, that the actual incidence of initiatives, referenda, and recall petitions may not be the best indicators of their effectiveness in the exertion of citizen control. It is entirely possible that the *threat* of these measures is a very useful means by which the public can influence the behavior of their representatives and others in state government.

Many political researchers have argued that, given the problems of citizen control in a mass democracy, political parties are the most effective and efficient means of communicating citizen intent to, and exerting programmatic control over, elected officials.[4] If this is indeed the case, then the discussion presented in chapter four does not provide strong evidence for Washington state's political parties being agents of citizen control. From this chapter we see that there are numerous obstacles preventing the development of strong political parties in Washington. First and foremost, the blanket primary system allows voters to disregard the party affiliation of primary candidates, thus decreasing the party role in recruitment. Second, the lack of state party conventions to nominate state or local candidates diminishes recruitment. Third, authority is greatly diffused within Washington state government, meaning parties have a harder time controlling these diverse power centers and, thus, are less successful in enacting party programs. Fourth, Washington voters have a well-ingrained streak of independence that diminishes the parties' appeals to mobilize the electorate. The fifth reason for the lack of strong parties in the state results from the last two. Because Washington state voters tend to vote "the person, not the party," they tend to elect a partisan "hodgepodge." It is rare in Washington state to see either the legislative or executive branch dominated by one party. Given the fact that power is widely scattered, it is very difficult for one party to control enough of the government to enact its programs without some form of compromise and/or weakening of policy stands. All of these factors have produced a relatively weak party system featuring numerous vacancies in formal positions in party organizations and a high incidence of intraparty conflict and division. As the chapter concludes, "The parties of the 1990s face the prospect of being one set of players out of many in the political arena and not necessarily the most important set in many situations."

All of this means citizens cannot rely on political parties to serve as effective mechanisms of citizen control in the state. The reason for this comes from the very stuff of politics. If officials see parties as having only marginal impact on their chances of winning, then there is very little need for them to adhere to a party line while in office. The lack of programmatic control over office holders denies the political party the chance of being a "short cut" mechanism for citizens to use to influence elected officials.

William Allen White once observed that organized interest groups provide the *real* input into governmental decision-making. In essence White argued that the citizen who votes in isolation is "a pretty poor stick of a citizen," with real clout lying with those who use their organization to influence policy.[5] Interestingly, White made these observations in 1924, but they also hold true today, and, as chapter five noted, they certainly have relevance to the politics of Washington state.

As the chapter points out, Washington politics allows for *both* an important policy influencing role for interest groups and an effective method by which citizens can monitor interest group activity. Washington's fragmented political system, conjoined with a relatively weak party system, allows great opportunity for a widely diverse pattern of interest group activity and access. The initiative and referendum systems also provide opportunity for effective interest group influence.

The chapter also provides strong evidence as to the importance of interest groups in the conduct and financing of Washington state's election campaigns. Thus, the state's political system does allow views and opinions to reach legislators who may or may not be in touch with the many and varied aspects of society. While this pluralistic form of citizen control and input is theoretically valid, there are some problems in the actual operation of the representational system. The chapter indicates two of these. First, the disadvantaged and disenchanted, even the mass of the state population itself, are unlikely to form effective groups. The chapter presents data showing that established business groups and business-connected political action committees (PACs) undertake the majority of lobbying and campaign financing efforts. Money and organization are two vital resources for an effective interest group. Those segments of the public which lack either or both are unlikely to benefit from the pluralistic system. Second, "some groups are more equal than others" in their ability to gain a legislator's ear. There exist a few powerful and established interests in Washington state that continually win budget battles and have the resources to give continued support to specific candidates or causes.

Washington's "moralistic" political culture has allowed for the existence of greater restrictions on acceptable interest group tactics. Perhaps no other state organization captures the essence of this moralism more than the Public Disclosure Commission (PDC). The commission's duty, to disclose the financial records of lobbyists, allows for great potential in the area of public control. Information is power. The more information we have concerning lobbyists, the more power we have to control and, if the case demands it, limit their influence. However, while the PDC is fulfilling its function by collecting information and releasing it to activists and the news media, no strong evidence exists that the general public is aware of its activities. Again we see a public control device that engenders great promise but raises questions as to whether that promise is being fulfilled.

If you are not afraid of long periods of embarrassed silence, try the following experiment. Ask a friend to name their representatives in the Washington legislature. After the silence, ask them to name the most important leaders in either the house or senate. It usually becomes quickly apparent why legislators do not tremble in their shoes wondering how the public will react to their most recent actions. The reason for this lack of fear (although you would never find one legislator who would admit it) is that they *know* the majority of their constituents do not follow their actions closely. And, as chapter six reveals, members of the state legislature, like most other state legislatures, do not really "look"–in occupational, racial, age, or gender terms–like the people they represent.

The question to be asked here is "on whose behalf is the legislature exercising power?" The chapter shows that the question of constituency representation is difficult to unravel. It concludes that "occupational categories often come close to identifying a legislator's primary reference group on political issues. Some of these groups may be residents of his or her district, but others may not." In other words, and as impressed in chapter five, organized interests tend to be defined as relevant clientele groups. Certainly the discussion concerning "ulcer gulch" and the informational function of lobbyists gives a strong indication of who gets the legislator's ear. It also indicates who does not: "Interests lacking the advantage of group organization are less likely to be a part of legislative consideration when policy choices are made."

It is clear, then, that the concept of citizen control over the legislature can only be understood within a group context. The legislature has been shown to be responsive to the demands of groups, dependent upon them for valuable input into the legislative process, and hopeful of their monetary and vote-raising support in reelection battles. The result of this influence is a legislature that, more often than not, opts for the status quo. This rather conservative orientation towards change tends to fit the needs of established interest groups very well. For those citizens without organizational ties or with membership in a weakly structured group, the outlook for legislative responsiveness and control is less than bright.

From an early age we have been socialized to think of the chief executive as a commanding figure in government. Given this, the discussion of the governor's role in Washington state presented in chapter seven may be surprising. The portrait that emerges from this chapter is of an office without a sufficiently large power base even to oversee other elected executive office holders, much less the people who occupy the departments, agencies, and boards of the executive bureaucracy. Further, the rise of an established cadre of lobbyists in Olympia and the increased size and independence of executive staffs works against effective use of the governor's powers. Additionally, the governor is only nominally considered as head of his or her political party. This means that he or she is unable to effectively use party mechanisms to influence legislative activity. Once again we see that a weak party system works against effective citizen control. So while a dynamic and aggressive personality could wield much influence from the governor's mansion, in general the office is not a position from which citizen opinion can exercise a great deal of influence.

It is important to differentiate the powers of the chief executive officer of the state from that of the state executive bureaucracy. We are the recipients of bureaucratic rule-making, ranging from policies involving crime in the streets to the qualifications of the person who cuts your hair. Much of this rule-making results from bureaucratic interpretation of legislative acts. While the legislative act may say "we want this done," exactly how and by what means it will be done is often left to executive agency interpretation. Thus, the executive bureaucracy can have enormous interpretive power. Since most of the occupants of these agencies are not elected, the degree to which citizens can control their activities is always in question.

Many people are surprised to learn that the judicial branch of government, at both state and national levels, has an important policy-making role. By settling disputes between contending parties—sometimes state policy makers themselves—judges' decisions serve as policy. The principle of judicial review serves as a basis for judicial lawmaking. By their powers of interpretation, judges influence all other actors in the state political system. Such policy-making power, combined with the jurists' relative isolation from the political process, raises some problems for effective citizen control. For state judges, the central dilemma is how to settle disputes objectively while remaining accountable for those settlements that have public policy implications.

At first glance, it would seem that Washington's system of an elected judiciary is more than adequate to fulfill the needs of effective citizen control. Chapter eight, however, points out weak spots in such a belief. Initially, the selection process for jurists narrows the list of possible candidates and, in many cases, chooses the most likely winner long before the voters get a chance to participate. A second reason for weak citizen control comes because the majority of jurists first gain office via political appointment. They then face their first electoral exposure as incumbents – a very useful and beneficial position in terms of holding onto one's office. Third, since judicial elections tend not to emphasize discussion of legal issues and because the races are nonpartisan, election is often due to incumbency and endorsement by interest groups. While the judicial electorate is select in that it tends to be aware of the qualifications and stands of the candidates – especially in primary elections – it cannot be said to represent the state's citizenry. Judicial elections, therefore, hardly serve as models of democratic and effective citizen control.

As chapter nine points out, while important decisions are indeed made at the national and state levels, they most often impact us at the local level. This chapter tells us that the arrangement of local governments in Washington provides both an opportunity and a hindrance to citizen involvement. On the positive side, we know now that the governmental structure in our state is far from monolithic. Matters germane to large cities, small towns, counties, and even to specific policy areas such as education, are all influenced by governing agencies tied to local jurisdictions. Because we are most affected by local policies, and because the administrating agencies are tied to local communities instead of being located in some distant and faceless seat of power, we have a better chance of gaining access to and influencing those in a position to do something about our concern.

But as the discussion in this chapter on growth management reveals, the trans-boundary nature of many social problems, and the overlapping and sometimes conflicting nature of the state's local government hierarchies, present huge obstacles for the average citizen. It takes considerable time and effort to discover the proper person to whom to voice one's concerns. Because of this, only a small portion of the population, usually from the higher socioeconomic ranks, takes the time to learn *how* to get involved at the local level. The irony of all of this is that by providing so many different points of access, the system winds up discouraging all but the most committed.

Chapter ten provides a clear picture of how money is spent in our state and where it comes from. Three areas of expenditure account for the overwhelming majority of the state's money outflow: public education, human resources, and the cost of government itself. In comparison to other states, Washington spends more on public education, about the same on running the government, and slightly less on human services. All in all, the state cannot be said to be out of line in the way it spends money. Where the money comes from, however, is a different matter. While sales taxes average about 50 percent of tax revenues for other states, Washington receives 75 percent from this source. This, combined with property taxes much higher than the national average, classifies Washington as a high tax state with a regressive tax structure.

This, as the chapter points out, is due to the fact that Washington lacks a state income tax, thereby requiring that revenues be found somewhere else. It is very clear that state voters are not interested in instituting such a tax and, consequently, no politician will propose one. It seems, therefore, that the present tax system results from the wishes of the majority of the electorate. One problem, of course, is that the group upon whom the burden is disproportionately greatest, the poor, have little chance of changing the tax structure, and it is doubtful that other, more organized interests will find it advantageous to come to their aid. A second problem indicated by the chapter is that, as demands for state expenditures escalate, a revenue system based on sales and property taxes has no recourse but to increase these burdens, thus placing Washington further out of line with the rest of the country.

Political Linkage in Washington State: An Overview

Before we try to summarize the degree to which the citizens of this state can control the actions of their elected and non-elected officials, let us develop a snapshot of the degree to which Washington state citizens participate in the governing process. Austin Ranney[6] states there exist four types of participants in state government: *organizational activists*—those who donate a substantial investment of resources into influencing government, such as lobbyists and political party activists; *organizational contributors*—those who make some contribution, in terms of time and/or money, to political parties or interest groups; *opinion advocates*—those who try to persuade others to vote a particular way, but not as part of an organized interest group or party activity; and *voters*—those who vote in state elections. To Ranney's types of participants we add a fifth group of citizens: *non-participants*—those eligible to participate who do not. Ranney presents an overall estimate of the percentage of state citizens occupying each participatory type. If we add in an estimate of the percentage of non-participants, based on a six-year average of turnout in Washington gubernatorial races, we come up with an estimate of the breakdown of participation on the part of the Washington state citizenry. That estimate is presented in Table One.

The estimates presented in this table do not provide an overly optimistic view of the level of citizen control in this state. This is not, however, a problem limited to Washington, as Thomas Dye and Harmon Zeigler argue:

The masses play an even smaller role in state and local politics than they do in national politics. The news media emphasize national politics rather than state or community politics. Very few citizens know who their state Senator or state Representative is or who their council members or county commissioners are.[7]

So what does all of this mean in terms of political linkage in Washington state? Political scientist Norman Luttbeg argued that there were five "models" of political linkage.[8] The first three he labeled "coercive" because they represent ways in which the public can force their representatives to behave in line with their wishes. The *rational-activist model* assumes that the public plays a direct role in influencing representative behavior. The representative, knowing that the public is scrutinizing him or her, votes his or her perception of what the public wants. The *political parties model* focuses on the role parties play in forcing representatives to behave in accordance with their party membership's desires. The *pressure groups model* sees interest group activists as pressuring officials to act in ways beneficial to the group's membership. There are two other "non-coercive" models of linkage. By non-coercive, Luttbeg means that the official is not forced to represent the wishes of the citizenry, but does so nonetheless. The *sharing model* posits that since elected officials come from the districts they represent, they will share the important beliefs prevalent in the constituency. As Luttbeg states, "Certain policies abhorred by the electorate will be equally abhorrent to the representatives, causing them to satisfy public opinion merely by acting on their personal opinions."[9] The final model Luttbeg suggests is the *role playing model.* In this model, representatives vote in conformity with prevalent public opinion, believing that, as elected representatives, they *ought* to do so.

The earlier discussions in this chapter concerning the institutional resources of public control and the breakdown of the state's population in terms of participatory categories can now allow us to ascertain which model of linkage best captures the patterns existing in Washington state. There is little evidence to support the *rational-activist model.* While Washington provides a great deal of institutional access, by means of the initiative, recall, and the existence of the Public Disclosure Commission, there is little evidence to indicate that the majority of citizens take advantage of these means of control. The *political parties model* is inappropriate to Washington. Parties are not a strong source of power within state government, partially due to the level of citizen distrust of their activities. The *pressure groups model* also is inadequate in explaining political linkage. Interest groups have an important impact on state politics, but there is a real question concerning the degree to which these interest group elites *represent* their membership. In addition, many citizens are excluded from group membership altogether. Table One suggests that only a very small percentage of the state's population—6 percent—actively participates (.6 percent) or contributes (5.4 percent) to groups that try to influence policy. So while the political clout of interest groups is not in dispute, their role as linkage mechanisms is.

Table One

Estimate of the Percentage of Each Participation Type in the Washington State Public

Participation Type	Estimated Percentage in Washington State Public
Organizational activists	.6%
Organizational contributors	5.4%
Opinion advocates	17.0%
Voters	33.0%
Non-participants	44.0%

This leaves the explanation of political linkage to the non-coercive models of *sharing* and *role playing*. While data do not exist that could help us find out which non-coercive model is most important, that question is of less consequence because, by narrowing the choice down to these two models, we have achieved our goal. While the institutional structures of the state government of Washington provide the *opportunity* for citizen control, *in actuality* a good deal of the political linkage existing in this state is due to the values and beliefs of the representatives themselves. This is not to say the coercive forms of citizen control have not been used successfully in the past. A representative is always concerned about the possibility that his or her position will be threatened by a concerned and informed majority of the citizenry. But such movements, as important as they may be, are more the exception than the norm in Washington state politics.

In essence, political linkage, the fundamental principle of a democracy, is preserved not by the general public, but by the political and social elites themselves. This phenomenon has been termed by Dye and Zeigler as the "irony of democracy":

> Democracy is government "by the people," but the survival of democracy rests on the shoulders of elites. This is the irony of democracy: elites must govern wisely if government "by the people" is to survive. If the survival of the American system depended on the existence of an active, informed, and enlightened citizenry, then democracy in America would have disappeared long ago, for the masses of America are apathetic and ill informed about politics and public policy...the American masses do not lead; they follow. They respond to the attitudes, proposals and behavior of elites.[10]

In a very real sense, Washington state's political and economic environment exacerbates the domination of elites. Dye and Zeigler point out that states with political parties with little cohesion and unity,[11] where one or two industries prevail,[12] yield a more cohesive elite system. The more cohesive the elite system the more there is "a lack of political confidence among residents and a widespread belief that political activity is useless."[13]

So, Washington has a great potential for strong citizen control. But it is not utilized to any great extent. There appears to be an acceptance of letting officials take the responsibility for the conduct of state affairs—unless something goes seriously wrong. It has been argued in this book that citizens can reinstate control by making use of the procedural devices outlined earlier. But this reassertion is generally *reactive*. Voters usually take advantage of it to redress a wrong, not to keep a wrong from occurring. One can think of many areas, especially those involving the environment and health care, where such "crisis response" can have very damaging, and perhaps permanent, impacts. For example, it is certainly preferable that citizens debate the possible ecological effects of nuclear waste dumping in the state *prior* to the actual dumping. If the public reacts *after* the policy is underway, after-effects could be devastating.

The Obligations of the Citizen

Only a few things in life can be categorized as "right" or "wrong," but there are some such things. If a friend tells us that "Politics is all bull—it's not important," she is wrong. As discussed in the opening to this chapter, "politics" has very real consequences to our lives, every day. If another friend says "Politics is just too complicated. No one can figure out what's going on," he is wrong. To be sure, politics is complicated, but in this modern society almost everything is complicated. We hope this book has demonstrated that while Washington state politics is complex, that does not mean it is beyond understanding. Finally, if a chorus of friends tell us "Government is too big. An individual can't have an impact," they all are wrong. We have discussed the many different procedures an individual could use to influence government. There is far too much emphasis given to "just voting," and too little given to other forms of participation. Government leaders are real people! We can write to them, call them on the phone, submit petitions to them, and see them in their offices. These contacts, if well organized and articulated, can dramatically impact an official's actions. We can join and participate in political parties and interest groups. Through an active commitment to a political and/or issue group, our power as a citizen is magnified many times over.

We are left to ponder the commitment we have as citizens. We, as citizens, have an obligation and a choice. Are we content to let others dictate our physical and social environment? Or would we prefer having a hand in determining the quality of our own lives?

Notes

1. Philip E. Converse, "The Nature of Belief Systems in Mass Publics," in David E. Apter, ed., *Ideology and Discontent* (New York: Free Press, 1964), p. 224.
2. Warren E. Miller and Donald E. Stokes, "Constituency Influence in Congress," 57 *American Political Science Review* 46-56 (March 1963).
3. *Modernizing State Government* (New York: Committee for Economic Development, 1967), pp. 19-20.
4. For some empirical tests of this theory see Norman Luttbeg, ed., *Public Opinion and Public Policy*, rev. ed. (Homewood, Il.: The Dorsey Press, 1974), pp. 109-186.
5. William Allen White, *Politics: The Citizen's Business* (New York: The Macmillan Co., 1924), pp. 15-16.
6. Austin Ranney, "Parties in State Politics," in Herbert Jacob and Kenneth N. Vines, eds., *Politics in the American States: A Comparative Analysis, 3rd ed.* (Boston: Little, Brown and Co., 1976), p. 52.
7. Thomas R. Dye and L. Harmon Zeigler, *The Irony of Democracy*, 5th ed. (Monterey, Ca: Duxbury Press, 1981), p. 432.
8. Luttbeg, *Public Opinion and Public Policy*, pp. 4-10.
9. *Ibid.*, p. 7.
10. Dye and Zeigler, *The Irony of Democracy*, p. 4.
11. *Ibid.*, p. 451.
12. *Ibid.*, p. 442.
13. *Ibid.*, p. 452.

About the Authors

Greg Andranovich (Ph.D., University of California, Riverside) is an assistant professor in the Department of Political Science and local government specialist in Cooperative Extension at Washington State University. His interests include urban and regional policy making, comparative and cross-cultural public administration, and body surfing.

Hugh A. Bone (Ph.D., Northwestern) is professor emeritus and former chair of the Department of Political Science at the University of Washington. He has also taught at the University of Hawaii, Stanford University, and Columbia University. He is a former president of the Pacific Northwest and the Western Political Science Associations. Bone has written numerous scholarly articles and is the author of *American Politics and the Party System* (1971) and *Party Committees and National Committees* (1968). He has co-authored *Politics and Voters* (1971) and *Public Policymaking, Washington Style* (1980).

Terrence E. Cook (Ph.D., Princeton University) is an associate professor of political science at Washington State University. His areas of specialization include political thought, democratic theory, and comparative politics. The former concerns are reflected in his book, *The Great Alternatives of Social Thought: Aristocrat, Saint, Capitalist, Socialist* (1991), and the latter will emerge in books on philosophy of social science and a theory of political choice.

Paul R. Hagner (Ph.D., Indiana University) is an associate professor in political science at Washington State University. He is the co-author of *Dynamics of American Public Opinion* (1982) and has published papers in the area of political behavior and media effects in numerous scholarly journals.

Nicholas P. Lovrich, Jr. (Ph.D., University of California, Los Angeles) is professor of political science and director of the Division of Governmental Studies and

Services at Washington State University. His areas of teaching and research are public administration and state and local government studies. He has written a number of articles and co-authored several books on public administration and environmental problems affecting local government, including *Public Choice Theory in Public Administration* (with Max Neiman, 1984), *Water Resources, Democracy and the Technical Information Quandary* (with John Pierce, 1986), and *Public Knowledge and Environmental Politics in Japan and the United States* (with John Pierce, Taketsugu Tsurutani, and Takematsu Abe, 1989).

Herman D. Lujan (Ph.D., University of Idaho) is president of the University of Northern Colorado. He previously held positions as vice provost and vice president for minority affairs at the University of Washington, and as director of the Institute for Social and Environmental Studies and chair of the Department of Political Science at the University of Kansas. Lujan has taught graduate courses in American politics and public policy analysis, and undergraduate courses in state government. A former state planning director and consultant, he is familiar with state educational planning and budgeting in both the executive and legislative branches.

David C. Nice (Ph.D., University of Michigan) is professor of political science and chair of the Department of Political Science at Washington State University. His areas of teaching and research are American politics and public policy. He is the author of numerous articles on state politics, Congress, the presidency, and public-policy making, as well as *Federalism: The Politics of Intergovernmental Relations* (1987) and *Policy Innovation in the States* (scheduled for publication in 1993).

Linda Louise Blackwelder Pall (J.D., University of Idaho; Ph.D., Washington State University) practices law in Lewiston and Moscow, Idaho, and teaches at Washington State University. A frequent contributor to continuing legal education seminars, her special interest is civil liberties, particularly First Amendment issues. She is past chair of the Idaho State Bar Family Law Section, is chair of the Research Committee of the American Bar Association Family Law Section, and vice chair of the Historic Preservation Committee of the Real Property, Probate Trust Section of the ABA.

John C. Pierce (Ph.D., University of Minnesota) is professor of political science and dean of the College of Sciences and Arts at Washington State University. His areas of teaching and research are public knowledge and political values. He has written a number of articles and is the co-author of several books, including *Water Resources, Democracy and the Technical Information Quandary*

(1986); *Public Knowledge and Environmental Politics in Japan and the United States* (1989); and *Information, Individuals and Interest Groups in Canada and the United States* (forthcoming).

Debra L. Sanders (Ph.D., Arizona State University) is associate professor of accounting and business law at Washington State University. Her area of teaching is federal income taxation. She has written a number of articles on individual taxation, corporate taxation, and taxpayer behavior. Her current area of research interest is state and local taxes.

George W. Scott (Ph.D., University of Washington) has taught college classes and served as a medical school administrator and bank vice president. He is now director of public affairs for the Washington State Bar Association. Scott was elected to the Washington State House of Representatives in 1969 for northeast Seattle's Fourth District. He served in the state senate from 1971-1983 and chaired the Republican caucus and the Ways and Means Committee.

Charles H. Sheldon (Ph.D., University of Oregon) is professor of political science at Washington State University. His areas of teaching and research are public law and judicial behavior. He has written a number of articles and books on courts and judges, including *A Century of Judging: A Political History of the Washington Supreme Court* (1988) and *The Washington High Bench: A Biographical History of the State Supreme Court, 1889-1991* (1992).

Elizabeth Walker (Ph.D., Washington State University) served for four years as assistant professor of political science at Washington State University with teaching and research interests in state and local government, political parties, interest groups, and gender politics. Walker is currently a candidate for the Washington State House of Representatives for the Ninth District.

Kay Gausman Wolsborn (Ph.D., Washington State University) is associate professor of government at the College of Saint Benedict/Saint John's University in St. Joseph, Minnesota. Her areas of teaching are public policy, bureaucracy, and political parties. Her research and writing projects have focused on program assessment and electoral behavior.